Thomas Hardy and the Folk Horror Tradition

Thomas Hardy and the Folk Horror Tradition

Alan G. Smith, Robert Edgar and John Marland

BLOOMSBURY ACADEMIC
NEW YORK • LONDON • OXFORD • NEW DELHI • SYDNEY

BLOOMSBURY ACADEMIC
Bloomsbury Publishing Inc
1385 Broadway, New York, NY 10018, USA
50 Bedford Square, London, WC1B 3DP, UK
29 Earlsfort Terrace, Dublin 2, Ireland

BLOOMSBURY, BLOOMSBURY ACADEMIC and the Diana logo are trademarks of Bloomsbury Publishing Plc

First published in the United States of America 2023

Copyright © Alan G. Smith, Robert Edgar and John Marland, 2023

For legal purposes the Acknowledgements on p. x constitute an extension of this copyright page.

Cover design: Eleanor Rose
Cover image: Robert Edgar, 2022

All rights reserved. No part of this publication may be reproduced or transmitted in any form or by any means, electronic or mechanical, including photocopying, recording, or any information storage or retrieval system, without prior permission in writing from the publishers.

Bloomsbury Publishing Inc does not have any control over, or responsibility for, any third-party websites referred to or in this book. All internet addresses given in this book were correct at the time of going to press. The author and publisher regret any inconvenience caused if addresses have changed or sites have ceased to exist, but can accept no responsibility for any such changes.

Library of Congress Cataloging-in-Publication Data
Names: Smith, Alan G., 1951- author. | Edgar, Robert, author. | Marland, John, author.
Title: Thomas Hardy and the folk horror tradition / Alan G. Smith, Robert Edgar and John Marland.
Description: New York : Bloomsbury Academic, 2023. | Includes bibliographical references and index. |
Summary: "Examines the recent resurgence of folk horror and argues that Thomas Hardy is one of its progenitors by analysing his prose (in particular his rarely examined short fiction) and its adaptations as foundational in the development of folk horror in literature, film and television"– Provided by publisher.
Identifiers: LCCN 2022048181 (print) | LCCN 2022048182 (ebook) | ISBN 9781501383991 (hardback) | ISBN 9781501384035 (paperback) | ISBN 9781501384004 (ebook) | ISBN 9781501384011 (pdf) | ISBN 9781501384028 (ebook other)
Subjects: LCSH: Hardy, Thomas, 1840–1928–Criticism and interpretation. | Hardy, Thomas, 1840–1928–Influence. | Hardy, Thomas, 1840–1928–Adaptations–History and criticism. | Horror tales, English–History and criticism. | Folk horror fiction–History and criticism. | Folk horror films–History and criticism. | Folklore in literature. | Folklore in motion pictures.
Classification: LCC PR4757.H66 S65 2023 (print) | LCC PR4757.H66 (ebook) | DDC 823/.8–dc23/eng/20221103
LC record available at https://lccn.loc.gov/2022048181
LC ebook record available at https://lccn.loc.gov/2022048182

ISBN: HB: 978-1-5013-8399-1
ePDF: 978-1-5013-8401-1
eBook: 978-1-5013-8400-4

Typeset by Integra Software Services Pvt. Ltd.

To find out more about our authors and books visit www.bloomsbury.com and sign up for our newsletters.

This book is dedicated to the NHS and the Snickleway Inn, York. Without the assistance of both of these fine institutions this manuscript would never have been completed.

Heredity

I am the family face;
Flesh perishes, I live on,
Projecting trait and trace
Through time to times anon,
And leaping from place to place
Over oblivion.

The years-heired feature that can
In curve and voice and eye
Despise the human span
Of durance – that is I;
The eternal thing in man,
That heeds no call to die.

Thomas Hardy (1917)

CONTENTS

Acknowledgements x

Introduction: 'Down their carved names the rain-drop ploughs' 1

1 Foundations: Towards a Hardyan folk horror 5
2 Haunted Hardy 21
3 Cultural bereavement 47
4 Re-enchantment 65
5 Hardy constructed and re-constructed 87
6 Hardy's range of narrative perspectives 99
7 Wessex on page and screen 127

Conclusion: 'Teach me to live that I may dread the grave as little as my bed' 159

Works cited 164
Index 173

ACKNOWLEDGEMENTS

The authors would like to thank Amy Martin and Hali Han at Bloomsbury for all their support and guidance in bringing this project to publication. The authors would also like to thank colleagues and students in the York Centre for Writing in the School of Humanities at York St John University. Special thanks to Dr Jo Waugh.

Alan would like to thank Robert Edgar for his patience and Joyce for many, many years of her patience.

Robert would like to thank Julia for being from Dorset and Evan for being Hardy. A special thanks to the cover star, Merry, who is sadly lost somewhere on Egdon Heath. Very special thanks to my best friend Agatha, who would have eaten my heart out of a biscuit tin given half a chance.

John would like to thank John Joseph and Annie M. for their forbearance. He would also like to thank Marian and Mamma Rita for their lack of forbearance. Both were vital.

Introduction: 'Down their carved names the rain-drop ploughs'

There is an ever-growing academic interest in folk horror with journal specials and books being produced at an ever-increasing rate. This has yet to match the pace of the creative folk horror infused output of fiction writers and film and television makers. Folk horror fan sites sweep the internet; the *Folk Horror Revival and Urban Weird Network* reaches a wide audience and *Helleborzine* grows in popularity with every new edition. This renewed interest in folk horror, or perhaps an interest in a renewed folk horror, arguably gained recognition in the academy in 2014 with the *Fiend in the Furrows* conference at Queen's University in Belfast and in 2016 with *Otherworldy: Folk Horror Revival* at the British Museum. Further folk horror-inspired conferences have been held at the University of Bristol, Leeds Metropolitan University, Falmouth University and York St John University. Recent academic texts have been written to meet the popular interest in the genre, most particularly Adam Scovell's ubiquitous and defining 2017 text *Folk Horror: Hours Strange and Things Dreadful* and the special issue of *Revenant* Journal, edited by folk horror studies pioneer Dawn Keetley in 2020. There is a forthcoming comprehensive *Routledge Companion to Folk Horror* (Edgar and Johnson), a text on folk horror from Louis Bayman and Kevin Donnelly and Dawn Keetley and Jeffrey Tolbert's edition of *Horror Studies* journal.

This book seeks to add to these ongoing discussions by tracing a line of folk horror whose roots can be found in Britain in the late nineteenth century, most specifically in the work of Thomas Hardy. Although popular research suggests that the definition of folk horror starts in 2010 in reviewing the popular artefacts of the late 1960s and early 1970s, this book suggests that there is a much deeper history and lineage to be considered. Whilst foregrounding folk horror as a genre in the opening chapter, this is a book about Hardy and how he can be viewed through the lens of a genre which is formally defined more than a century later. This is not to suggest that this book provides a new and totalizing view of Hardy's work; as is evident from this text there is a clear recognition that Hardy's work and in particular his novels represent variety in form and content. There are, however, particular motifs that run throughout and are perhaps most clearly seen in his short fiction – the work that is less studied, less adapted and is perhaps less familiar. However these themes are also present to varying degrees in some of his novels and later poetry. Whichever the form being analysed, part of the power of Hardy's work is in his totalizing creation and conception of Wessex – a topography which uneasily and eerily maps over ours. Tracy Hayes and the Hardy Society are currently leading on this work with a symposia and publications on the darker side of Hardy's work. What is most striking in Hardy's work is the tension between tradition and innovation, the rural and the urban, folklore and enlightenment, a landed class and working class, folk belief and Christianity. However these are not narrative dialectics, sources of conflict which raise drama to then be overcome with subsequent narrative conclusion. Rather the unease so central to his work is created by the perpetual co-existence of two states.

Of Hardy's short fiction it is only *The Withered Arm* that has previously been embraced by those interested in folk horror, most recently in Richard Wells' *Damnable Tales* and Edward Parnell's *Ghostland*. Hardy's presence is however most keenly felt and referenced by Andrew Michael Hurley in *Starve Acre*, the title itself a reference to *Tess of the d'Urbervilles*, and in the work of Benjamin Myers, both of whom discuss Hardy in interviews. As Myers suggests in his introduction to *Damnable Tales*, Hardy is not normally associated with horror; indeed an aspect that is central to this book is that his work is far more unsettling than it is horrific (although there are elements of the latter). This is why his work is so significant to a folk horror lineage and one of the reasons that he has been previously sidelined. His work is suggestive of an early form of the genre, what might be identified as 'Hardyan Folk Horror', exactly because it seeks to unsettle and disturb rather than invoke a horrific response. This is a strand of folk horror which takes place in the daylight, in broadly ordinary circumstances which are made strange by the people who inhabit Wessex and particularly Egdon Heath.

Hardy's 'achievement' as an artist was to remain open to both reason and unreason, belief and disbelief, Gods and gods, the magical and the mundane. He can be found responding to the loss of a single over-riding religious meta-narrative with a rehabilitated paganism which imbues the landscape with its own inherent meaning. As Charles Taylor says: 'In face of the opposition between orthodox and unbelief, many, and among them the best and most sensitive minds, were cross-pressured, looking for a third way' (C. Taylor, *Sources of the Self: The Making of Modern Identity* 302). Hardy was of this number. Hardy embodies many of the complexities of the modern mind, and nothing in Hardy was more modern than his nostalgia for the pre-modern. In response to this tumult of social, cultural, philosophical and religious change, he invested himself in materials that remained beyond its reach.

Chapter 1 establishes the contextual framework of folk horror and establishes the characteristics of the genre through analysis of foundational critical works and the analysis of contemporary examples. This establishes key ambiguities in the definition and how the view of a 'Hardyan Folk Horror' functions. In many ways Hardy epitomized his age. He was caught in the intellectual and cultural crosscurrents, pulled by the competing claims of Christianity and Scientific Materialism, mourning his lost faith, haunted by the loss. Hardy was between intolerable extremes, most specifically between the 'picture-book Christianity' to which he could not return, and an atheism that rendered only a cold grey flat image of the world. One represented an unsupportable excess of meaning, the other threatened its total loss. Hardy may not have confessed to suffering dark nights of intellectual crisis but he did struggle to keep the disparate sides of himself together: the religious and the 'enlightened', the romantic and the realistic, the intellectual and the non-intellectual.

Hardy held these tensions in a rather unstable, that is, inconsistent, equilibrium. Whichever side of himself, Hardy cared to reveal its opposite could still show through. It is surprising to suggest that Hardy, often thought of as the most 'localized' of nineteenth-century English novelists, was in fact profoundly affected by a severe case of dislocation. Chapters 2, 3 and 4 debate the philosophical and theological context in which Hardy emerged: the contextual analyses, the context in which he worked. The focus in these chapters is to analyse how Hardy was haunted by his past and then how this manifested itself in his work. The contemporary concern with Hauntology is identified as something not so contemporary in that it is applied to Hardy's concern with the social structure and belief system of his past. That Hardy was 'time-torn' is developed in Chapters 4 and 5 and these debate Hardy's narrative form, and how this reflects his philosophical position. Even though Hardy's delivery of narrative at times anticipated the traits of twentieth-century literary modernism, Hardy was comfortable in his use of it in conveying the folkloric beliefs and practices of nineteenth-century Wessex. Hardy asserted that the subject matter of folk belief, often embodying the tropes of (what would later be defined as) folk horror, existed beyond and above traditional modes of literary representation. Chapters 4 and 5 analyse the darker elements of Hardy's work, his creation and evocation of landscape in Egdon Heath and the function of Wessex as a haunted county. Chapter 7 examines hardy in adaptation and in particular how that which can be seen to be connected to folk horror are supressed in the 1980s and 1980s as his work is subjugated by politicized manifestations of heritage. The presence of Hardy can still be felt in a contemporary line and the conclusion draws out parallels in P. J. Harvey's *Orlam* (2022).

1

Foundations: Towards a Hardyan folk horror

Folk horror is, in definition, a curiously modern concern. It is impossible to attempt a definition of the genre without reference to Mark Gatiss' 2010 documentary *A History of Horror* (Jardine) where he interviews director Piers Haggard who, it is often claimed, first uses the phrase. Although, as Dawn Keetley identifies, the 'two central designations of folk horror – in 1970 in *Kine Weekly* and in 2010 in Gatiss' documentary – helpfully mark what can be seen as the two waves of folk horror, each with their own representative texts' (Keetley, 'Defining Folk Horror' 1). This identification of two periods of folk horror, the latter defining the former, is the starting point for a contemporary understanding of the nature of the genre. The argument herein is, however, that there is a further preceding moment where folk horror, as it is defined in contemporary terms, can be seen. This is not a lineage which identifies its roots in M. R. James, Arthur Machen et al., although this strand is important and debated in other analyses. This is a line of folk horror which can be seen in the work of Thomas Hardy, which is more akin to a line of contemporary texts. [Many of the socio-political circumstances in which Thomas Hardy was writing are replicated in the 2020s.] As Keetley further notes in considering a definition:

> The first wave of folk horror extended from roughly 1968 to 1979 … The second wave began in roughly 2008 … [and] has moved in two directions – forward, shaping new incarnations, as well as backward, revisiting and reworking the defining folk horror texts from the late 1960s and 1970s.
>
> (Keetley, 'Defining Folk Horror' 1)

It is the vital function of looking back and reconsidering earlier texts as a methodological approach to considering the work of Hardy, where a further understanding of the context in which he was working and the form his work took benefit from a recognition of parallels.

There are inevitable differences between Hardy as a progenitor of folk horror and the burgeoning number of texts that appear in the late 1960s and 1970s or the volume of work being produced now, with a mass audience in mind. Looking forward there is much work being done on the international and transnational dimension of Folk Horror, particularly in New England (Walsh) (Hauke) and beyond (Thurgill, 'Strange Permutations, Eerie Dis/locations: On the cultural and geographic specificity of Japanese folk horror') (K. M. Johnson), but in origin the genre is peculiarly British. The political scene of the later 2000s arguably gave rise to what Andy Paciorek and Darren Charles would define and in turn promote as the 'Folk Horror Revival'. It is significant that much of the current interest in the form stems from a 'folk' interest which in turn can be identified as relating to class. The recurrence of class and social distinction as central to folk horror is paralleled in the context in which Hardy was writing and was something that affected him personally. This is an instance of a theme which is central – existing on borders and never quite belonging with a resultant sense of perennial unease.

Topographies

Hardy is a 'time torn man', as referenced in the title of Claire Tomalin's expansive biography and there is a similarity in the change in society that existed in the late nineteenth century. This is a period of dramatic social and philosophical upheaval with shifting patterns of rural to urban dwelling alongside rapid urbanization. The socio-political situation for many people in the early nineteenth century was unstable, where there was a clear separation between the rural and the urban, and subsequently away from tradition. The post-Empire world of the late 1960s proved to be equally unstable with Britain's place as 'the sick man of Europe' throwing political discourse about nation and status into doubt. In a period of slow economic and industrial decline, the representation of the past, and in terms of Britain this was a rural past, became a dark place. In the new millennium the question of Britain's status in the world has once again become a national concern and political tool. The resurgence of right-wing nationalism has given the past a more dangerous character in how it can be and is used. Whereas for some there is comfort in tradition, or at least a version of tradition and the past which suits, much writing about contemporary folk Horror in Britain refers inevitably to shifting notions of class, status and Britain's place in the world and particularly Europe. In these terms Brexit looms large. As Dan Coxon writes:

> Of course, these days it's almost impossible to discuss Britain, past or future, without Brexit rearing its scaly head ... Little did we know that two years later ... we would be shackled to it nonetheless. I'm reminded of a ride at Alton Towers called The Black Hole that I rode when I was a teenager, plummeting down through the darkness at such speeds that my stomach felt as if it was rising into my throat. That sensation of being in blind, rudderless freefall scared the shit out of me then – much as it does now.
>
> (Coxon, 5)

Folk horror, in whatever manifestation it might be, can include tea and scones but only if they precede a human sacrifice. This identifies something fundamentally political in a genre that has rarely been seen in such terms. As Todorov and Berrong identify, 'Genres, like any other institution, reveal the constitutive traits of the society to which they belong' (160). The political is being drawn into contemporary examples of the genre for example in *The Third Day* (HBO) which explicitly draws out the issue of race in relation to tradition in twenty-first-century Britain. However, to suggest that folk horror has only recently entered the political field would be to misunderstand its origins. It deals with fractures in belief and the overwhelming pressure of tradition as potentially malevolent and destructive. As Coxon states, 'The notion of "Britishness" is all too often marred by reactionary nationalistic sentiments, the chest-thumping of the far right or the "tea-and-scones" tweeness of Theresa May' (5). This has manifested itself into online campaigns of 'folklore against fascism', perhaps most notable in David Southwell's creation of 'Hookland' ('Hookland: High Weirdness from Britain's Lost County') which regularly rallies against reductive notions of tradition. (Southwell, 'Re-enchantment is resistance.') The function of folklore is central to this 'historical belief system'. Dawn Keetley identifies that whilst the:

> function of folklore in folk horror texts is complex but it is nonetheless critical to the task of defining folk horror ... One must not, however, take the 'traditions' of folk horror at face value. They are typically not 'authentic' traditions, although they may well be presented as such in the text.
>
> (Keetley, 4)

Many popular adaptations of Hardy confer a level of authenticity to the representation of folk culture and folk practices in his work. This is perhaps a symptom of the passage of time with authenticity ascribed by his being associated with (if not firmly in) the literary canon. Whilst it is without question that Hardy was part of a rural community as a child and would have absorbed some of these practices and beliefs, there is less clarity on what he has in turn created, or at least embellished. The passage of time grants authenticity to folklore as having authority, and the writer's presence in that time furthers this. There are contemporary parallels in the way that texts of the 1970s are now given the same status by their use by contemporary writers, as sources of the origin of contemporary folklore (Rodgers). A further level of credence is provided to this folklore precisely because the author was present and, at the time of publication, the audience also had it within living memory. This is to say that the present is being haunted by what went before, and recently. As Andy Sharp comments:

> Our perennial ruminations on war mean we are always just a heritage open day away from a sandbag and bunting re-enactment, overseen by the military gimp of an air-raid warden role-player. Rather than the faux pagan festivals of straw bears and hobby horses, the new land rites are happening on our D-Day visits to coastal forts.
>
> (Sharp, 51)

The cosy representation set in play by a thousand war films and endless reruns of *Dad's Army* (David Croft) on the television has taken a darker turn. There is a sense of us being haunted by our own past and by virtue of this 'spectral presence' the past has become distorted. This is something that this work will return to as a central theme and issue in Hardy's work.

Folk horror exists on philosophical fault lines between the recent past and the present and this manifests itself in topographical and ideological instabilities. This identifies a nuanced lineage of contemporary folk horror literature where the philosophical underpinning that informed Hardy's work is replicated, in a manner, towards the end of the twentieth century and into the twenty-first century. This can be seen by an increase in the references to Hardy in texts which draw on a landscape in which the eerie dominates and can be seen in Edward Parnell's *Ghostland:*

> In the geography of his imagined 'partly real, partly dream country' of Wessex it's a wild expanse, stretching much further than the actual heathland areas, known as Black Heath and Duddle Heath, that were within easy walking distance of the cottage in which he was raised in the hamlet of Higher Brockhampton, three miles east of Dorchester.
>
> (Parnell, 397)

In addition to Parnell visiting 'Wessex' in his braided memoir possibly, the most direct connection between Hardy and contemporary folk horror fiction is Andrew Michael Hurley's *Starve Acre* (2020). Hurley's work makes specific reference to *The House of Silence* (1886) in its preface. In 2019 Hurley discusses his technique and how he draws directly on Hardy (Liu). As does William MacGregor in the discussion of his debut film *Gwen* (2019),

> I love Thomas Hardy, and I love folk horror. I love suspicion, folklore, tradition, beliefs – how all that affects us. I love the gothic, and I love landscape and the sublime, and all of these things just compressed themselves into this one film.
>
> (Slater-Williams)

Genre tropes

It is impossible to discuss the genre without reference to Adam Scovell's *Folk Horror: Hours Strange and Things Dreadful*. Scovell's highly reflective text remains a foundational text for many reasons, chief amongst which is his identification of the 'Folk Horror Chain'. Most writing on the genre will in some way use or comment on this conceptual framework for the analysis. This is in part as his book seeks to cover a range of texts which, in generic terms, have a 'family resemblance' (Frow 59). These are rooted in the oft-quoted 'Unholy Trinity' of *The Wicker Man* (R. Hardy), *Witchfinder General* (Reeves) and *The Blood on Satan's Claw* (Haggard), where there are similarities but significant although subtle differences. The 'chain' provides an essential starting point in the reconsideration of aspects of Hardy's work.

1. Landscape: In this Scovell discusses topography as an essential part of place where there is a correlation between aspects of the landscape and the character of the people that inhabit that landscape. This is the function of Egdon Heath, a space which allows for isolation but also for a population which are at one with their environment. This evocation of space allows for the emergence of a key folk horror narrative trope – the appearance a stranger amongst strange people. The physical space of Wessex occupies what might be seen as a proto-generic space in which the rules are created and developed by the generation of more texts by Hardy himself. This is Scovell's application of psychogeography in his analysis of Arthur Machen, who was himself split between rural Wales and London; 'not only is Machen a writer of place but also a writer of time, both his own and that of "deep time", the vertigo-inducing expanse of the prehistoric past' (Coverley 59). This is a statement that could easily be made of Hardy in his construction of Wessex who was writing decades before Machen. Wessex is a place which could be seen to be part of an alternative history timeline, where Alfred

perhaps kept his power and the political future of Britain took a different line. Wessex derives some of its power to unsettle by the slippage between the real and the fiction. There is a feel of the Simulacra (Baudrillard) in Wessex and its relationship to Dorset; the two fade between each other. This instability of space between the real and the fictional extends to the potential for readers to feel as if their world intersects with the fiction; this is identified as the 'Spatial Hinge' by James Thurgill (Thurgill, 'Literary Geography and The Spatial Hinge' 152), where the topography of Wessex in a conceptual sense spills out into our world. This is furthered by a philosophical and theological connection as noted below in point 3 of the folk horror Chain.

2. Isolation: Andy Paciorek identifies that 'in considering isolation we have to remember that whilst it may in some instances relate to being out in the wilderness alone, it could also relate to being culturally or socially isolated for instance being a stranger among strange folk' (Packiorek) and this is evident in Hardy's evocation of Wessex. His description of landscape allows for the moments of isolation but there is a population ready to appear at any moment – in essence the plot of *The Three Strangers*. Outsiders can appear in a community, for example, in *The Fiddler of the Reels* with Mop Ollamor, but their presence is entirely accepted. The physical landscape also furthers the sense of isolation. Egdon Heath has to be crossed in order to enter this other world, to move from Dorset to Wessex and into this isolated place. This is the seaplane to Summerisle or the causeway in *The Loney* or *The Third Day*.

3. Skewed belief system: Whilst relatively self-evident in meaning there is variation in practice and is a further place where the two strands of folk horror can be seen to diverge, '.. forging a divide between tradition and modernity' (Keetley 5). This division in narrative form and particularly in cinema's rich folk horror tradition works as a perpetual opposition rather than as a dialectic. In *The Wicker Man* this is evident in the moment where, when confronted by a scientific challenge from Sergeant Howie, Lord Summerisle blinks. In this fleeting moment there is the acceptance of the creation of the rituals that have been used to underpin the rituals of Summerisle:

> CLOSE-UP – LORD SUMMERISLE
> His eyes reflect utter conviction.
>
> LORD SUMMERISLE
> (Shouting)
> But I know it will. It is the only way.
>
> He makes a gesture to the flambeaux bearers
> who step forward and light the brushwood

from huge buckets and barrels of flaming tar, and the flames leap upwards at The Wicker man. We:

CUT TO:

CLOSE-UP – HOWIE'S FACE
In front of which smoke is already beginning to drift.

HOWIE
(Shouting)
If the fruit fails again it will have to be a more important one than this one. Next year it may not be a stranger – no-one less than the King of Summerisle himself will do. Do you hear me Summerisle? If the crops fail your people will see to it that it is you who will burn next May Day.

CLOSE-UP – LORD SUMMERISLE'S FACE
For a fleeting moment it wears an expression of doubt and fear.
Miss Rose regards him speculatively.

(Shaffer)

still doesn't explain enough

In this moment there are questions about what belief system is skewed. For Lord Summerisle the facade slips and yet the belief system he has promoted continues for the islanders. It would be easy to see that this is the skewed belief; however, it is Sergeant Howie's Christian belief that also remains compromised. The two strands of belief continue to co-exist. Keetley suggests that this defining film, a member of the 'Unholy Trinity', is actually something of an outlier in the definition of the form. There is a strong line of folk horror where tensions exist in the co-existence of two contrary positions. In conventional narrative form the conflict, that is so fundamental at the heart of drama, is never resolved and this in itself has an unsteadying effect. This is perhaps why the forms that utilize this uneasy and unresolved narrative structure are notable in folk horror – short fiction and novellas with a restricted narrative forms and film and one-act television drama with time-based restriction on form. In Hardy's work there is a debate about how 'skewed' the value system is, as presented by the inhabitants of Wessex. However this is not simply a case of the rural folk believing something different to us. Hardy doesn't allow them to feel as alien as the Summerislanders; they are not even Lord Summerisle in his wavering belief system. They are people who, potentially like Thomas Hardy, hold two possible contradictory positions at the same time. The fear is in part engendered by the potential or even inevitability that this is reflective of us.

4. Summoning/happening: Whilst Scovell's work provides a fundamental framework for analysis, it highlights a crucial point of difference in the representation of summoning/happening. This is something that Scovell himself notes is the least consistent of the aspects of the chain. Hardy's work and subsequent 'Hardyan Folk Horror' texts operate through the belief in the summoning or the act or practising a system of belief where the efficacy of this has no material or verifiable outcome. This is clear in *The Withered Arm* and in practices in *Return of the Native*. Nothing ever happens as a result of the summoning; yet, the skewed belief system remains consistent in and for the characters. In his 2018 historical folk horror infused novel *The Gallows Pole*, Ben Myers evokes a similar approach. The novel has a 'rational' third person narrator and the folklore-infused perspective of David Hartley, a man literally of the earth:

> A Malkin an all I seen malkins stows of times up ont moors A Malkin been the man that's made of shirts stufft with straw to scare the crowes I seenum moving about thrae or for at a time at nite Circlin they were just like the stagmen done circlin And dansin and laffen too Onse I saw a malkin with his feat and hans on fyre On fyre they were And he was runnen Runnen across the moor as was as if to reech a tarn or sluice ditch to save himself from the friteful burnin And I say with my hand on the book I did heer that Malkin man scream becors even though he were maydde of straw and cloth there was life in him too and oh the sound he made it was like no man or annymul yoove ever heard Friteful it was.
>
> (Myers, *The Gallows Pole* 77)

In this moment the co-existence of two sets of beliefs IS clearly present. Hartley has no problem in believing he has seen scarecrows dancing on the moors and to prove this piece of incredible folk belief he suggests he is happy to swear on the Bible. These two systems of belief co-exist. This is the landscape that Hardy evokes in *The Return of the Native*:

> It seemed as if the bonfire-makers were standing in some radiant upper story of the world, detached from and independent of the dark stretches below. The heath down there was now a vast abyss, and no longer a continuation of what they stood on; for their eyes, adapted to the blaze, could see nothing of the deeps beyond its influence.
>
> (Hardy, 54)

This line of folk horror is then a subtly but fundamentally different one from that which stems from what might contentiously be identified as a line stemming from M. R. James. The discovery of the skull in *The Blood on Satan's Claw* (Haggard) draws on similar themes to the archaeological discovery in *Oh Whistle and I'll Come to You, My Lad* (1904) and has hints of the supernatural or of the 'old gods' (Hutton, 'Ronald Hutton on Folk Horror'). What both of these texts conjure is a sense of impending threat and violence. As James Thurgill suggests of folk horror authors, they:

> approach the rural (British) landscape as a commonly understood and singular entity, a process mirrored in their portrayal of the folk who inhabit it; these 'folk' are unmodern, superstitious and, above all, capable of enacting extreme violence in order to conserve the rural idyll.
>
> (Thurgill, 'A Fear of the Folk: On topophobia and the Horror of Rural Landscapes' 33)

Yet as they are portrayed in fictions, these 'folk' have certainties that are dangerously appealing. This is the 'ghost in the machine', the dangerous and alluring 'primitive' state that lurks in our psyche (Koeslter). As Derrida suggested, the collapse of the Berlin Wall didn't herald a new egalitarian future, rather the philosophical 'safety' of simple binarisms disappearing. The politically dangerous result would be to return to the security of an imagined past or a present 'Imagined Community' (Anderson) with all the certainties that this claims to provide. A Hardyan line of folk horror doesn't provide safety but instead provides succour in the evocation of perpetual unease: our past was no pastoral idyll and in turn the future will be no technological utopia.

'Wherefore is light given to him that is in misery'

In the preface to the *Wessex Tales*, Hardy discusses the narrative function of a character being 'Hag Ridden'. 'To my mind the occurrence of such a vision in the daytime is more impressive than if it had happened in a midnight dream' (XXI). In this he identifies what would later become a core feature of folk horror – it happens in daylight. Whilst not the only writer to have used this, the convention with horror was to use the fear of darkness or at least shadow. This can be seen carrying through to contemporary folk horror texts with a 'foundation' in *The Wicker Man* and a use in concurrent backwoods horror films in the 1970s in films such as *Deliverance* (Boorman) and

The Hills Have Eyes (Craven) (although these latter two lack other folk horror characteristics). The trope can be seen in the second wave *Midsommar* (Aster) where not only is the horror played out in daylight but it is bright idyllic sunlight. This is the aspect of the 'impressive' that Hardy identifies and uses throughout his depiction of Wessex. This serves to unsettle on a number of levels. Firstly it is unexpected, we little expect such horrors to occur in daylight. However one clear differentiating factor in, say, Michael Henchard selling his wife and daughter in the *Mayor of Casterbridge* or in Mop Ollamor disappearing with Ned and Car'line's child at the conclusion of *The Fiddler of the Reels* is that these behaviours are horrific precisely because they are pictured as ordinary. This is the essence of the skewed belief system; it is distorted by our measure, not by the measure of the people who accept it as natural. This is the context in which we are placed, we are the ones with the wrong belief system.

That which is horrific doesn't have to be graphic and is a further differentiating between a text such as *Deliverance*, as a piece of backwoods horror and Hardyan folk horror. *Deliverance* does share some folk horror traits with other texts but here the perpetration of the violence is seen and known to be wrong by the perpetrators; in fact, their pleasure is partly in their transgression. To the populous of a folk horror text, the skewed belief system is ours and therein lies the horror. In contemporary folk horror fiction such as *Water Shall Refuse Them* (L. M. Hardy), these traits continue. The world is painted as ordinary:

> Lying there, with the sunlight streaming into my bedroom, I wished I hadn't taken down the curtains, but I allowed myself to savour the early-morning sunshine before the temperature rose to an unbearable level. I lay there for a bit until the clamminess of the sleeping bag got too much and I swung myself out of bed.
>
> (McKnight Hardy, 32)

The light is both literal and metaphoric; the 'light of the world' has reached these places but has not superseded Beltane. The function of folklore as historic and the presence of a form of reality and regularity confirmed through the presence of daylight give folk horror a sense of authenticity which is central to its unsettling quality. This is where the timeslips so beloved of first wave folk horror become important, particularly in reference to either children's fiction (for example, *Astercote* (Lively)) or much of the work of Nigel Kneale or intersectional science-fiction folk horror that he inspired (for example, *Sapphire and Steel* (Hammond)). In many contemporary folk horror books, the timeslip is generated by our engaging with a text that is set in the recent past (within living memory) and by virtue of this forcing the two periods to co-exist.

This connection to that which is within living memory confers a sense of expressive authenticity:

> Champagne is authentic if it comes from a certain region of France ... By extension, the same is true for individuals. I am authentic if I am true to my heritage and if my life is a direct and immediate expression of my essential being, that is, if I am true to myself.
>
> (Lidholm 363)

In these terms the connection of Hardy to the work not only as author but as author who had direct experience of that of which he writes provides a sense of nominal authenticity to his work and by extension to writers now who appear to recall the work that they are writing about. In short they have provenance. This is something that connects Hardy to some contemporary folk horror writers. However, a sense of expressive authenticity is conveyed through 'a true expression of an individual's or a society's values and beliefs' (Dutton). The sense of expressive authenticity confers a different status on the reception of the text in addition to and beyond a sense of provenance. Its power to unsettle lies in relation to the work's proximity to lived experience or at least to the belief in this. As J. Barre Toelken identifies in his foundational work on folklore, 'Assuming the validity of the proposition dynamic variation is perhaps the most distinctive characteristic of folklore, I submit that any particular traditional item may be viewed very much as an animal in the evolutionary process' (98). Folklore is consistently evolving and that which has emerged in recent years has as much status and validity as that which emerged in the seventeenth century. Arguably it has more status given that it exists within living memory and that experience gives the impression of conferring status.

Hauntology and hauntings

Hardy's work is significant in that there is an uneasy co-existence of tradition and modernity and the pagan and Christian that is unsettling by their very co-existence. In these terms there is a lineage of contemporary folk horror writing which moves away from the dramatic conflict of the 'unholy trinity' and of the overtly spectral in favour of two worlds which bleed into each other and exist in perpetuity. The present is haunted by the past by virtue of it being within living memory. M. R. James and Hardy are both concerned with hauntings, but only one writes about ghosts as manifest. As contemporaries it is evident that they knew of each other's work. Edward Parnell notes that Florence Hardy recalls the sending of a Christmas card from Thomas to M. R. James after the former has read one of his ghost stories with enthusiasm. However, this appreciation of the work does not translate into Hardy emulating James, and the absence of the supernatural is a central trope in the definition of what can be defined as a Hardyan lineage of folk horror, where the themes and socio-philosophical context for Hardy's writing are in part replicated in the early 2000s onwards and where the narrative tropes that Hardy used fit contemporary concerns.

Tracy Hayes opens up a discussion of the gothic motifs running through Hardy's work. Her project to analyse the correspondence between M. R. James and Hardy is in development and she notes some of the differences between the two:

> Hardy's diffusion of Gothic motifs and taste for macabre folktales meant that he was able to provide much more concentrated instances of the bizarre and improbable than he could in his novels. Withered arms, devilish fiddle players and hideously defaced statues which make wives scream and faint are not the fare of general popular fiction.
> (Hayes, 'When Thomas Hardy Met M.R. James: An Evening of Ghosts and Gothic' 141)

These are people haunted by the world that exists around them; they are not haunted by ghosts but by the circumstances of their existence and belief. The Thomas Hardy Society organized a live performance of a meeting between the two authors. In terms of live performance there is something 'comfortable' in the tradition of the ghost story told around the fireside than does nothing to diminish its literary effect but has the potential to consign it to its Victorian roots. There is something to current, to prescient in folk horror that would make it too unsettling for an evening's entertainment.

In the Hardyan line, folk horror can be seen as relating explicitly to the human and where that which is supernatural is present only insofar as it is believed to exist by the characters in the text. This is something that is being lost by the extension of the definition of the genre into that which is clearly supernatural. It is therefore of note that there has been much work undertaken on the James, Machen and Algernon Blackwood as antecedents to the genre. There is clearly a lineage in their work through weird fiction, which also incorporates reference to H. P. Lovecraft, but these writers also tend towards the fantastic and/or supernatural, and this is where there is a fracture between what is now defined as folk horror:

> Folk horror has gained greater traction in a new century defined by financial crises, terrorist attacks and digital threats. It offers a double dose of nostalgia – not only for those wonderful novels of Alan Garner or Susan Cooper, which invited children to exist in worlds neither adolescent nor adult but simply other, or *Play for Today* episodes such as *A Photograph*

and *Penda's Fen,* or the uncompromising public information films of the 1970s – but also for a Hardy-esque idea of an England of foaming ale and romps in the hayricks during harvest, perhaps this time with the benefits of modern medicine and multiculturalism.

(Myers, 'Folk horror, a history: from The Wicker Man to The League of Gentlemen')

As Myers comments there is a feel of Hardy in the presentation of the rural in some 1970s British television. The adaptation of the Wessex Tales in 1973 saw the development of a series which allowed for a darkness in the stories to be presented to an audience with an appetite for the same. This was an era where the 'Unholy Trinity' was on screen at the cinema, where *Robin Redbreast* (McTaggart) had been shown as part of the Play for Today series and where Nigel Kneale's *Beasts* was in pre-production (Kneale). The 1960s had ended as a 'bad trip' and the retreat to the rural had taken a dark turn. 'The initial swathe of folkloric television texts in the 1970s was catalysed by the occult revival in the late 1960s' (Rodgers).

It is this world that in turn has inspired a generation of writers who are now engaged in the same process as Hardy – looking back to a childhood which was plagued by power cuts, economic strife and the rise of political extremism. They are writing about that which is in living memory. Some of this material has a level of humour and satire – *Discovering Scarfolk* (Littler) or *Scarred for Life*. Some of this is for a generation who grew with mass consumerism which grew in the 1950s and reached dizzying heights in the 1970s. Whilst global products were available, there was still a clear sense of national boundaries to many popular cultural texts. As Katy Shaw identifies, 'Culturally, odes to 1970s and 1980s culture comminated television, film, music, and fashion while, politically, the death of former Prime Minister Margaret Thatcher drew attention to the unresolved conflicts of those decades still active in English society' (13). Part of the 'haunting' is then a reconsideration of the change that was intended to happen at a moment of historical fracturing. Shaw identifies an 'end of the century' thinking that philosophers and critics such as Lyotard and Jameson had been predicting but in the end it was never realized. There are clear parallels with the world in which Hardy was writing. It is perhaps no accident that towards the close of the nineteenth century, in 1893, Hardy publishes *The Fiddler of the Reels*. In this the narrator casts his mind back to his youth and the Great Exhibition of 1851 features at the centre of the story. That great symbol of progress, industry and innovation has no effect on Wessex and the malevolent magic therein.

The rural Dorset focused world that Hardy grew up in and gave rise to his fiction is paralleled for a generation on a national scale: defined by Bob Fischer as 'The Haunted Generation'. In generating this concept, a culture 'addicted to its own material past' (Sweeney). This is the essence of Hauntology as identified by Derrida and defined by Mark Fisher (*Ghosts of My Life: Writings on Depression, Hauntology and Lost Futures*) and Simon Reynolds (*Retromania*). Whilst prevalent in its reference to television products and present in popular television programmes such as *The League of Gentlemen* (Bendelack) and *Inside Number 9* (Pemberton), these ideas have found a place in popular fiction, themselves referring back to a time of seeming innocence. Will McLean's *The Apparition Phase* makes direct reference to the 1970s classic children's book *The World of the Unknown: Ghosts* (Maynard), Andrew Michael Hurley pays reference to *Commando* comics, beloved of many '70s youths (Hurley, The Loney) and Lucie McKnight Hardy's *Water Shall Refuse Them* takes us back to a visceral hot summer where childhood belief is made real. Richard Littler's creation of Scarfolk includes narrative texts, a 1970s annual (Littler, *The Scarfolk Annual*) and a map (Littler, *Scarfolk & Environs: Road & Leisure Map for Uninvited Tourists*) furthering the authentic sense of place. There is an overlaying of Scarfolk and a 'real' 1970s in the same way that Hardy overlays Wessex on the Dorset of his childhood. Part of being 'haunted' by this period is the belief that the horrifying drawings present in *Usborne World of the Strange: Ghosts* might just possibly be real. This haunting is present in Hardy's work. The objects of belief are perhaps less tangible; they exist on the edge of an oral tradition rather than reprinted and sold in bookshops, but the effect is very similar. The object that haunts contemporary folk horror, the popular culture of the 1970s and 1980s, is that which was intended to be disposable and is arguably that which is the preserve of a largely urban working class. This is a parallel to Hardy's evocation of his Wessex childhood where there are tensions between the rural working class, urban working class, a traditional land owning class and an educated urban middle class. In these terms the former holds 'traditional' beliefs. Where, for a 'haunted generation' in the twenty-first century, the material culture is captured in plastic and recording of television for Hardy, the material culture was the soil and the loam of his upbringing.

In 2010 when Folk Horror was being defined his work was still held back by a 'Merchant Ivory' heritage representation, the world of adapted fiction was becoming darker but Hardy had yet to receive this revision to their representation. Indeed Hardy's presence was perhaps most keenly felt on road signs heading into Dorset where we are welcomed to 'Hardy Country'. In recent years there have been signs that this view is changing. The world of contemporary fiction has embraced the dark potential of 'haunted landscapes' (Heholt) as is present in much contemporary literature and is exemplified in a text such as Jenn Ashworth's use of Pendle Hill in *Old Trash* which functions in terms of both topography and myth. The implied reference to the witch trials is clear and sits behind a troubled relationship between mother and daughter.

Hardyan folk horror

The strands that emerge in the twenty-first-century British folk horror revival each have a subtly different character. All in some form conform to the folk horror chain as devised and exemplified by Adam Scovell and exemplified by the *Folk Horror Revival* website and series of Wyrd Harvest published books. What this suggests is the potential emergence of sub-genres of folk horror which, given the length of its existence (regardless of definition), is no surprise. This is not just then an exercise in categorization but rather a recognition that these distinct sub-genres have emerged in an interrelationship between context, discursive practice and artistic endeavour. As Todorov suggests of genres, 'They are not, however, merely meta-discursive entities – not just arbitrary names – since they have properties that can be described' (17).

Hardyan Folk Horror then builds on the principles as outlined by Scovell. This includes:

- The perpetual co-existence of two or more different states of being or philosophical positions.
- The absence of the supernatural or 'summoned' but the perpetual belief in this. Folklore is given equivalent status to science or established religion.
- The landscape as threatening because of its pastoral quality.
- The creation of a story world as a simulacra, where not only is there a difficulty in seeing the line between the real and the fictional but where the two fade between each other.
- People haunt themselves by engaging with the recent past – that is within living memory.
- The creation and legitimization of an 'authentic' world by reference to some form of personal 'provenance', which can include personal and/or cultural memory.
- There is an inclusive narrative where the boundaries of the world exist beyond the edges of the text.

These traits can be seen in the work of many contemporary writers. This is not to say that all the work of particular writers fits within a folk horror categorization but rather there are particular works which exemplify the identified traits and contribute to the development of folk horror as a parent genre in the twenty-first century. These include texts such as Max Porter's *Lanny*, Zoe Gilbert's *Folk*, Tom Cox's *Help the Witch* and some of the stories in *Hag* (Larrington). These texts create a world in which folktale becomes real. This is the invented landscape that, whilst rooted in recognizable folklore, is fantastic in presentation. Stories such as 'Sour Hall' (Booth) carry their power in part by the reuse of folktales and their presence becomes foregrounded in the text; by the very nature of the collection *Hag* is deftly politicizing folktales not weaving them into its background. This is equally true of hybrid genre work such as *Melmoth* (Perry), *The Essex Serpent* (Perry) and *The Gallows Pole* (Myers). These texts might be very broadly described as historical folk horror fiction and are where the 'authentic' past is created/evoked but where it sits outside living memory.

It is in texts where the present and past co-exist and where the conflict of differing belief systems perpetually exists that it is possible to see the presence of a form of Hardyan Folk Horror: *Devils' Day* (Hurley), *The Loney* (Hurley), *Pine* (Toon), *Water Shall Refuse Them* (L. M. Hardy), *How Pale the Winter Has Made Us* (Scovell), *Fell* (Ashworth) and *Fen* (D. Johnson). What is of note is how many of these texts appear in and around 2016, perhaps being conceptualized around the defining moments of the genre in question. As there is increasing confirmation that the promise of the future isn't going to materialize and that the old battles still rage, it is perhaps no surprise that we remain haunted by our recent past. There seems no slowing of appetite for folk horror, and many of the aforementioned are being adapted for television series and as audio dramas. New works continue to be produced which follow in this line, for example, *Witch Bottle* (Fletcher), *Villager* (T. Cox) and the graphic novel, *Lip Hook* (Stafford). Audiences at large seem comfortable with drama that reflects the world in which we live in, given that it seeks to unsettle and provide no answers. As for Hardy, we are split between different times and belief systems and as such we are drawn to fiction where this is not debated but rather where it is reflected.

2

Haunted Hardy

The title of Claire Tomalin's 2006 biography of Thomas Hardy encapsulates her subject in a single phrase: *The Time-Torn Man*. The image it presents is of someone painfully stretched across the span of years, a mind straining to hold together past and present, wholly inhabiting neither. In many ways Hardy existed between worlds, his identity forged in his transit across boundaries of class and culture. Born into a poor rural family, he rose to literary eminence drawing on his experiences of the deep-rooted but precarious agricultural world he had left behind. The son of a builder, he built fictional worlds inspired and shaped by the memories stored up in childhood. This presence of the past in the contemporary may seem like a mere function of memory, a use of experience in the construction of fiction. However, it is far more central to Hardy's work given the experiences he had and the context in which he had them. There are parallels with contemporary folk horror writers working in a 'Hardyan' manner and drawn on the essentially hauntological in the construction of the work. The manifestation of the past in the present is not via literal hauntings but rather by the opening of a portal through which the past can be seen. The sense is of being haunted by yourself, or at least by a cultural past that is specific and in which you were involved. For Hardy this is his rural past and for the contemporary writer a 1970s past which is more broadly shared by virtue of the expansive nature of consumer culture.

Spectres of the past

Hardy was not merely nostalgic for the past. He was haunted by it, and by the longing for something eerily familiar, yet endlessly strange. His sense of self was constantly in danger of slipping between selves old and new. As a writer he was predisposed towards what is ghostly in human experience, the gaps in established reality, the frisson of otherness found even in the most ordinary things. The imagination itself has a ghostly agency, with the power to relive the past and summon up the dead. With his predilection for hanging around with ghosts, Hardy effectively haunted himself. This is the essence of Hauntology as preliminarily outlined by Jaques Derrida:

> It [the specter] affects and bereaves it in advance, like the ghost it will become, but this is precisely where haunting begins. And its time, and the untimeliness of its present, of its being "out of joint." To haunt does not mean to be present, and it is necessary to introduce haunting into the very construction of a concept. Of every concept, beginning with the concepts of being and time. That is what we would be calling here a hauntology.
>
> (Derrida, 5)

This is a definition reiterated and refined by arch critic of hauntology, Mark Fisher, in the new millennia. In Fisher's terms to be haunted is to have sense of the 'spectre' without its physical presence being felt. This is a moment of distinction from forms of supernatural fiction where the ghost is manifest. In hauntological fiction the spectre is felt by characters but not seen by the reader. As Merlin Coverley identifies:

> For Fisher ... there are two opposing temporal currents intrinsic to hauntology: the no longer and the not yet. The former haunts the present from the past, an event, idea or entity whose moment is past but which continues to make its presence felt. The latter haunts the present from the future, through the unfulfilled promise of that which never comes to pass but which may yet do so.
>
> (Coverley, 11)

At the heart of this conception of Hauntology is the presence of the recent past, indeed to exemplify the nature of the spectral Derrida draws on Hamlet and in particular the ghostly presence of his father (5). This personal connection to the recent past is something that contemporary critics cite as the intrusion of the 1970s and 1980s. However, the drawing in of the recent past in times of social and economic change is a feature of Hardy's work and a further manifestation of him being 'time torn'. The spectre then becomes a metaphorical manifestation. Hardy was no poltergeist chaser, nor was he drawn to the Victorian craze for spiritualism. He was a realist, but a realist for whom reason had its limits, for whom reality retained a halo of uncertainty. Hardy was no fantasist, and yet the mundane world continued to carry the possibility of the fantastic. Something remained potential in life that neither Enlightenment reason nor Romantic idealism quite captured – something he found expressed in the folk idiom of story, song and ritual in which he was immersed as a child. It was a haunting music playing continually in the background. It echoes through his Wessex tales.

Hardy the stranger

Thomas Hardy wasn't expected to live. Born in 1840, into a poor family in the rural Dorset village of Bockhampton, he was a sickly child, and not thought likely to survive. As he grew up, his bookish and solitary nature continued to set him apart and made him something of an exception within the family and the wider village community. Physically unsuited to the rigours of manual labour, but exhibiting a marked aptitude for learning, unique opportunities and wider horizons opened up for him. At the age of sixteen he was given an early taste of freedom, living and working independently in Dorchester, as an articled trainee in John Hick's architect's office. From then on Hardy lived something of a double life, straddling the distance between 'village boy' and 'young-man-about-town'. The distance only increased with time. In 1862 he made the bold decision to leave Dorset and find work in the capital. He became a self-professed 'Londoner' and for five years immersed himself in the very different sights and sounds, rhythms and routines, of the teaming metropolis. The professional middle-class milieu of Blomfield's architectural business was another clear step away from Bockhampton. As a young woman, Hardy's mother had also known life in London, but as a servant. This humble background probably remained obscure to his new colleagues and acquaintances (Tomalin 69).

In 1870, Hardy's courtship of Emma Gifford opened a new front of potential discomfort. Meeting her in distant Cornwall, in a professional capacity, he seems to have been less than fully frank about his family circumstances. The need to keep these various worlds apart continued well into married life. Fidelity to one side always ran the risk of disloyalty to the other. Hardy never disowned his family, but his personal situation had changed beyond all recognition, whereas theirs had not. His father and brother remained working men, and he still had cousins in domestic service. On holidays in Bockhampton, the would-be novelist worked on manuscripts in the cramped confines of a shared bedroom. Even when he was earning large sums from international publishers and winning earnest respect from senior literary figures, Hardy's social status remained anomalous. Without a university education, he never felt at ease in establishment circles. Emma's own lack of refinement frequently gave rise to embarrassment. When calling on the eminent critic Leslie Stephens or visiting his parents, Hardy's wife was equally unwelcome. Issues of identity and place never ceased to be tender. Having migrated from the rural working class into the professional ranks, and then into the strange condition known as 'being an author', Hardy's sense of self was understandably attenuated and under strain. For a man who became renowned as a major 'novelist of place' he had reason to feel remarkably unsure of where he truly belonged. There is a striking entry in Emma's diary of 18th June 1876, following a trip to Germany: 'going back to England where we have no home and no chosen country'.

It suggests Hardy was less securely rooted in his native environment than might typically be imagined.

In addition to class insecurity, Hardy was troubled by the spectre of estrangement: not just the prospect of separation from his beloved rural landscape and its people, but alienation from an essential part of himself. His fiction repeatedly reveals a fascination and acute sensitivity to the melancholy condition of 'the returning native':

> The figure of Mr Lackland was seen at the inn, and in the village street, and in the fields and lanes about Upper Longpuddle, for a few days after his arrival, and then, ghost-like, it silently disappeared. He had told some of the villagers that his immediate purpose in coming had been fulfilled by a sight of the place, and by his conversation with its inhabitants: but that his ulterior purpose – of coming to spend his latter days among them – would probably never be carried out. It is now a dozen or fifteen years since his last visit was paid, and his face has not again been seen.
>
> (Hardy, *A Few Crusted Characters* 224)

Hardy was haunted by the notion of coming home to find himself a stranger. Mr Lackland is a modern prodigal in search of an idealized past and a place of homecoming, but finding only disconnection and emptiness. Absence has severed the ties that bound him to the 'inhabitants' of the village. Othered by time, he both can and cannot 'return'. It isn't possible to step twice into the waters of Upper Longpuddle. Like a tourist, he mysteriously appears and disappears. He's a lost soul, ghosting in and out of their lives, fading from sight, leaving behind him no more than vague puzzlement. The allegorical explicitness of his name places him in the realm of abstraction. Hardy's fear of finding himself 'a foreigner at home' was more existential than filial, an aspect of the wider crisis of identity brought on by the shifting uncertainties of modernity. Once freed from the limits of nature and custom, free to choose oneself, what remained to bind an individual to the world?

If 'Lackland' is a fate Hardy avoided, it may be because his vital connection with the past didn't really depend on anyone else. He maintained it creatively, by private imaginative means, erecting memorial defences against any loss of material attachment. Nevertheless, the fear stalks his writing. In the effort to become 'someone' to the world it was possible to become 'no one', unrecognized by those you left behind. Hardy was a man betwixt and between, left painfully exposed in a middle ground, neither a man of earthly toil nor one of college learning. Worldly success meant he could no longer share in the rhythms and customs of his childhood. Recollection of that childhood, and the life it had showed him, sat uneasily with the values and attitudes of the educated elite into whose company he increasingly advanced. This manifested itself as a pull towards the past, both his own and that of his forebears. There are eerie future echoes of this in Mark Fisher's idea of 'The Slow Cancellation of the Future' (*Ghosts of My Life: Writings on Depression, Hauntology and Lost Futures* 2). In this Fisher recasts the recent past as being forever locked in battle with the future. What he describes as a 'familiar narrative' is established in the late nineteenth century and captured by Hardy; 'it is a matter of the old failing to come to terms with the new' (7). This transition was, for Hardy, profound. This is not as simple as the complexity of moving from one class to another by virtue of his job. His early life was spent in a situation where there was a separation between the urban and rural working classes and the emergence of urban middle classes as distinct from the landed classes of his rural Dorset background. Hardy was therefore an author who had to negotiate a number of social positions and class distinctions at once. This in itself suggests perpetual conflict.

The answer to the problem of preserving the past and moving into the future was to be a writer. Inevitably, the workingman's cottage and village life became increasingly 'remembered', but those memories could be reconstructed and revivified in words. The architect could return home through fictions of his own construction. There the past could reappear in ghostly fashion, affirming what had once been, mourning what was now lost. Underlying the theme of the returning native is the disappearance of a way of life. Leave it and it might be gone forever. Look away and it might be gone. Hardy's Wessex is located in this haunted space, suspended between worlds of past and present, innocence and experience. It is a liminal zone where ancient and modern meet, where the divergence between imagination and reality is negotiated. Life ghosts into memory, memory into art; and the art becomes an alternative reality, an otherworldly realm partaking of both, limited by neither. If Hardy's identification with the people and landscape of rural Dorset remained unbroken, it was because he was so adept at living across these divisions, and then releasing the psychological pressure into his characters, country people living lives both rooted in necessity and yet inwardly propelled beyond its constraints. If we often find them struggling to reconcile the contradiction 'between custom and education, between work and ideas, between love of place and experience of change' (Williams 197), it's because their author had to wrestle with the problem in his own being.

For Hardy the writer there were other stresses to reconcile, as he found himself pulled between the twin poles of realism and romance. His need to appeal to a genteel readership was a steady inducement to produce dreamier versions of the world he knew. His first and greatest commercial success, *Far from the Madding Crowd* (1874), indulges in more than a little idealization of labouring life, and he isn't above making his country-folk comical. He may have had direct knowledge of the hardships and precariousness of rural life, and he couldn't fail to register the fluctuating economic fortunes of agricultural communities, but he also knew how little his readers relished serious analysis of social realities or the working conditions among the country poor. There are parallels in contemporary discourse in relation to the past where the evocation of hardship is one of honour, sacrifice and authenticity. This can be seen in some of the discourse of the twenty-first century with reminiscence of the Second World War in particular taking a prominent role. The hardships of the middle of the twentieth century are re-created with rosy nostalgia and the far right's evocation of a mythic isle where everyone knew their place is perpetuated. This can be seen in the evocation of 'the folk' in classic examples such as *The Wicker Man*, where there is deference to Lord Summerisle because of his class status.

Hardy's attachment to local lore and legend has been represented as quaintly antiquarian, merely devoted to the preservation of tradition recollected in 'the Mead of Memories', but he fully understood that he was living through a moment which would see these age-old patterns and practices pass away. Hardy's imagination dwelt on the pre-industrial past, but he neither opposed the steam engine nor imagined that 'progress' it could be halted. He upheld tradition against the menacing encroachment of the outside world, bearing witness to the sympathetic quality of time-worn things, but he didn't delude himself or his readers about the direction the world was travelling. Implicitly or explicitly, Hardy's fiction expresses a profound cultural tension between a heartfelt attachment to tradition and a fascination with its inevitable demise. His fiction has always promised readers a reconnection with something antique or primal, but it also presents the dramatic human struggle within time itself: the continual conflict between continuity and change. What is more, he gives this ghostly drama a local habitation and a name: Wessex.

In Hardy's most positive mood, the description of sheep-shearing in *Far from the Madding Crowd* (1874) celebrates a living energy capable of surviving an age of change:

> The old barn embodied practices which had suffered no mutilation at the hands of time. Here at least the spirit of the ancient builders was at one with the spirit of the modern beholder. Standing before this abraded pile, the eye regarded its present usage, the mind dwelt upon its past history, with a satisfied sense of functional continuity throughout – a feeling almost of gratitude, and quite of pride, at the permanence of the idea which had heaped it up. The fact that four centuries had neither proved it to be founded on a mistake, inspired any hatred of its purpose, nor given rise to any reaction that had battered it down, invested this simple grey effort of old minds with a repose, if not grandeur, which a too curious reflection was apt to disturb in its ecclesiastical and military compeers ... This picture of today in its frame of four hundred years ago did not produce that marked contrast between things ancient and modern which is implied by the contrast of date.
>
> (Hardy, *Far from the Madding Crowd* 195)

The curious continuity of the past, secretly and silently persisting in the present, is another spectral dimension in Hardy's imagination. The ancient barn enshrines an animating spirit binding together a common culture of thought and action. An idea erected the building, and the building carries forward the idea. Its survival justifies that idea, and attests to the healthy ecology of thought and action, builder and barn, sheep and shearer, history and habit. It does not stand outside time, but expresses a relationship with time that stands in contrast to an age of social revolutions and rapid technological change. Observing the mass migration of the working population during decades of unprecedented urban expansion, it was radical *dis*continuities that preoccupied the Victorian Age. Nevertheless, the idea or image of a life-force, maintained in practice or memory, or merely in fiction, had a strange power to seize the mind.

The pathos of Lackland has a semi-comic counterpoint in *The Mayor of Casterbridge* (1886), where Donald Farfrae, the ingenious Scot, is forever 'giving the impression to a song of his dear native country that he loved so well as never to have revisited it' (78). Farfrae appears as if out of nowhere. He is just passing through, his ultimate intention being to emigrate abroad. The reforming energy that triumphs over Casterbridge and its mayor is related to his inherent rootlessness, his entirely voluntary relation to time and place. He is his own man, belonging to nothing greater than himself. Home everywhere, and nowhere. He is an image of modernity, essentially detached from the land and traditional patterns of engagement, a spirit moving in across the surface of things, transient, restless, ghostly.

The spirit of place

As the title suggests, *The Return of the Native* (1878) bears directly on the abiding themes of place and belonging, continuity and change. The novel re-tells the archetypal story of the special child who, having left home to find his fortune, returns with big and improved ideas, a prophetic message from the world beyond. Clym Yeobright turns his back on Paris and a successful career in the diamond trade to become a schoolmaster ministering to the local poor of Egdon. He represents a modern intellectual type, sensitive to tradition, but committed to social improvement. However, his idealism is frustrated, not so much by human antagonists, as by the innate hostility of the place itself. The central character of the novel is the Heath, the background against which everything takes place. As 'home' it's curiously inhospitable and peopled with strangeness. Its spirit is embodied in the bizarre figure of Diggory Venn, 'the Reddleman', stained from head to foot by the substance of his trade, the red ochre used by farmers to mark their sheep. Dyed like the beasts of the field, red as the devil, he is an emanation of the landscape, imbued with a natural resourcefulness and instinctive aboriginal assurance, at one with the terrain in knowledge and feeling. Eustacia Vye, reckoned by many to be a witch, roams the Heath with her spyglass and hourglass, symbolic instruments of unnatural vision and deathliness. Driven by desire or desperation, these and other characters move across the landscape (variously heat-exhausted or snake-bitten, frantically signalling or recklessly in pursuit of one another) in a tangled knot of tragic misunderstanding and mischance. The Heath resists enlightened change and reduces Clym to eking out a living with his bare hands, reabsorbing him into itself. The human drama seems of less importance than the idea of a place animated by a spirit that claims, possesses and works through the people living there. One of the unsettling features of this and other novels is the spectacle of characters utterly assimilated to the landscape.

At the same time, Hardy's greatest novels leave a sinister impression of a hostile and alien terrain, soaked in hardship and suffering. Hardy has some claim to be the national poet of pessimism. He may have been blessed with a twinkling eye for 'life's little ironies', but he was also possessed with the gloomiest view of the world. His most celebrated novels exude a notoriously bleak outlook. Some early works, like *Under the Greenwood Tree* (1872), are jolly and bucolic enough, but for that very reason they seem less 'authentically Hardy' than the later doom-laden narratives of *The Mayor of Casterbridge* (1886) and *Tess of the d'Urbervilles* (1891), in which hopes are briefly kindled precisely for the purpose of seeing them cruelly dashed. Most notoriously *Jude the Obscure* (1895) plumbs the depths of despair, expressing the nihilistic desire 'not to be'. It proved too dark even for his most loyal readership, and the criticism he received caused him to abandon the novel form altogether. There are perverse pleasures in pessimism. At a psychological level it can represent something of a refuge. It provides the comfort of feeling 'undeceived' and the security of being braced for the worst. But in his last novels Hardy goes beyond the realist obligation to look things squarely in the face. He seems intent on menacing his central characters. They go entirely unprotected, not only from the harsh realities of the prevailing social order, but from the author's own savage imagination. To most readers, the suffering heaped on Tess and Jude feels gratuitous and wilful. The treatment metered out to them is well in excess of that required to make them victims of tragic misfortune. Hardy seems intent on sacrificing them on the altar of a sadistic God to enforce a moral point about the Universe. Faced with the spectacular cruelties of *Jude the Obscure*, even a seasoned critic like Edmund Gosse, a fervent friend and admirer of the novelist, could reasonably ask: 'What has Providence done to Mr Hardy that he should rise up in the arable land of Wessex and shake his fist at his Creator?' (Gibson 107). Given the context in which he was working this suggests that Hardy was interested in building in a 'skewed belief system' (Scovell, *Folk Horror: Hours Dreadful and Things Strange* 18). This is rooted in a philosophical gulf where misfortune is heaped upon characters as a result of an absent God and where the manifestation of folklore becomes a belief in something far more tangible and, given its provenance, something much more real.

In shaking his fist at the heavens Hardy strikes a suitably Shakespearean pose. His imaginary landscape often resembles King Lear's Blasted Heath. Both are symbolic spaces for the figuration of a metaphysical vacancy, for radical abandonment in a barren and Godless world. Tess upon Salisbury Plain is like Lear wandering amid ancient stones, orphaned and unhoused. The space that Hardy creates is one which is isolated and where the moral framework therein furthers the sense of isolation. This is not necessarily the creation of a natural space which is threatened by lightening or other forms of physical danger. The potential for horror is furthered precisely because the space is, at first glance, an idyll, but the 'implication is actually that it is an inhospitable place because it is in some way different from general society as a whole and not simply because of a harsher topography' (Scovell, *Folk Horror: Hours Dreadful and Things Strange* 17). Both Shakespeare's Globe and Hardy's Wessex stage human dramas ringed by an annihilating darkness. There are unclear boundaries to these spaces, edges to the world which cannot be seen and by virtue of that they blend with our world; however, these are places where different rules apply. This allows the expansive presentation of Wessex to become claustrophobic and oppressive – a place where horrors can take place; '… elements of its topography have adverse effects on the social and moral identity of its inhabitants' (17).

It's striking then to reflect on Hardy's popular image as 'a man of place'. No English writer is more intimately associated with a specific portion of the English landscape. His name will be forever associated with this particular and intensely observed geography. The sights and sounds of his Dorset childhood echo throughout his writing in prose and poetry. The physical landmarks and behavioural patterns of ordinary country life that structure his novels belong to his earliest experience and sense of identity. These realities are re-orchestrated and aestheticized out of novelistic necessity, but they represent the foundations of his sensibility. The Wessex that Hardy forms from these memories is essentially a simulacra. The unsettling effect is not in the differences but rather in the similarities. Very much like China Mieville's creation of Beszel and Ul Qoma in *The City and the City* (2009), Wessex and Dorset slip into each other, the uncanny giving way to the weird, to 'the conviction that this does not belong' (Fisher, *The Weird and the Eerie* 13). Critics and biographers have sought to answer Gosse's question in terms of the private stresses and frustrations within the author's own psyche, in terms of a 'raging, wounded inner self who chastized the values of the world he inhabited' (Tomalin 218) Some have attributed Hardy's 'inner rage' to his own social displacement. Despite his fiction being richly imbued with 'a sense of place', in many ways Hardy was a highly dislocated figure.

Socially speaking he was an awkward anomaly, neither one thing nor the other; the son of a Dorset builder turned celebrated author and household name. Yet neither his remarkable creative genius, nor his commercial success made him eligible for comfortable inclusion into the highest society, and he knew that lacking the polish of a university education he would never be fully accepted as a gentleman. In him too, the past governed the present, ineradicably exerting its arbitrary force.

Hardy was certainly alive to inequality and injustice, but the stories of Michael Henchard, Tess d'Urberville and Jude Fawley reflect more than the distorting values of conventional society, they speak to something misshapen in the universe. Like their author they are embedded in a traditional environment and yet subject to the characteristic modern sense of abandonment within it. Hardy wasn't the only major nineteenth-century novelist to cast a cold and distrustful eye on the workings of the modern world. What distinguishes him is that unlike a Dickens or a Wells he wasn't taking his readers into the industrial or commercial labyrinth of the city. Instead, Hardy reveals the dark heart of the English countryside, nakedly exposing the physical hardships of the landscape. Hardy was no naïve arcadian. He resisted the Romantic notion that Nature itself provides spiritual support. In his poem 'In the Wood' (*Wessex Poems and Other Verses* 56), Hardy expresses this anti-Wordsworthian feeling. Having sought relief from the oppression of the city, the poet reports finding the realm of nature even worse. All he can see is furious competition. All nature is embroiled in a wild Darwinian struggle. He ends cheerlessly:

> Since, then, no grace I find
> > Taught me of trees,
> Turn I back to my kind,
> > Worthy as these.
> There at least smiles abound,
> There discourse trills around
> There, now and then, are found
> > Life-loyalties

The 'now and then' is not exactly a resounding endorsement of human society, but it represents the only source of light in the face of Nature's disinterest.

Such a view has its melancholy consolations. But Hardy's notorious negativity was more than a dismal personal temperament securing for itself a layer of psychological insulation. It reflects in dramatic form the profound trauma of his age. Hardy's gloom was Victorian pessimism writ large. His reverence for place and custom always co-existed with a personal scepticism regarding humanity in general. Like the milkmaids he describes in *Tess of the d'Urbervilles*, Hardy 'had been reared in the lonely country nooks where fatalism is a strong sentiment' (203). At a personal level his gloomy outlook came directly from witnessing the privations of the rural poor. There were those who owned land, and those who worked it. And the one often treated the other as an inferior species.

A hanging

[handwritten: good job setting the scene]

Victorian England was a violent place. It retained the stocks and invented the workhouse. The brutal spectacle of public hanging continued its double function as legal deterrent and public entertainment. Hardy's father remembered when 'he had seen four men hanged only for being with some others who set fire to a rick, one of them a half-starved boy who had run up to see the blaze and who weighed so little that they had to put weights on his feet to break his neck' (Tomalin 22). The idea stuck in his son's mind and is a detail woven into 'The Withered Arm' as an alarming example of arbitrary injustice.

Hardy himself remembered how, as a boy of sixteen, first working in Dorchester, he had witnessed the execution of a woman called Martha Browne. In a letter written in 1926, he could still vividly recall both the image and the shame he felt at having witnessed the event: 'I remember what a fine figure she showed against the sky as she hung in the misty rain, and how the tight black silk gown set off her shape as she wheeled half-round and back' (*The Collected Letters Vol. 2 1893–1901 VII 5*). Hardy's account has drawn comment from critics like Robert Gittings, reacting to the way his memory aestheticized the image of the dying woman. But in responding to her appearance, Hardy is registering what made the image multiply incongruous to him. The haunting confluence of death and beauty heightens the poignancy of the scene. A young mind disturbed by its implications would seize on details it could deal with. Witnessed with a mixture of horror and fascination, and with the feeling of being implicated in the ritual, the woman's 'crime' is less prominent than the collective iniquity shared by all present. The image scarred his memory and remained a source of shameful regret for the rest of his days.

Hardy's imagination developed a correspondingly macabre streak that comes out most clearly in his short fiction. In 'The Three Strangers' (1883) a man on his way to work just happens to be a hangman. In 'The Withered Arm' (1888) a woman suffers an infirmity that only a hangman's victim can cure. In *Barbara of the House of Grebe* (1891) a man torments his wife by creating and destroying an effigy of her lover. Each tale is dramatized to bring out the strangeness lurking within ordinary things and reflects Hardy's lifelong fascination with hanging, deformity and emotional bewitchment.

The case of Horace Moule

Most biographers agree that Hardy's friendship with Horace Moule was the most influential intellectual relationship of his life. Hardy was seventeen when he became acquainted with the Moules, a highly respected, deeply conventional and staunchly religious Dorset family; the father was the country parson in Fordington near Dorchester, his sons mostly churchmen. But it was the fourth son, Horace, who 'took virtual control of Thomas Hardy's life in the year 1857, not only as a teacher but as a friend' (Gittings, *The Young Thomas Hardy* 37). Only eight years Hardy's senior, he was already an accomplished musician, a gifted classical scholar, a published critic and poet: 'Horace Moule's impact upon Hardy was immense. He was handsome, charming, cultivated, scholarly, thoroughly at home in the glamorous worlds of the ancient universities and of literary London' (Millgate, *Thomas Hardy: A Biography* 67).

Acting as unofficial tutor, Moule brought Hardy into contact with the academic learning denied him by his social circumstances. He helped Hardy grapple with Greek, and introduced his protégé to new books and the latest ideas (Millgate, *Thomas Hardy: A Biography* 66). In education and class Moule had advantages which Hardy lacked, but as a local man he stood as proof that a connection could be made between a remote provincial setting and the literary metropolitan world beyond. Moule was a window onto a larger, otherwise inaccessible world. But that window also offered a dark prospect. Moule had his demons, surfacing in recurrent cycles of depression and drink. The rotation of misery and self-medication on whiskey and morphine must have contributed to his academic frustrations. Moule was fully aware of his own precarious condition, but unable to control his behaviour: 'By 1861 Horace was lecturing on temperance in his own district, but he could not conquer his own predisposition' (Seymour-Smith 48). So, Hardy's mentor and role-model was himself terribly 'torn' between lofty ambitions and plunging spirits, pulled agonisingly between polarities of dazzling potential and morbid self-destruction. Pitched perilously between triumph and disaster, Horace introduced Hardy to Greek tragedy, and then embodied one himself.

In September 1873, Moule died, aged forty-one. He had spent the evening in his rooms in Queens' College, Cambridge, evidently drunk and deeply dejected. After a three-hour conversation with his brother Charles, he retired to bed. Minutes later a 'trickling' sound was heard coming from the bedroom, and Charles found Horace covered in blood. After uttering the words 'Easy to Die' and 'Love to my mother', he never spoke again. He had slashed his windpipe with the razor that he kept under his pillow. At the coroner's inquest the jury returned a verdict of 'suicide whilst in a state of temporary insanity', a form of words that allowed the man's body to be respectfully buried in consecrated ground. His friend, no doubt shocked and bewildered, paid his respects in advance:

> On the previous evening, 25 September, Hardy, according to a later poem, went to Fordington churchyard, and contemplated the mound of chalk dug from the newly-prepared grave. It was this day, rather than the day of death, or that of the funeral, which he attended, that he always remembered.
>
> (Gittings, The Young Thomas Hardy 179)

According to Millgate, 'Tom went there on 25 September, the eve of the funeral, and drew a sketch of the mound by the side of the freshly dug grave; he would continue to visit Horace's grave for the rest of his life' (*The Life and Work of Thomas Hardy, by Thomas Hardy* 155). Hardy's private visit suggests a heightened sensitivity to ritual. That he should wish to preserve the image of a heap of earth beside an empty grave suggests a mind already moving beyond the immediate shock, delving Hamlet-wise into the universal questions surrounding the end (and the ends) of existence. It seems an oddly redundant and ghoulish thing to do at a moment of bereavement. Why draw a picture of a mound of earth? In 'Before My Friend Arrived' (*Collected Poems* 782), a poem penned many years later, Hardy asks the question himself:

> Why did I pencil that chalk?
> It was fetched from the waiting grave,
> And would return there soon,
> Of one who had stilled his walk
> And sought oblivion's cave

Displaced earth, and a hole waiting for a body to fill it, is a sight that raises a profound question over all human schemes. With this as the destination, what point the journey? The answer, if Hardy offers one, is in the rituals of sketch and poem. These remain to mark the mortal passage from one darkness to the next, and share the common fate they commemorate.

In so many ways Horace Moule was the pattern to which Hardy aspired. His gruesome death, by his own hand, was both an almighty jolt and a sharp warning regarding the hidden hollow beneath the vanities and ambitions of the world. Horace had been granted great gifts, together with the irresistible impulse to squander them. His advanced consciousness only enhanced awareness of its own imminent eclipse. He had been living with death. It was an open secret that he slept with that razor.

The suffering and waste attached to the circumstances of Moule's death, together with the haunting image of the beckoning grave, vividly evoke a sense of the void over which all life is absurdly suspended. But another mournful image attaches to the memory of Horace Moule, one that perfectly illustrates Hardy's characteristic impressionability, and his fascination with the secret signs that life seems to transmit. Hardy was well acquainted with Moule's rooms in Cambridge, and his last visit there remained vivid in his memory, even to being described in great detail decades later to the second Mrs Hardy. As Gittings tells it:

> On that evening of 20 June, as they talked in Moule's rooms in Queens', the conversation between the two men went on deep into the summer night. Moule stood by the mantlepiece of his keeping-room, with the candles guttering behind him. As he spoke on and on excitedly, he seemed to Hardy to be pointing unconsciously at the long trailing overflow of wax that was gathering on the candle. This, in country-superstition terms, was known as the 'shroud', and it was held to foretell the death of the person to whom it applied.
>
> (Gittings, The Young Thomas Hardy 181)

This is the factual basis for late poem 'Standing by the Mantlepiece', subtitled 'H.M.M., 1873' (*Collected Poems* 846), which begins and ends with the same compound image:

> This candle-wax is shaping to a shroud
> To-night. (They call it that, as you may know) –
> By touching it the claimant is avowed,
> And hence I press it with my finger – so.
>
> [...]
>
> And let the candle wax, thus mould a shape
> Whose meaning now, if hid before, you know,
> And how by touch one present claims its drape,
> And that it's I who press my finger – so.

There are revealing disparities between the story as told and the poem as written. In 'reality' the guttering candle, shaping itself into a portent symbol of death, was only noticed by Hardy as he watched his friend's animated performance before the fireplace. In the poem it is Moule who acknowledges it, and 'avows' the portentous significance of the candle-wax, bringing on himself the death it foretells by deliberately touching it 'so' with his finger. The poem also places the image within a larger narrative, featuring a woman who takes the place originally occupied by Hardy. Furthermore, the woman seems to have just announced the end of their affair. Here, Hardy folds in another layer of Moule's legend, another rumour hovering over his friend:

> ... the story of his engagement to a governess, 'highly cultivated' and of 'sterling character', whom his sister-in-law, Frederick Moule's wife, thought a 'splendid person', perhaps capable of solving Horace's

difficulties. But the governess broke off the engagement, probably because of Horace's drinking – the reason cited in another version of the same story, which speaks of the fiancée as a 'lady of title'.

(Millgate, *The Life and Work of Thomas Hardy* 154)

Stories within stories. Ghost upon ghost. This cascade of rumour and surmise elaborates the horrific facts of Moule's final crisis into a concentrated tangle worthy of a Hardy novel. Whatever the factual basis for this scenario it presents a complex blend of elements, all suggestive of a 'skewed belief system' and unconventional morality: local superstition, frustrated desire, self-harm, abandonment and despair ('Above but shade, and shadier shade below') topped by the prospect of a Freudian reading that couples mutually enhancing intimations of desire and death. All that is missing is a whiff of sexual scandal and misdirected moral outrage.

So here it is. Another story circulating around Moule is one that Hardy's second wife, Florence, heard directly from her husband: 'According to the story, Horace got a Fordington woman (and therefore one of his father's parishioners) pregnant, and she was shipped off to Australia where (doubtless vindicating Hardy's view of the malign workings of fate) the son she bore was in due time hanged' (Seymour-Smith 50). The concatenation of tragedies is indeed Hardyan, and so too is the conflation of cultures. The 'country-superstition' acknowledged and validated in a university study. By having Moule both 'own' and participate in the candle-ritual, Hardy draws together the opposed cultural spheres of Dorset and Cambridge.

In 'Standing by the Mantlepiece' the pointless horror of Moule's suicide is reimaged as the inevitable conclusion of a tragic fate. Like the sketch of Moule's grave, it points towards an impenetrable dark. Nevertheless, in both cases memory and art collaborate theatrically to reassert meaning as a pattern of symbols and gestures. Art may not expel the dark, but it can act as a stay against nothingness. Moule's history belongs to a morally formless and chaotic universe, but poetically reframed in terms of fateful signs and mysterious forces it rescues order from meaninglessness. Like the folklore it re-enacts, the poem unifies random events into a sustainable whole that can be imaginatively governed, held up and passed on. Secret signs provoke equally powerful feelings of attraction and repulsion. They enfranchise the initiated, but frighten those for whom collective identity represents a threat to the self. Hardy never altogether relinquished his country affiliations. Amid the influx of modern ideas, including those of his great friend, Hardy retained a respect for the arcane and the timeworn. They retained or restored something that could be held against the chaos. The pattern of ancient superstitions and folk customs may have been overlaid by the conceptual schemes of orthodox religion and enlightened science, but their efficacy in securing a sense of 'meaningful participation' in the unfathomable mystery of life and death assured their survival as a valid dimension of the reality he acknowledged.

Weird wife

Claire Tomalin opens her biography with what she describes as 'the moment when Thomas Hardy became a great poet' (xvii). In 1912 Emma Hardy died. Their marriage of over forty years had not been a happy one. (This is the premise for Elizabeth Lowry's novel *The Chosen*, where Hardy is literally haunted by Emma.) He had long ago cut himself off emotionally, neglecting her interests, retreating into his work. She had grown disappointed and resentful. There had been no children, and the two seventy-year-olds cohabited in mutual isolation, sharing the house he built, Max Gate, but little else. Yet despite the collapse of their relationship, Emma's unexpected death plunged Hardy into a dark and turbulent place. His curious behaviour during the first few days of widowhood suggests a profound shift in his consciousness. After years of domestic separation, Hardy gave orders for Emma's body to be brought down from her attic room, and for her coffin to be placed at the foot of his bed, 'where it remained for three days and nights until the funeral' (Tomalin xviii).

If this was an episode from a Hardy novel, it would submit to various interpretations: as the suspiciously stagey performance of a man belatedly adopting the part of a broken-hearted lover, or the pious gesture of a repentant husband looking to atone for past indifference and neglect, or the morbid act of a professional novelist gathering first-hand material. Regardless of the motives, Hardy creates a ritual for himself as clearly as if it had been concocted for a piece of short fiction. This shares qualities with the presentation of the lore and rituals of 'summoning' in many folk horror texts. As Dawn Keetley notes, 'One must not, however, take the "traditions" of folk horror at face value. They are typically not "authentic" traditions, although they may well be represented as such within the text. Instead, they are highly mediated and often expressly fabricated' (5).

There may be something true in each 'reading' of Hardy's motives in claiming Emma's coffin, but they shouldn't disguise the very real shock and confusion occasioned by his grief at her passing. Just as it had, nearly forty years earlier, the raw fact of mortality confounded the reasoning self, nakedly exposing the ultimate meaninglessness into which life can instantly dissolve. By 1912 Hardy had long-since abandoned fiction as his preferred medium. His tales of the grotesque and eerie were well behind him, and he had altogether forsaken the novel for the more intimate spaces of poetry. Nevertheless, in the months that followed, he gave a singular illustration of his personal imaginary in a great outpouring of verse, published as *Poems of 1912–13*, 'one of the finest and strangest celebrations of the dead in English poetry' (Tomalin xx). Largely composed 'in sorrow and remorse for their estrangement' (xvii), the volume represents a remarkable act of imaginative reclamation, restoring Emma to the centre of his life. With the living woman missing, vivid memories of happier times flooded back, re-arousing old tenderness and prompting bitter self-reproach. The aching poignancy of poems such as 'The Going', 'After a Journey' and 'At Castle Boterel' comes from contrasting the bright promise of their courtship with the marital gloom that eventually overtook them. What is clear is that having lost any meaningful connection with Emma while she still lived, Hardy now formed a new and intense relationship with her ghost.

Poems of 1912–13 is an extended conversation with the dead in which Hardy manages to be both fanciful and excoriating. He travels back in time to watch himself watching her, and stages posthumous encounters that have her standing in judgement on him. But this unflinching self-examination offers no balm of consolation. The poems are borne out of an inescapable emotional bind, a condition beyond healing, beyond anything but deepening pain. They tend to a personal wound, yet leave it painfully exposed. What makes them more than private confessions are their relevance to the central paradox of memory, its fragile lightness and its unbearable burden of subjective meaning. These poems of later life demonstrate an impulse characterizing all his imaginative work, a reaching back into memory, into the emotional 'atmosphere' of the past, in order to establish the reality (or otherwise) of the present. More than that, they exhibit a common feature of Hardy's imagination: vertical time. The vivid present does not lead back to the distant past along a horizontal line. Both are rendered equally concrete and visible, like overlaid transparencies. This telescoping of time reflects an anxiety of orientation, and a radical readjustment of established images of the self, that is more than individual. Hardy reached back not with some nostalgic view of the past but to a time which had been, and remained, troubled and inconclusive.

In 'The Spell of the Rose' (*Collected Poems* 336), Hardy reproaches himself through Emma's perspective. As a husband he provided the outer form of married stability, but left the human relationship untended: 'He built for me that manor-hall,/And planted many trees withal,/But no rose anywhere.' Having failed in life to cultivate 'the flower of love', the task is left to Emma to 'end divisions dire and wry' by planting it herself. In a sense, the poem itself is that flower, a moment of refreshed vision, only attained in the face of Emma's death:

> But I was called from earth – yea, called
> Before my rose-bush grew;
> And would that now I knew
> What feels he of the tree I planted,
> And whether, after I was called
> To be a ghost, he, as of old,
> Gave me his heart anew!

Under Hardy's hand the gesture of giving your heart to the dead is more than a romantic trope. Familiarity had made the poet blind to the real person in his life. Death, and the renewed affection it kindles, restores his sight from 'the mis-vision that blurred me', but leaves him staring into an abyss: 'He sees me as I was, though sees/Too late to tell me so!' Giving these thoughts to Emma adds an extra degree of separation to the ontological gap between them. They exist either side of an impenetrable barrier that leaves each in devastated solitude. She will never know of his restored feelings for her. His words do not reach her. The poem sits in ghostly limbo in the void between them. Many more poems enact this double death. The imagination retrieves something long lost in Hardy himself, some depth of living connection, only to see it fade again, and again. The poet throws an imaginative bridge across the gulf between past and present, but once constructed it melts away leaving him more exposed and bewildered than before. As recollections of lost relationship, they briefly retrieve the past, only to make it feel immeasurably more distant; the most intimately familiar made misshapen and strange.

In this time-torn condition Hardy again returns to his great theme – the persistence of the past. It does not let go. Nor does it cease to speak to him about what has been, and what he made of it. What were they before they grew apart? What has he since become? Memory as interrogation; it stares back at him posing insoluble questions. The poems are epiphanies, visionary windows through which the poet can glimpse the possibility of a different, unrealized and now unrealizable history. Hardy the novelist was always fascinated by twists of fate, the play of chance and necessity, the way an entire history can hang upon a momentary thread. If he had held fast to what these memories reveal, if he had not been distracted, not 'looked away', their matrimonial estrangement might have been averted. Mr Lackland, again. The images that return to him not only occasion a sense of guilt, disturbing his settled self-image, they also open up a channel into the abiding mysteries of selfhood, otherness and time. The pictures that arise are more than mental mementos of a happier, more hopeful period. Their meaning is immediately pressing and urgent. They inflict themselves upon him like wordless accusations, or signs to be deciphered. Just as he might have sought a suitable image to capture the tragic essence of a fictional character's life, here Hardy discovers the true nature of his own story. The essential meaning of his life is being played back to him. Emma's death didn't merely force Hardy to review his life, it pushed him further out into the precarious psychological terrain of the remembered past, and forced him to ask where, as narrator of his own life, he would have to stand in order to survey the narrative in its entirety. It gave him the opportunity to explore the painful mysteries of lost time, and the haunting effect of the past upon the present. This was Hardy at his most fruitful – riven by time, haunted.

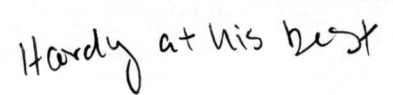

The celebrated poem 'The Voice' (*Collected Poems* 325) was one of the first in the volume to be completed. Its opening line straddles the divide between the commonplace and the transcendent, the natural and the supernatural, the earthly and the otherwise:

> Woman much missed, how you call to me, call to me,
> Saying that now you are not as you were
> When you had changed from the one who was all to me,
> But as at first, when our day was fair.

The convoluted syntax tangles the reader on a knot of time, enfolding the bereaved present ('much missed'), the distant romantic past ('first' and 'fair') and the in-between of dull domestic dissatisfaction ('when you had changed'). This woman changed in life and continues to change in death is in fact still very much 'alive', returning to what she had originally been, and calling to him to acknowledge something defying change and time. This disembodied voice has a presence that, imposing itself, has an autonomy and authority to which the poet must harken and bend. As Tomalin points out, the poem is both 'a wail of grief' (Tomalin xx) and an attempt to understand a complicated communication coming from beyond the grave of his own complaisant good opinion. Hardy isn't conducting a séance; yet he is, through the medium of poetry, trying to locate what he has lost. But the 'she' of the poems is not to be pinned down or defined. She moves between identities, places and conditions. She is by turns the young woman he first met on the Cornish coast in 1870, the unhappy neglected wife of their final decades together, and the newly mourned creature who was both these things and neither. Hardy is 'summoning' Emma through the ritual of his poetry, bringing forth her ghost in vertical time. Indeed, her image is more vivid in death than in life. Age and experience altered her, but death and burial have changed her back. Like a revenant, she comes and goes between worlds with a message for the living. The poem holds them tantalizingly close yet forever apart. Even as the distinction between past and present seems to collapse, she remains still just out of reach. Emma is both teasingly imminent and tormentingly distant, as tangibly absent as any phantasm. The published poem is flatly elegiac ('Woman much missed …'), but in earlier draft form it began in a different, more disturbing vein ('O woman weird …'). Hardy's first impulse was evidently to cast Emma in the role of an eldritch wife, bewitching his imagination. Even in the finalized version something unearthly clings to her. She is not confined to her grave. He begs her to appear to him as she did long ago, when it was she who waited upon him:

> Can it be you that I hear? Let me view you, then,
> Standing as when I drew near to the town

> Where you would wait for me: yes, as I knew you then,
> Even to the original air-blue gown!

Emma is transformed from earth to air. The shroud which cloaks her mortal remains is replaced by a spectral garment that gives her image flight. As a disembodied voice she has become as ethereal as a breath of wind. The whole poem dematerializes and destabilizes time and space too. Solidity has melted away, leaving the poet, himself revealed as a frail uncertain presence, stumbling through an emptiness. The voice is all that remains, all that retains any meaning for him. The poem ends:

> Thus I; faltering forward,
> Leaves around me falling,
> Wind oozing thin through the thorn from norward,
> And the woman calling.

Ambiguity dissolves the binaries of here and now, past and present, real and imaginary. Her voice is both seduction and judgement – the poet's motion both 'forward' and 'falling'. Is he being drawn trance-like towards reunion and a posthumous reckoning, or lured towards mere oblivion? This wrath-woman takes on a double aspect, both desired and dreadful. He is called towards something terrible and true. The past will speak and deliver its sentence, a final verdict on his former unresponsiveness. There is no protected inner space from which the poet can mount a defence for what he has been or has failed to be. Drawn on by a palpable but invisible force, he himself is fading into impalpability. What is 'much missed' can indeed exert a 'weird' bewitching influence, reducing what remains to shadow and doubt.

Hardy takes the everyday melancholy business of wondering where time goes, and fills it with existential wonder. In 'The Phantom Horsewoman' (*Collected Poems* 332) he once more telescopes time, revisiting the period of their courtship on the Cornish coast, and the memory of Emma on horseback. Born lame, and always walking with a limp, Emma took added pleasure in riding, aware of herself cutting an elegant and fearless figure atop the cliffs of *her* native landscape. The poem is framed by the poet observing himself from the outside; as Tomalin says, imaging himself as 'old, half mad and obsessed with something only he can see as he gazes over the ocean' (Tomalin xxi):

> A ghost-girl-rider. And though, toil-tried,
>   He withers daily,
>   Time touches her not,
>   But still she rides gaily
>   In his rapt thought

> On that shagged and shaly
> Atlantic spot,
> And as when first eyed
> Draws rein and sings to the swing of the tide.

Here Emma is mythologized as a dangerous siren, not so much luring her man onto the rocks as abandoning him there to wait hopelessly for her return. Again, she is both there and not. Again, it is he who tires, dwindles and decays. Again, it is the present that seems insubstantial. The spur for the poem is both a remembered moment and an image outside time, both fleeting and indestructible. Her compelling majestic presence symbolically redresses the injustice of his diminishment of her in real life. She is restored to glory, magnificently commanding the scene, triumphantly riding the waves. Time cannot touch her; but neither can he. Again, in bringing the past agonisingly close, memory emphasizes a distance that can never be crossed, both time and man, unredeemable.

The eighty or so poems Hardy eventually addressed to Emma are the late flowering of a distinctive impulse in him to affirm and demonstrate how the past returns, clings and overwhelms. You cannot simply cast it off. It makes demands. The past isn't even 'past'. It lives on, capable of interrupting the flow of life, making repeated claims, frustrating the desire for control of the here and now. A constant rebuke to ego and reason, the past is suspended over the present in condemnation and a certain sort of grim mockery. What never left Hardy, and is crystalized in these intimate poems, is his sense of the radical indeterminacy at the still centre of the lived moment, something spectral within the material life. Encounter with this fluidity of experience melts the boundaries conventionally established between modes and agents. Hardy often reimagines the women in his life as ghosts.

Nowhere in these verses is Hardy encountering the supernatural. Emma's 'ghost' is purely textual. Her ghostly form to give shape to thoughts and feelings that lie outside easy conceptualization lies off the mind's map of itself. Ghosts escape conceptual captivity, defy logic (past *and* present, here *and* there, alive *and* dead), come and go independently, resist finality and closure. Hardy in these poems is haunted by the meaning invested in Emma's image, a meaning hanging over his life like the questions asked beside Moule's grave. As the archetypal 'embodiment' of paradox and indeterminacy, the ghost represents whatever might be beyond the conventional range of perception and language, a counter to all that modernity is built upon. The ghostly in Hardy is a sign that the past has not finished with us, that in us past and present cohabit.

But even as Hardy wrestles with the phantom call of the past, he can acknowledge the material facts of the present. In the poem 'Lament' (*Collected Poems* 323), he reflects on how much Emma would have enjoyed a day like today, a summer party with friends, but he also knows that the mistress of Max Gate lies at that moment 'In the clodded shell/Of her tiny cell'. In Hardy the spectral and the mortal co-exist. The omens surrounding their life together at Max Gate were not altogether good from the start. While digging a well he discovered three skeletons in three separate graves dating from the third or fourth century. Most unnaturally, all were identically arranged, lying on their right side, curled up in a foetal position, with their arms stretched down so that their hands rested on their ankles. He gave a description of them in a paper entitled 'Some Roman-British Relics Found at Max Gate, Dorchester', delivered to a local antiquarian society in 1884: 'Each body was fitted with ... perfect accuracy into the oval hole, the crown of the head touching the maiden chalk at one end and the toes at the other' (Tomalin 202). He described them as looking like chicks tightly packed into their shells or, one might elaborate, like babies in the womb.

Here there are some parallels with M. R. James and the unearthing of antiquity, bringing the past into visceral view in the present. However whilst James makes this manifest in his fiction as spectral figures emerging from the landscape, Hardy uses these as a method of rooting his characters in a deep tradition. They are both hauntological in their references but the fundamental difference is in their engagement with the past. 'Trapped or willingly interred within the landscapes of his own endlessly recreated youth, James was able to finesse the rules of his hauntological miniatures, establishing a template for future practitioners of the ghost story' (Coverley 95). For James the past is something which can be touched, or rather something which may reach out and touch you. For Hardy it is something which is perpetually present with us and can make its way to the surface at any point.

Hardy was no stranger to disturbing exhumations. When in his former career as trainee architect Hardy was responsible for overseeing work on London's St Pancras Station, workmen unearthed disintegrating coffins spilling their contents in a jumble of bones. One coffin contained a single body, but two skulls. In contrast it is the very orderliness and care with which the bodies were buried beneath Max Gate that makes the find so unnerving. Having just bought a plot on which to build your dream home, you find, just three feet beneath the surface, evidence of lives lived, and a civilization extinguished, without any other visible trace. Or rather, there are bones everywhere: 'the workmen making the drive to the house found they had decapitated five more skeletons' (Tomalin 203). Hardy was already imaginatively drawn to the ancient past – its bones and stones. In his mind, as in his landscape, it seems to have had an irresistible influence, exerting an underlying pressure that was always on the point of rising up to reveal an unpalatable truth. Mortality was a constant in Victorian experience. More than perhaps any writer of the age, Hardy was as aware of the thin veneer that cloaks 'civilized' consciousness.

Pre-posthumous Hardy

In 1888 Hardy described a rather curious and disturbing game he liked to play:

> If there is any way of getting a melancholy satisfaction out of life it lies in dying, so to speak, before one is out of the flesh; by which I mean putting on the manners of ghosts, wandering in their haunts, and taking their views of surrounding things. To think of life as passing away is a sadness; to think of it as past is at least tolerable. Hence even when I enter into a room to pay a simple morning call I have unconsciously the habit of regarding the scene as if I were a spectre not solid enough to influence my environment.
>
> (Millgate, *The Life and Work of Thomas Hardy* 218)

Hardy sounds here like a man in haste to dematerialize. This melancholy pastime seems to be a deliberate exercise in dissociation, reducing the pains of living by imaginatively disengaging from the world. Hardy's fantasy of ghosting through the world, affecting nothing, affected by nothing, doesn't sound like a productive strategy for a novelist and poet devoted to realistic social and psychological representation. But distance and impassivity do serve the interests of the observer's art, and insofar as this inclination of Hardy's was a 'habit' it speaks of something more profound than a mind game. It suggests that despite all his social and professional success, despite a solid reputation and solid accomplishments, Thomas Hardy, approaching fifty, could feel as insubstantial as an apparition. Claire Tomalin quotes Hardy's description of his game of dying, in relation to the poem, 'The Dead Man Walking' (1896) (*Collected Poems* 202) that casts the poet as a paradox, an animated corpse. Hardy placed it as the last poem in the volume *Time's Laughingstocks* (1909), making for a chilling last chuckle:

> They hail me as one living,
>   But don't they know
> That I have died of late years,
>   Untombed although?
>
> I am but a shape that stands here,
>   A pulseless mould,
> A pale past picture, screening
>   Ashes gone cold.

The process of zombification proceeded by incremental stages. When he finally died, he cannot say. Little by little his faith in life crumbled, leaving him an empty husk. Life began in freedom, song and passion:

> - A Troubadour-youth, I rambled
> > With Life for lyre
> The beats of being raged
> > In me like fire
>
> But when I practised eyeing
> > The goal of men,
> It iced me, and I perished
> > A little then.

The first death blow was discovering the indifference and self-interest that lurks beneath the cloak of civility. Such knowledge both killed his innocence and imbued him with an alienating gaze that 'sees through people'. Seeing while being unseen confers a secret power, and perhaps all writers are ghostly in this way, looking at the world from a vantage point beyond the limits of common perception. But standing back and apart from the 'fallen world', the habit of distance and objectification ('practised eyeing'), played a part in turning the poet cold ('iced' and 'perished'), placing him in frozen suspension above his fellow creatures.

More blows followed. Moule's suicide. The loss of Emma's love.

> When passed my friend, my kinsfolk,
> > Through the Last Door,
> And left me standing bleakly,
> > I died yet more;
>
> And when my Love's heart kindled
> > In hate of me,
> Wherefore I knew not, died I
> > One more degree.

Other blows follow, but the posthumous poet concludes:

> And if when I died fully
> > I cannot say,
> And changed into the corpse-thing
> > I am to-day.
>
> Yet is it that, though whiling
> > The time somehow
> In walking, talking, smiling,
> > I live not now.

Time devouring. The fire of life put out. Disillusionment. Abandonment. But the final point that Hardy wants to make is that no one knows him. He goes through the motions of healthy sociability, but it is pure performance, the presentation of a 'pale past picture' of himself, hiding a dead soul: an uncomfortable fore-echo of *The Portrait of Dorian Gray* (1890) perhaps, or simply another example of the older trope of Life-in-Death, 'dying ... before one is out of the flesh'. In these moments, in memoir and poetry, Hardy is mourning himself. The young troubadour has become the weary ghost of a man singing over his own grave. And the last line says more. He lives not now, but in the past: not in this world where time is whiled away 'walking, talking, smiling', but elsewhere, with his 'kinsfolk'.

There is self-pity here. The writer is playing with death in a self-theatrical way. But the morbid self-theatricality is perhaps a surface effect of a deeper darkness into which Thomas Hardy was liable to sink throughout his life. Hardy suffered from prolonged bouts of the severest depression. Writing to Edmund Gosse in 1887, he confessed to lengthy periods of desolation: 'You would be quite shocked if I were to tell you how many weeks and months in bygone years I have gone to bed wishing never to see daylight again' (Tomalin 203).

3

Cultural bereavement

Cultural context

In the middle and late decades of the nineteenth century, Victorian Britain was seized by fears regarding the validity and survival of the very ideas and values that formed its cultural foundations. Assumptions about the universe and humanity's place in it were put into question as never before. Intellectual optimism and spiritual confidence were being steadily eroded by a succession of alarming modern theories that cast unprecedented doubt on the most cherished beliefs. A revolution in scientific thought was systematically threatening the settled conception of reality, and a great wave of anxiety engulfed the educated class, leaving it disorientated and confused. Thomas Hardy grew up under this darkening shadow, and interiorized it to a remarkable, almost unprecedented, degree. We can reasonably ask whether these conditions, and the consequent rift in consciousness, were responsible for the imaginative distortions of the horror genre. At the very heights of late Victorian self-confidence, its sense of solidity and permanence was being revealed as little more than an illusion. Beneath the settled surface lay troubling doubts and fears, and a shadow began to prevail over British society's sunny self-image.

Doubting Thomas

Hardy was born into a committed Christian family with numerous Church connections. He enthusiastically attended services as a child and taught Sunday school as a young man. His inherited faith seems to have survived into his mid-twenties, when he was still vaguely contemplating a career in the Church (less perhaps out of doctrinal conviction than the hope that it might afford him a university education).

The first twenty years of Hardy's life coincided with the great religious turbulence surrounding the 'Oxford Movement' and its dissent from the theological liberalism of the established Church of England. More disturbing still were the developments in scholarly research provoking increasing doubts about the material reality behind Church teaching, and particularly about the literal truth of scripture. The Bible was not to be treated unquestioningly as the unmediated word of God, but as a cultural artefact, a book like any other, and therefore open to different interpretations. The impetus for interpretive revision came from comparative historians, mostly German, and chief among them the theologian David Friedrich Strauss (1808–74). In *The Life of Jesus, Critically Examined* Strauss interrogated the Gospels, deploying standard scholarly techniques to separate fact from fiction, and identify a 'historical Jesus' stripped of the metaphysical projections of traditional theology. The elimination of the miraculous and the supernatural amounted to a denial of the divinity of Jesus, and effectively recast Christ as a figure of myth. The shock wave sent across Europe can be measured in one eminent reader's response to the 1846 translation in English by Marian Evans (yet to become the novelist George Eliot) calling it 'the most pestilential book ever vomited out of the jaws of hell' (Hesketh 97).

The Hardys in Bockhampton felt none of this, but the Moules in Fordingham most certainly did. Horace might not have stepped far beyond what his clerically orientated family would have tolerated, but this fresh and exhilarating climate of thought had shocking implications for a young gentleman with his class background. In comparison Hardy was insulated from the impact of these new ideas. His native community had a relatively relaxed attitude to religion in general, it being more a matter of culture than concepts, more about established custom than theological dogma. Nevertheless, notions that suited a young man in rural Dorset came under pressure when his training as an architect took him into the professional circles of the great metropolis. In fact, Hardy's religious faith was an early casualty of his entry into the wider world. That Moule unwittingly played a major part in this is painfully ironic, but in this (as in much else) Hardy was nothing other than a typical Victorian, torn between tradition and modernity, struggling to accommodate old practices and new perspectives.

The collective 'loss of faith' experienced by many in the period is a familiar story. At the institutional level it was a process of gradual decline. For particular individuals, it was a crisis of identity amounting to a profound rupture and reorientation of life's fundamentals. Men like Matthew Arnold felt themselves in the midst of a catastrophe that threatened both the soul and civilization. Arnold's 'Dover Beach' (1867) perfectly expresses the cold feeling of confusion that attended this turning of the intellectual tide. The poem famously ends:

> The sea of faith
> Was once, too, at the full, and round earth's shore
> Lay like the folds of a bright girdle furl'd;

But now I only hear
Its melancholy, long, withdrawing roar,
Retreating to the breath
Of the night-wind, down the vast edges drear
And naked shingles of the world.

Ah, love, let us be true
To one another! for the world, which seems
To lie before us like a land of dreams,
So various, so beautiful, so new,
Hath really neither joy, nor love, nor light,
Nor certitude, nor peace, nor help for pain;
And we are here as on a darkling plain
Swept with confused alarms of struggle and flight,
Where ignorant armies clash by night.

The waning of Christian sentiment was experienced as a cultural bereavement. For men like Arnold its weakening hold on the modern imagination profoundly threatened the social and moral order. Nothing but chaos could ensue. The figures in the poem are not unlike characters from Hardy, stranded in a world of blind conflict. There is no shared reality that can protect or sustain them. The only thing standing between the poet and utter oblivion is a private bond of love (Arnold wrote the poem on honeymoon). All else is stripped of value and meaning, eroded by the inexorable forces of modernity. The light is dwindling. Life is being clawed back into the dark. Arnold represented a generation of educated, austere and conscientious intellectuals working in a state of spiritual despair to salvage something meaningful from the wreckage of their faith. And it was into this disorienting environment, both invigorating and full of self-doubt, that men like Moule and Hardy were trying to find their way. Moule seems to have followed something like the standard pattern of the free-thinking Victorian, suffering a profound struggle of mind and conscience. If Hardy experienced agony over his fading faith, very little showed on the surface. Certainly, when he later came to ghost write his autobiography, he declined to dramatize it as any kind of existential crisis. He dissociates himself from the Sunday pieties of his youth, casting them as 'the old transcendental ideals' and 'dogmatic superstitions', but there is no narrative of religious conscience under siege, no tale of counter-conversion or intellectual epiphany. Old ideas just fell away under the influence of new ways of thinking. What Hardy gives us is not a story of gradual and inexorable (all-but-inevitable) growth into realism.

Presented with the perfect opportunity to recount in full detail his intellectual development, and attest to his mature convictions, Hardy was somewhat evasive. However, in private correspondence he could be less guarded. Approaching his fiftieth birthday, he wrote to a friend, making it clear that there was no place in his 'philosophy' for traditional Christian belief: 'I have been looking for God for fifty years, and I think that if he existed I should have discovered him'. The remark encapsulates Hardy's studied ambivalence around the subject of religion. The tone is gently mocking of all concerned. The 'search' was serious enough, but ultimately futile; compelling, but fruitless. The kind of God that Detective Hardy was hoping to track down was of a particular kind; nothing less than 'an external personality [...] ... the only true meaning of the word' (Millgate 189). Hardy evidently lost faith in the sort of 'personal God' with whom Christians hope to have a living spiritual relationship. But the wasted effort prompted as much sadness as cynicism.

The sadness expresses itself in the aching nostalgia of popular poems like 'The Darkling Thrush' (1900) (*Collected Poems* 137). Something like religious 'hope', hope against hope, perhaps, evidently remained with him. The 'darkling' comes directly from Arnold's 'Dover Beach' (Hardy originally entitled the poem 'By the Century's Deathbed'). Nevertheless, something 'blessed' is not quite finally extinguished. Hardy still entertains the possibility that some meaning unknown to him might yet exist in the song of the bird: 'Some blessed Hope, whereof he knew/And I was unaware'. Likewise, in 'The Oxon' (1915) (*Collected Poems* 439) Hardy confesses his ultimate inability to relinquish the comforting childhood picture of the Nativity, the animals kneeling in adoration of the Christ-child. Unable to finally rid himself of the hope that it might yet be true, Hardy is again between things, at home neither in belief nor in unbelief, agonisingly suspended between the two. If not exactly a yearning for God, it nevertheless conveys the persistent ache of His absence.

In the fiction of his middle years, a streak of cynicism is easier to detect. It runs through his last novels. His childhood affection for the Church of England turns remarkably sour, and his antipathy towards its principles and personalities spills out everywhere. Christianity is little more than licensed moralizing, busy distorting and maiming natural human affections. Nor does religion provide the comfort or protection it promises. Hardy's heroes and heroines are marked by abandonment, or worse. It is easier to fit Henchard, Tess and Jude into a pattern of studied malevolence, than to imagine them creatures of a benevolent and forgiving Father. No such divine 'person' survives in Hardy's mature imagination; there can be no 'personal' appeal to the gods, or fate, or the circumambient universe.

Darkness revealed

While the latest Biblical exegesis was dispelling the magic of Christianity 'from within', the emerging theories in the physical sciences were assailing it from every other direction. What had seemed beyond question now succumbed to detailed interrogation in the light of material evidence. A paradigm shift from faith to reason seemed about to carry the entire culture beyond the claims of tradition or faith. All that once was solid seemed on the point of melting away. Hardy may not have enjoyed an Oxbridge education, but he had access to the most challenging ideas of his day. Moule introduced his protégé to a wide range of reading, including periodicals like *The Saturday Review*, the leading London weekly which played a major part in reshaping Hardy's basic attitudes and beliefs, and which he subscribed to for the rest of his life. Books that were unwelcome in the parsonage were passed on to Hardy. Horace Moule never declined from formal adherence to the Church, but it's clear that within the context of his profoundly orthodox family environment he was something of a 'free thinker', and that 'Hardy soon absorbed Horace Moule's own habits of mind' (Gittings, *The Young Thomas Hardy* 42). In tandem with Biblical scholarship, new ideas in the physical sciences were shaking faith in Christianity as a credible explanatory framework. In his *Principles of Geology* (1830–3), Charles Lyell (1797–1875) had described processes of rock formation extending over immensities of geological time, well beyond the calculations of those attaching literal significance to Scripture. Contrary to the timescales of Genesis (six days) and the genealogical deductions from the Old Testament (6,000 years), the Earth was immeasurably older than anyone had imagined. Fossil material deeply embedded in geological strata revealed a story of life going back, not thousands but millions of years, and contained evidence of species after species that had just disappeared. The implications of such a pre-history of development and destruction were shocking and enthralling to poet and naturalist alike: mankind was part of a natural system that could see humanity extinguished in the same way. On this view, what characterized the Earth was not stability and permanence, but instability and flux.

Archaeology advanced the same picture. To dig beneath the Dorset countryside was to uncover unimaginable depths of time. The surface was strewn with the litter of 'lost civilisations', once as vibrant and confident as the British Empire itself, but now visible only as wreckage and ruins – the skeletal remains of Roman Britain, and more ambiguous signs of still more ancient pre-historical inhabitants. This was a landscape both haunted and haunting. Cold remnants of extinct cultures stood like headstones, in silent rebuke to the might and pride of the present age. To a mind, like Hardy's, that could vividly imagine past generations in all their warmth and vitality, the landscape was itself like a graveyard of vanities, a constant reminder of fragility and impermanence. This perspective on the past had a chilling effect upon the present. Past and present are revealed as merely different points in a shared history of decline and defeat, death and decay. This perspective is manifest in the observance of calendar customs that embody and express the tension that exists between a continuity of practice with a larger condition of change. This can be seen as manifest in ritual, which itself is so central to a conception of folk horror, as Merlin Coverley writes '[the] cycle of eternal recurrence as time returns periodically through the observance of sacred ritual is experienced positively as significant and celebratory. This only remains the case, however, as long as the beliefs which underpin such rituals are maintained' (54). This can be seen in the domineering presence of the Rainbarrow in *Return of the Native* or Stonehenge in *Tess of the d'Urbervilles*. The megalithic and ancient is part of the landscape of Wessex in a pre-heritage age. The characters that Hardy creates easily inhabit the ancient and the modern as they both co-exist. People and the land are indivisible.

Just as geology and archaeology were busy problematizing the Earth, modern astronomy was steadily estranging the heavens. In Hardy's short poem 'The Comet of Yell'ham' (*Collected Poems* 138), the poet's upturned eye witnesses a lump of rock in its silent passage across the night sky, briefly illuminating the landscape beneath. When it next passes in its orbit, the poet will be long gone. Nor will it shine on his beloved, 'that sweet form of thine'. The expanse of the physical universe prompts melancholy thoughts of non-existence. Wonder at the mysterious vastness of time and space is shadowed and bedevilled by the fact of human transience. In common with the comet, the unimaginably distant stars are on their inevitable path, entropically bent towards oblivion. In the face of such bleak immensities, human hopes and designs are relativized into irrelevance. Huge advances in knowledge are gained at the expense of 'meaning'.

Typical of the culture at large, Hardy was caught between enthusiasm for the advances in enlightened reason, and a pervasive gloom at its philosophical implications. The intellectual optimism and positivism of the new sciences yielded answers to questions many wished had been left unasked. It opened vast territories, which the mind struggled to inhabit. Revised perspectives in religion and science confirmed a common vision of a universe oblivious to human existence and human suffering. Hardy's novels set human activity against cosmological time and archaeological time. The tangible evidence of 'deep time' is strewn across the physical landscape and across the heavens. The static pre-modern picture of the cosmos centring on the fixed presence of God had given way to an image of continual flux into which the human being briefly rises up and disappears, without point or purpose. Hardy was haunted by this loss of meaning brought about by the death of God. His absence was everywhere.

The last nail in the coffin of human exceptionalism was hammered home when Charles Darwin published *On the Origin of Species* in 1859. Inspired by Charles Lyell's expansion of the geological record, Darwin added the 'deep time' of *biological* evolution, a process equally mindless and dictated only by forces morally blind and impersonal. His theory that organisms had slowly evolved into their current forms through countless generations revolutionized human self-understanding in a way that no serious Victorian could ignore. Ideas pertaining to evolution had preceded him, but Darwin's more detailed picture of biological processes emphasized nature's ruthless pursuit of its own interests, 'red in tooth and claw'. Hardy had little difficulty embracing the implications of Darwin's work. His last novels are dramatizations of the fact that those who do not adjust to their environment do not endure. What happens to Michael Henchard in *The Mayor of Casterbridge* is precisely this. Failing to adapt, he fails to survive. In Darwin's *The Origin of Species* Hardy found confirmation of his own observations on the wasteful horrors of the natural world. Darwin's theory was disturbing enough, even shattering to those who began to think through its deeper implications, but it entered an arena already haunted by religious doubt.

[margin note: Hardy's work in result]

The poem 'Nature's Questioning' (1898) (*Collected Poems* 58) expresses Hardy's own bewilderment in the face of deep time. It imagines all living things, animal and vegetable, collectively puzzling over their existence: 'We wonder, ever wonder, why we find us here!' They ask whether they are the product of some 'Vast Imbecility' or 'an Automaton/Unconscious of our pains'. Is there 'some high Plan', not yet understood, or gone horribly awry? The poet responds: 'No answer I'. Neither art nor intellect can frame a reply: 'Meanwhile the winds, and rains, / And Earth's old Glooms and pains / Are still the same, and Life and Death are neighbours nigh.' No meaning or purpose, nothing but a bleak struggle for survival, and the uncomfortable proximity of Life to Death. New knowledge only reveals the human tragedy afresh, playing itself out in an even-greater darkness. Humans are expendable. Human virtues are alien to the fabric of reality. Human consciousness is both a gift and a curse – to be made sentient enough to suffer, and to learn that the suffering is to no avail. The human condition is 'absurd', inimitable to happiness or harmony of any sort, irony on a cosmic scale.

The nether world

Darwin's theory sharply conflicted with the Victorian picture of social progress. If evolution was the rule, and the human animal was still in the process of being formed by its environment, then what guarantee was there that it would always be change in the direction of something higher and finer? It seemed equally plausible that society could sink back into the sort of chaos and anarchy educated class most feared. Few were in any doubt that within the growing populations of the modern industrialized cities lurked destructive regressive impulses that could overwhelm civilization.

Novels of the period frequently entertained the horrifying possibility that humankind might devolve, degenerate into something 'less than human'. In *The Strange Case of Dr Jekyll and Mr Hyde* (1886), Robert Louis Stevenson gave form to the intellect's fascination with the irrational, and to the fantasy of releasing the pent-up primitive energies and appetites suppressed by social norms. In due course Freud would make his own interpretive contribution to this gathering dystopian nightmare. The arcane substrate of the mind was not dormant, but actively seeking expression. Repression only strengthens what is denied. Attempt to live by reason alone and irrationality will overwhelm. Nature will rebel. In *The Time Machine* (1895) H. G. Wells imagined an entire world stratified along similarly 'Freudian' lines, with a literal underclass living underground. Wells' enormously popular novel directly addressed the fears of degeneration fuelled by Darwinian images of the beast within.

In contrast to his 'futuristic' contemporaries, Hardy's response to this schizoid threat was to tap into his folklorist roots. This is a point where there is a further split for Hardy. He is, in part at least, drawing on his working class/rural background with its associated 'lore' but at the same time exercising his power as an author and adapting and creating stories he may have heard earlier in life. The two blur in Hardy's work and perhaps for the writer himself. This gives the sense of something beneath the surface, outside our control, which emerges again and again. As Dawn Keetley argues of folk horror, there is a constructed quality to the rituals that the 'folk' perform and this is in part where the horror lies. When Hardy was asked for his opinion on the problem of evil and the prospect of reconciling human suffering with the image of a benevolent God, he responded in the third person: 'Mr. Hardy regrets that he is unable to offer any hypothesis which would reconcile the existence of such evils [...] with the idea of omnipotent goodness', and pointed his correspondent in the direction of Darwin, Herbert Spencer 'and other agnostics' (*The Life and Work of Thomas Hardy, by Thomas Hardy* 214).

Herbert Spencer (1820–1903) was the most influential English philosopher of his day. Already in the 1840s and 1850s, and before publication of *The Origin of Species*, he was reflecting on the general concept of evolution, and applying it beyond the realm of biology. Spencer believed very firmly that human societies were just like natural organisms and developed according to the same process of selection and struggle that Darwin described. It was Spencer who coined the phrase 'the survival of the fittest', subsequently used by Darwin, to characterize the hidden logic operating through history. But Spencer's philosophy offered an ameliorating gloss on Victorian pessimism. For all the unpleasantness involved, including war and famine, civilization was on an inevitable path of progress. Competition among humans was unavoidable, but beneficial, because it ensured the triumph of the healthiest and most intelligent. Nothing should be allowed to interfere with the natural processes at work. But there were clear signs that this 'progress' came at a terrible cost. Industrialization had caused a huge change in population patterns. London had already reached its peak, and the Thames had become a sewer. The poverty and squalor that came in the wake of mass urbanization were a new and alarming phenomenon. The 'teaming masses' of uneducated people, collected in over-crowded, squalid and insanitary conditions, created fevered nightmares of an inflamed and uncontrollable mob:

> In 1801, the proportion of the population of England and Wales living in towns and cities was just 17 per cent, but by the close of that century, as landowners were displaced and industry boomed, it had jumped to 72 per cent. The most recent UK census showed that 81.5 per cent of the population of England and Wales now live in urban areas, with less than 10 per cent residing in what would qualify as villages or hamlets. This mass movement from agricultural to post-industrial life has detached us from the land that fed and clothed us for thousands of years, with the countryside becoming increasingly alien territory, avoided or misunderstood by those who have little contact with mud, dead animals, or the stench of excrement. Such urbanites have scant knowledge of farming or food production and patronise ancient local traditions. They are unnerved by the space, the silence. They fear their countryside, their own past.
>
> (Myers, 'Folk Horror, A History: from The Wicker Man to The League of Gentlemen')

The Italian criminologist Cesare Lombroso (1835–1909) claimed that cities bred degeneracy, and set about proving it using the pseudo-science of phrenology to identify 'the criminal type' by examination of their cranial features. Unlike the health-giving properties of the countryside, cities harboured a semi-vicious underclass breeding their way to ultimate victory over decent people. Hardy had his own bumps read – the results are unrecorded.

This image of an underground culture is one that arises in numerous contexts. In London it took physical shape in the form of the underground railway system. Begun in 1863, it provoked equal quantities of exhilaration and fear. Cultural anxieties around the urban poor were manifest in the mixture of terror and excitement created by the Whitechapel Murders of 1888, credited to 'Jack the Ripper'. The previous year had seen the publication of the first Sherlock Holmes story, *A Study in Scarlet*, with its unique window on the same underworld milieu of criminality and violence. The 'underclass' to which the Ripper's victims belonged received realist treatment in the work of George Gissing (1857–1903). Gissing offers a picture of the poor 'in their own right', without reference to their masters. Theirs was a world unto itself. Gissing wrote to Hardy of his evening 'ramblings about Clerkenwell', researching his subject. The title of his 1889 novel, *The Nether World*, uses a phrase in recurrent use at the time. An early review described Gissing as 'a modern Dante', and the notion of London as a contemporary Hell was not new. Report had it that in the mid-1880s a local clergyman had compared the noises emanating from the earthworks dug for the underground railway to the 'shrieks and groans of the lost souls in the lowest circle of Dante's *Inferno*'.

In *The Time Machine* (1895) Wells fantasizes the 'underclass' into a separate species, the subterranean Morlocks, giving emblematic form to Marx's warning in the *Communist Manifesto* (1848) about the lumpen proletariat, and the alienation of the working man from the product of his labour. The basic fear among the middle and upper classes was that the birth-rate of the urban poor would lead to their outbreeding them. But another facet of this 'crisis' emerged in the context of Empire, in circumstances which could be said to demonstrate what Spencer and others merely theorized about. In the act of colonial expansion those who perceived themselves to be 'intellectually advanced' races were defeating, if not exterminating, what they defined as 'non-intellectual' industrially undeveloped people. The spectacular growth and power of the British Empire stood as a powerful argument for the strength of British culture, proof that it was the most 'fit' among the evolving nations. But the First Boer War (1880–1) had been a great reversal to this confidence. The fact that it had gone very badly for the British Army was immediately blamed on the poor physical condition of the men coming forward for recruitment.

To Social Darwinians like Spencer, this apparent diminishment in masculine vigour presented a material, spiritual and theoretical problem. If the birth-rate of the urban poor constituted an existential threat to the superior social classes, then in evolutionary terms these 'inferior specimens' could hardly be regarded as inferior at all. Whether they revolted against their upper-class masters or simply outbred them, the eventual triumph of the lower orders would prove them to have been more 'fit to survive'. The logic of this was massively troubling to Spencer. Indeed, issues of heredity and recidivism began to press on the Victorian imagination generally. Class became an imagined field of existential conflict: the question being whether the cultivated intellectual or the uneducated common man would inherit the future. One 'solution' to the problem offered itself in the form of the 'science' of eugenics. The term, meaning 'beautiful heredity', was coined by Darwin's cousin Francis Galton (1822–1911) to imply that human improvements could be achieved through selective breeding that illuminated unwanted characteristics and maximized the health of the species. The first real practical attempt to engineer the genetic make-up of the population was many years in the future, but the aspiration to encourage only the beautiful, the intelligent and the moral to marry and reproduce was in the air. The fact that the state sought to address these demographic changes via mass education and widening democracy only further alarmed the cultural elites, Arnold, Darwin and Galton among them. The year 1870 saw the introduction of universal state-funded education, of which Hardy was a beneficiary. The vote was extended to working men in Reform Acts in 1867 and 1884. The advent of steam and electrical power opened up the world in new ways, bringing benefits to vast numbers of people. The developing consumer society was of course viewed with snobbish disdain, but it also struck fear into those already worried that they were being out-populated.

The anxieties about degeneration and decay that preoccupied the cultural elites were not only an urban phenomenon. Agriculture suffered a collapse in the 1880s and 1890s, and the countryside became dangerously *de*populated. Grain pouring in from the vast prairies of North America and Eastern Europe made domestic farming uncompetitive. Food prices fell, but so did rural employment. Rail transportation cut costs. Increasing numbers of city dwellers could suddenly afford luxury items, smart clothes and decorative furniture. They benefitted from a fall in the price of land and could even put money down on a house. The modern consumer society, ironically the focus of many contemporary hauntological texts, so has its origins in the collapse of agriculture. All this caused another sudden burst of pessimism among the establishment. For centuries the countryside had been talismanic for English culture. Now the average Englishman was an urbanite, and could live detached from the land, indifferent to its woes. At the end of the century the nation had an identity crisis. What it meant to be English changed. Who or what determined its character? Was it still the property of an aristocratic landholding class? Was it defined by the pronouncements of philosophers, churchmen and poets, a few well-educated, well-connected intellectuals who claimed responsibility for its continuing traditions and values? Or was it now to be handed over to the democratic will of the masses? The cultural despair expressed by Arnold et al. was the shadow side of the immense positivity that accompanied the unprecedented technological progress and imperial grandeur of the era. The last word on this mood of pessimism is that it was popular. Pessimism became the intellectual fashion, particularly among that class of men who may not have been born into great privilege, but who felt their role and influence in society under threat. Hardy lived on the very fringe of that world, but shared its profound intellectual unease.

Unholy spirit

Hardy refused to subscribe to any school or theory, remaining sceptical of large philosophical schemes and totalizing formulas. By his own admission he was no systematic thinker, but a man who gathered ideas which then organized and solidified themselves in their own organic way. At the end of his life Hardy confessed 'I have no philosophy', but only 'a confused heap of impressions, this those of a bewildered child at a conjuring show' (Millgate, *The Life and Work of Thomas Hardy* 441). Nevertheless, Hardy was a keen student of contemporary thought and filled his Literary Notebooks with material captured from innumerable sources including the growing body of critical journals, like the *Fortnightly Review*, *Edinburgh Review* and the *Cornhill Magazine*, that challenged conventions and disseminated new philosophical, scientific and political ideas. He encountered the thought of materialists like Ludwig Feuerbach (1804–72), attracted by the way they repudiated conventional Christian morality, seeking the common good through renewed social forms (Man invents God). Likewise, Hardy was drawn to August Comte (1798–1857) and his system of altruistic virtue (Christianity without Christ).

But if Hardy had a philosophical disposition of his own, it was towards determinism: 'No creature in the universe, in its circumstances & according to its given property, can act otherwise than it does act' (*The Literary Notebooks of Thomas Hardy Vol 1 and 2 Vol 1* 114). Life is governed by forces, like Darwin's law of evolution, that exert a fierce and inflexible control over individual destiny. Human beings sit within a fundamentally deterministic universe, which only affords them the dubious privilege of just enough self-awareness to appreciate their captivity. Seen in this light, the self is epiphenomenal, merely a by-product or secondary symptom of more fundamental activity, the 'last transformation of the great natural forces of light & heat & electricity, passing through the mysterious involvements of the human nervous system' (*The Literary Notebooks of Thomas Hardy Vol 1 and 2 Vol 1* 88). This redefinition of the self from entity to relationship, from substance to process, was articulated at length in Spencer's *Principles of Psychology*. The self is not a site of coherent agency transcending its material composition, but rather a succession of 'psychical states' promoted in accordance with physical laws, creating the illusion of a point of view outside the automatic processes of stimulus and reflex.

Such a conception inevitably informed Hardy's fiction. His characters are often presented as bodies of feeling, prone to sudden seismic fluctuations. Tess and Sue Bridehead are frequently described in physiological rather than psychological terms, not as individuated thinking and feeling creatures, but as the location of sensations passing through them. They resonate with their surroundings as though they were aeolian instruments played into passionate life by the other lives they encounter. Tess herself describes the life of most women as 'tremulous', and under Angel's influence she becomes 'such a sheaf of susceptibilities that her pulse was accelerated by the touch, her blood driven to her finger-ends, and the cool arms flushed hot' (28–9). Of Sue Hardy writes, 'the fibres of her nature seemed strained like harp-strings' which 'the least wind of emotion from another's heart could make to vibrate' (*Jude the Obscure* 228). Both are passive recipients and channels of vibration travelling through them, reaching the outer surface of their lives as experiences of pleasure or pain. In this, and so much more, Hardy's creatures are disempowered and derided. He places them in a Godless universe, but one pervaded by an inscrutable extra-human agency.

Hardy's conception of the human predicament found philosophical support in the work of Arthur Schopenhauer (1788–1860). Although Hardy didn't read German, and Schopenhauer's great work, *The World as Will and Idea* (1819), did not appear in English translation until 1883, he was a regular point of reference within the novelist's reading and notetaking. The philosopher's ideas and idiom percolated through the academic and intellectual publications of the 1870s, and he became a familiar subject for reviews and commentaries. Hardy may have been no more a philosopher than a biologist, but the outline and drift of Schopenhauer's thought were just as distinct and communicable as Darwin's central ideas. Schopenhauer's metaphysics explained why the human subject, being primarily no more than a tremulous and quivering bundle of fragmented sensations, held together as any kind of coherent unity. The answer was that one force gives form to everything, human bodies as much as stars and bacteria, one force with a single drive. All things are manifest expressions of the same singular cosmic impulse, the 'Universal Will to Life'. This Will courses through existence, throbbing and pulsating, striving to realize itself through all means, animate and inanimate alike. Hardy found in Schopenhauer an idea that clearly chimed with his own intuited grasp of the unifying energy that brought rock and tree and human together into one common condition of being. When Hardy came to read Schopenhauer's *Studies in Pessimism*, he made notes relating to 'the reasonless Will', the underlying motive force working through all things. It had been long at work in Hardy's fiction too, surging through the Wessex landscape and the creatures inhabiting it. Schopenhauer's vision gave formal and systematic expression to otherwise inchoate thoughts arising in the surrounding culture. The Death of God created a philosophical vacuum which needed to be filled. What Schopenhauer offered to Hardy was the replacement for the discredited idea of a personal God. The 'Universal Will' provided an alternative all-embracing Absolute that 'at a stroke' unified the disparate facets of contemporary life. It could be seen at work in the physical processes of evolution and the social struggle for life and liberty. It preserved a metaphysical dimension to existence, while avoided the embarrassments of anthropomorphism. But more, it retained a thrilling air of mystery, something of the sublime.

What governed human affairs was not an omniscient consciousness, not a concerned Creator invested in human welfare, but something even more 'other', more alien, even more mysterious, without discernible qualities or narrative dimensions. What Hardy arrived at under Schopenhauer's influence was not something less 'supernatural' than the God of traditional worship, only less biddable, and even more indifferent to human suffering. Such a metaphysics suited the image increasingly implied by science. Change occurs and patterns unfold, but there is no plan that bears reference to humanity. The processes of life and growth merely express the blind energy of the Universe. Schopenhauer did raise the prospect that the Will to Life was in the business of progressively growing into awareness of itself. It might then be hoped that it would ultimately become more sympathetic, but the current signs are not good. If the consciousness allotted to human beings is an aspect or foretaste of the Universal Will, then it is a tragic gift. To be human is to be granted riches with one hand, and have them snatched away with the other. The force presiding over existence is pretty well indistinguishable from an Evil Spirit perversely kindling the light of consciousness, hope and desire, only to absent-mindedly snuff them out.

What underlies human action is nothing more than a state of compulsion; and once revealed as such, it bears the hallmarks of horror. To feel compelled by a will other than one's own, however grandly conceived, is to be threatened with utter annihilation and erasure. It suggests grotesque fairground images of puppetry or conditions of psychic 'possession'. The feverish struggles of sexual desire and social competition, distorting and enslaving enough as these can seem within the Darwinian context, are made all the more ridiculous and dehumanizing when seen as the operation at the furthest possible distance, of an impersonal irrational Other. As Hardy put in a letter of 1882, without some such conception of 'mind-stuff' existing at every material level of existence, organic and inorganic: 'there is no explaining how the mental universe is developed out of the physical' (*The Literary Notebooks of Thomas Hardy Vol 1 and 2 Vol 1* 148). Thought and action become expressions of inhuman energy passing like a virus through its host. Speculating on the origin of things Hardy suggested a 'consciousness, infinitely far off, at the other end of the chain of phenomena, always striving to express itself' (Asquith 291).

Tragic consciousness

Developing his idea of a Universal Will, Schopenhauer had taken the Hegelian concept of 'Spirit' and married it to something like Darwin's conception of the life-urge. The resulting metaphysic was stark and bleak. The personal God of Christian faith is replaced by an impersonal 'irrational' force, a source of pure activity uninhibited by any consideration other than its own continuation. Hardy's vision of haunted places and pointless sacrifice is intensified by this sense of a cosmic current of indifference running through the entire human story. The bitter wind blowing over Hardy's fiction emanates from this cold metaphysical region, and this can be seen in the creation of Wessex, and Egdon in particular. A fatalism prevails over a helpless humanity, at the mercy of senseless irrational forces. This is Hardy's tragic vision. The horrific irony of the human predicament is to have sufficiently evolved to become conscious of its own insignificance.

Intimations of such knowledge divide persons against themselves. Hardy's fiction is full of characters suffering interior alienation. Henchard and Jude are baffled by their own behaviour, their choices driven by an alien logic, self-defeating and destructive, an intimate otherness that is sensed but inexplicable. They look at themselves without recognition or understanding, as if their actions belonged to another, as if their hands were not their own. There is no sacrifice that will free them of their bounded nature as 'creatures of fate'. Inevitable destruction awaits characters like Henchard, who strive to assert themselves in the face of an implacable foe. Hardy characteristically employed the metaphor of performance to convey the way the suffering soul must seek to align itself with the Universal Will, rather like an actor might throw themselves into their allotted role or a musician might make themselves an instrument to the music, whose 'fingers are free to go on playing the pianoforte of themselves when he talks or thinks of something else' (*The Life and Work of Thomas Hardy*, by Thomas Hardy 361). The image is not so far removed from those describing the contemplative Christian soul attaining a prayerful relationship with God, except for the unmistakable sense of disembodying weirdness. Rather than attaining union with the Godhead, one is being operated upon. Rather than suspending one's ego to gain a higher perspective, the implication is that one is being used, manipulated, handled. As will be discussed in *Wessex Tales*, short stories by their truncated nature radically reduce/strip away characters' consciousness, leaving exposed the workings of the Will. They also deny clear narrative conclusion and as such feed the instability that is so central to the inherent unease in folk horror.

The absent God

In his examination of Western secularization, the philosopher and intellectual historian Charles Taylor calls into question the image of reason triumphing over superstition. He challenges the commonplace assumption 'that science refutes and hence crowds out religious belief' and argues that this 'official story' fails to provide 'an adequate explanation for why in fact people abandon their faith, even when they themselves articulate what happened in such terms as "Darwin refuted the Bible"' (*A Secular Age* 4). The role of conscious rational debate in shaping our deepest convictions is greatly exaggerated, and the heroic narrative of solitary individuals reasoning their way towards a disillusioned atheism may amount to little more than a retrospective rationalization of changes in attitude fundamentally rooted in the lived cultural environment.

In the light of this Hardy's ambivalence around 'statements' of belief signifies less than his repeated orientation of mind around certain sources of meaning. Florence Hardy, his second wife, wrote:

> He said once – perhaps oftener – that although invidious critics had cast slurs upon him as Nonconformist, Agnostic, Atheist, Infidel, Immoralist, Heretic, Pessimist, or something else equally opprobrious in their eyes, they have never thought of calling him what they might have called him much more plausibly – churchy; not in an intellectual sense but in so far as instincts and emotions ruled.
> (Millgate, *The Life and Work of Thomas Hardy* 386)

This privileging of 'belief' ('agnostic', 'atheist'), as against 'unthinking practice' ('churchy'), is a prominent component of the modern mindset Taylor seeks to chart:

> We tend to think of our differences from our remote forbears in terms of different *beliefs*, whereas there is something much more puzzling involved. It is clear that for our forebears, and for many people in the world today who live in a similar religious world, the presence of spirits is no more a matter of (optional, voluntarily embraced) belief than is for me the presence of this computer and its keyboard at the tips of my fingers. Like my ancestors, I confront a great deal in the inner workings of this computer that I don't understand (almost everything, in fact) and about which I could be induced by experts to accept various theories. But the encounter with a computer is not a matter of 'belief.' It's a basic fact of my experience. (C. Taylor, *Dilemmas and Connections* 219)

In his context Hardy's deliberate religious ambiguity might be read as 'constructive', as an acknowledgement of the limited grip 'belief' has upon the reality it purports to endorse or reject. Lived experience and the affinities it creates are not captured in mental formulae or grammatical statements. In Taylor's view, religious belief or unbelief is not fundamentally about assent (or otherwise) to a set of explicit propositions; it comes from a vital sense of connection (or otherwise) to what is experienced as a supreme source of life. That 'source' can be conceived of as 'the presence of God, or the voice of nature, or the force that flows through everything' (C. Taylor, *A Secular Age* 6). What confers ultimate meaning and value is the promise of relationship with an unbounded all-encompassing 'fullness of being'. What constitutes 'belief' is not primarily an attachment to some mental abstraction, but a feeling of being embedded within a sovereign background reality. And its authenticating power is very much bound up with the radical otherness of its intangibility. The familiar spiritual language of 'presence', 'voice' or 'flow' conveys something that is both intimate and beyond our grasp.

Few would claim that Thomas Hardy consistently experienced this sense of 'fullness', but its absence is powerfully felt in writing which consistently gestured towards something beyond the propositional. When aligned with a 'source of meaning', through a relationship of obedience or participation, the experience is positive. But even if this connection is broken, the quality of meaning attached to it endures, negatively, experienced as loss. When the voice of God or Nature is silent, even when the source of living fullness appears emptied out, or faith in it drains away, its absence can still remain the primary point of human orientation. Even when 'revealed' as error or illusion, it remains an irradicable ideal presiding over the actuality of things. This was the case following the ebbing tide of Victorian pessimism. Even as inherited certainties collapsed, thought remained dominated by an absence, the loss of the divine. Thus, Hardy remained as God-haunted as any would-be atheist.

4

Re-enchantment

In his comprehensive study, *A Secular Age* (2007), philosopher and social theorist Charles Taylor traces the development of human consciousness in the West, passing through three broad phases from pre-history to the present. Borrowing the language of Max Weber, he characterizes the first of these as an 'enchanted' condition. Human beings existed in a state of 'original participation', utterly immersed in a totally animated world, shot through with meaning. Life was experienced as a continuous unimpeded flow of vitality passing between humans and the ambient environment, within which they were constantly assailed by gods and spirits, autonomous powers associated with the natural landscape, and integral to the ritual economy of tribute and sacrifice. In what Robert Bellah in his book *Beyond Belief* calls 'archaic religion', the primary agent of tribal activity was the group as a whole. The necessary tasks of invoking and propitiating the gods were conducted by the community not the individual. Within this *archaic imaginary*, self-consciousness barely existed.

The enchanted self

In this state, the mind was thoroughly porous, a realm without distinct frontiers, constantly subject to psychic invasion. The boundaries that eventually came to structure the modern psyche, distinguishing self and other, were not yet firmly in place. There was no sharp differentiation between 'inside' and 'outside', 'mental' and 'physical'. Whatever entered consciousness was experienced as 'immediate reality' (C. Taylor, *A Secular Age* 12). Thought and emotion permeated the environment and were encountered as objective facts. Stones, rivers and mountains were coextensive with the thoughts and feelings they evoked. The most powerful emotions were exterior to the mind. Meaning was not primarily a property of thoughts but of things. No-one could imagine themselves outside this condition.

This enchanted condition now seems no more than a naïve prelude to a proper conception of the world. The modern mind has largely dispensed with 'supernatural influences', reinterpreting them as psychological phenomena. But Taylor insists it would be wrong to view the content of enchanted experience as merely 'imaginary':

> These were not "theories" in any sense [...] They were objects of real fear, of such compelling fear, that it wasn't possible to entertain seriously the idea that they might be unreal. You or people you knew had experienced them. And perhaps no one in your milieu ever got around even to suggesting their unreality.
>
> (C. Taylor, *A Secular Age* 11)

This fear did not derive its potency from some collectively held body of metaphysical belief. These 'objects' constituted an integral part of the given cosmic background that determined the very possibilities of experience.

The second stage of Taylor's history begins with what the German philosopher Karl Jaspers called the so-called Axial Age, around the first millennium BCE. He follows other 'grand theorists' in identifying this moment as a seismic shift in human consciousness, when the advent of monotheism began to loosen the psychological connection to ancient forms of experience, causing a 'withdrawal of participation'. Meanings were no longer firmly embedded in the immediate environment. The spirits began to disappear. Philosophical enquiry started to challenge the authority of old myths. The diverse voices of the Axial Revolution (Buddha, Confucius, Socrates, as well as the Hebrew Prophets) spoke in the name of some transcendent Good beyond the tribe, beyond Nature. Gradually the idea emerged that ultimate significance resided in an exterior dimension remote from ordinary experience. These Axial figures started what Taylor calls a Quarrel with Life.

This quarrel deepened in the West during the mediaeval period. The pre-modern patterns did not entirely disappear. There was still plenty of enchantment, but it sat within a much wider horizon of Christian theology, mediated by socially authorizing institutions: 'The medieval ceremony of "beating the bounds" of the agricultural village, for instance, involved the whole parish and could only be effective as a collective act of this whole' (C. Taylor, *Dilemmas and Connections: Selected Essays* 217). Other practices for dealing with spirits and forces were delegitimized, not because they were believed to be empty or ineffective, but precisely the opposite:

> Rituals of this kind were supposed to have power in themselves and hence were blasphemous. All such rituals were put into a category of "magic." The category was constituted by the rejection, rather than providing a clear reason for rejection'.
>
> (C. Taylor, *Dilemmas and Connections: Selected Essays* 288)

In its attempt to subsume pre-existing cultures, the new religion had long ago appropriated existing sacred sites. The pagan landscape was effectively over-written, its stones and streams, wells and springs, were rededicated and repurposed. The old gods were replaced by a corresponding dispersal of spiritual power attributed to saints and other holy figures, whose shrines and relics offered protection and healing. In this way the numinous continued to reside in places and things, especially in association with human remains. A fragment of bone or cloth could become a locus of mystical energy and veneration:

> Catholic Christianity retained the sacred in this sense, both in its own sacraments and in certain pagan festivals suitably "baptized". But protestantism and particularly Calvinism classed it with idolatry and waged unconditional war on it. It is probable that the unremitting struggle to desacralize the world in the name of an undivided devotion to God waged by Calvin and his followers helped to destroy the sense that the creation was a locus of meanings in relation to which man had to define himself.
>
> (C. Taylor, *Hegel* 8)

This *mediaeval imaginary* still allowed for the coincidence of human and extra-human forces. The mediaeval self could still encounter wood-sprites and demons. Shakespeare was only reflecting the ingrained assumptions of his audience when he had ghosts rising from their tombs at the killing of a king. For the mediaeval mind these signs and wonders were not literary flourishes, they were reminders that the community was grafted onto an enchanted order of reality, a Great Chain of Being connecting all things:

> Embedding in society also brings with it an embedding in the cosmos. In early religion, the spirits and forces with whom we are dealing are in numerous ways intricated in the world. We can see examples of this aplenty if we refer back to the enchanted world of our medieval ancestors: although the God they worshipped transcended the world, they nevertheless also had to do with intra-cosmic spirits, and they dealt with causal powers that were embedded in things: relics, sacred places, and the like.
>
> (C. Taylor, *Dilemmas and Connections: Selected Essays* 218)

This 'social embeddedness' defines and delimits identity, such that 'from the standpoint of the individual's sense of self, it means the inability to imagine oneself outside a certain matrix' (C. Taylor, *Dilemmas and Connections: Selected Essays* 218). All societies, ancient or modern, are embedded within a particular background condition that governs what can be acknowledged as real.

Hardy folk

The rural folk traditions of Hardy's Wessex were essentially mediaeval remnants, pagan elements excluded or suppressed by the official faith. Their continued existence did not rest on a different structure of belief. What country practices and local ritual offered was a different *participation* in reality. In distant locations, within close-bound communities, vestiges of the archaic religion persisted as acts of resistance against a dominant orthodoxy intent on submerging diverse identities and repressing instincts. Hardy's representation of active folk tradition illustrates a hybridized paganized religious impulse, deeply embedded in the stuff of rural life, distanced from the controlling gaze of an officially regulating culture. These anthropological speculations are not introduced here to suggest that Hardy's Dorset harboured some lost pre-historic tribe languishing in primeval darkness. Hardy himself was living proof that modern ideas had penetrated the England countryside, but he was also aware that these modern ideas failed to entirely eradicate magical thinking. Something of the pre-modern animistic environment continued to survive, nurtured and nourished by folklore and custom. It's integral to Taylor's story that mere 'ideas' do not sweep away or displace the unreflective background of lived experience. That background is tenacious in being more than a mental construct. It is the context within which such constructs make sense or gain purchase on life.

The third stage of Taylor's framework sees Christianity steadily dissociate from the dark pagan imaginary: 'One of the main vectors over the last six or seven centuries in this civilization has been a steadily increasing emphasis on a religion of personal commitment and devotion, over against forms centred on collective ritual' (*Dilemmas and Connections: Selected Essays* 215). In particular, the Reformation and Counter-Reformation movements of the sixteenth and seventeenth centuries were systematic attempts to root out archaic remnants persisting in the popular imagination. Both Protestant and Catholic elites fought against what were now characterized as 'superstitions'. The suspicion was that the uneducated and illiterate populous concealed pagan sentiments beneath a cloak of respectable Christian observance. The common people might be just 'going through the motions', more out of cultural solidarity than right-minded belief, prompting 'attempts to regulate the lives of the laity according to more and more stringent models of practice' (C. Taylor, *Dilemmas and Connections: Selected Essays* 215). The aim of religious reformers was, in effect, to actively delegitimize everything outside the mystique of the Church, leaving no space for anything but catechized orthodoxy:

> The Reformation and Counter-Reformation repressed first magical practices and then those facets of traditional Christian sacramental

ritual that they began to deem magical ... practices that suppose and draw upon various intra-cosmic spirits, good or bad, and higher powers inhering in things (e.g. relics). I want to use the word *disenchantment* for this movement of repression.

(C. Taylor, *Dilemmas and Connections: Selected Essays* 216)

Religious elites bore down on the ordinary people from various directions, but each point of pressure producing unintended consequences. The concentrated insistence on 'personal commitment' to clear codes of explicit verbal assent meant that those who could not recite the prescribed formula or demonstrate the required rigour were pushed outside. Ironically, the stress on conformity created a marginalized, even outlawed subculture. The figure of the witch came to prominence, apparently steeped in a religiousness of the wrong sort. Where the Church preached a faith handed down from ivory towers, the Countryside performed a way of life sourced and sustained from below, from the earth itself. In parallel, the rise of science encouraged both individualism and the anxieties that accompany it. Empiricism prized a disengaged reason, capable of instrumentally applying itself to an essentially inert exterior world. The modern self steadily 'withdrew' more deeply into a private space. Immersive 'participation' in the cosmos gradually became the sole preserve of mystics and seers.

What made possible this transformation from the mediaeval to the modern was the development of what Taylor calls 'the buffered self', a mind having established limiting boundaries for the protection and control of its psychic territory, able to bracket off spirit dimensions and maintain a strong distinction between the surrounding environment and the human operation within it. The buffered identity has a radically different way of perceiving and being in the world. The self is not completely divorced from Nature, but is in a relationship determined by human constructs and projects mobilized to use it. Where the mediaeval mind still entertained the work of spirits in everything from 'the King's touch' to the cultivation of crops, the modern mind increasingly acknowledged only itself as the source of meaningful action. Where the porous self of the enchanted world was vulnerable to invasion by cosmic forces, and governed by fear of them, the modern 'buffered self' increasingly experienced them (if at all) as internal objects, eruptions or fluctuations of temper, to be diagnosed and 'treated':

For the modern, buffered self, the possibility exists of taking a distance from, disengaging from, everything outside the mind. My ultimate purposes are those which arise within me, the crucial meanings of things are those defined in my responses to them.

(C. Taylor, *A Secular Age* 38)

One such 'response' was the development of a rational materialism. The old idea of a reciprocal relationship of 'participation' in the cosmos became nothing more than a consoling or aggrandizing fiction. The universe is merely mindless matter. Consciousness, merely an effect of material processes. The language of 'soul' fragmented into a myriad anthropocentric spiritualities. The Christianity that survived the Enlightenment was a thoroughly 'rationalized' one, relegated to the status of a socially useful moral instrument. As the Christian wave receded, what was left on Dover Beach was the individual mind, buffered within its protective shell, looking in on itself.

The immanent frame

The standard anthropological 'grand narrative' states that the enchanted cosmos of the mediaeval world was, in its turn, destroyed by an Enlightenment rationality that redefined reality as a grid of material forces, obeying Newtonian notions of time (a homogeneous sequence of punctual moments) and space (matter in motion). For Charles Taylor, the rise of empirical science certainly has a place in this narrative, but it is not the full story. What has gradually replaced mediaeval cosmology and its attachment to the magical system of nature is what he calls 'the Immanent Frame'. This is more than an ideological context, more than the shift to a rational materialistic worldview. It is more than a body of ideas or precepts. The Western Mind has drawn around itself a new horizon, which confers meaning only on what lies within it. From within this *modern imaginary*, meanings are only mental phenomena. Human beings don't encounter meanings residing in nature or reality itself. All that exists is subject to historical time in plottable space.

All experience occurs within the context of that unspoken assumption. The Immanent Frame is not a body of beliefs or an all-embracing ideology. What Taylor describes is not the triumph of one description of reality over another. It was not primarily a matter of intellectual enlightenment, of an individual or group becoming 'better informed' about its environment. It marks a transition to an entirely different experiential background framework, a change in what it is possible for human beings to think and feel, and perceive: 'an unspoken boundary' or 'inarticulate limit' to experience itself (C. Taylor, *Hegel* 6–7). The *modern imaginary* is an altogether different existential condition, defined not by epistemology but by configuration within a radically altered horizon of possibilities.

Taylor is not making metaphysical claims. He is attempting to dismantle the 'official story' that science has (a) disabused us of an illusion and (b) done so purely by virtue of the truths it reveals. For Taylor, the modern Western worldview (the 'mature', 'objective', disengaged rationality epitomized by scientific method) went from being one available form of description, to being the frame through which all other descriptions are invalidated:

> What was once one possible construction among others sinks to the level of a picture, in Wittgenstein's sense; that is, it becomes part of the unquestioned background, something whose shape is not perceived, but which conditions, largely unnoticed, the way we think, infer, experience, process claims and arguments. From within the picture, it just seems obvious that the order of argument proceeds from science to atheism, through a series of well-grounded steps.
>
> (C. Taylor, *A Secular Age* 565)

And it is within this modern 'picture' that *belief* becomes the dominant intellectual focus, beliefs of the kind that find expression in linguistic propositions. The relationship between human and world is founded upon 'beliefs', potential statements of perceived fact, and the consequence of actions based upon these. In a sense the Immanent Frame gives birth to 'belief' as a defining state of mind. And with 'belief' is born its twin, 'unbelief'. As never before, modern identity occupies a space in which belief and unbelief co-exist as alternative possibilities from which the individual consciousness constructs (or imagines it constructs) its own reality.

Having evolved beyond 'original participation' and exposure to extra-human forces, the modern psyche has won for itself an autonomy that is both liberating and dreadful. The modern identity is exposed to multiple perspectives, the very existence of which argues against any ultimate foundation upon which life can finally rest. The burden of doubt is doubled by the burden of *choice*.

> The shift to secularity ... consists, among other things, of a move from a society where belief in God is unchallenged and indeed, unproblematic, to one in which it is understood to be one option among others, and frequently not the easiest to embrace.
>
> (C. Taylor, *A Secular Age* 3)

In the absence of a given 'meaning', the modern mind must achieve one for itself. The cultural shock of 'modernity' is not so much the shift in beliefs, from religion to science, as the fact that life must now be lived in the face of indeterminacies. The co-existence of belief and unbelief, both equally coherent, neither eliminating the other, speaks to the terrifying groundlessness of the enterprise. Taylor says the most important fact about the *modern imaginary* is that:

> ... it has opened a space in which people can wander between and around all these options without having to land clearly and definitively in any

one. In the wars between belief and the unbelief, this can be seen as a kind of no-man's-land; except that it has got wide enough to take the character rather of a neutral zone, where one can escape the war altogether.
(C. Taylor, *A Secular Age* 351)

It was this 'no-man's land' that swallowed so many of the notable Victorians who surrounded Hardy. And one might characterize Hardy's ambivalence and equivocation as a tactical retreat into that 'neutral zone'. When Taylor's history reaches the nineteenth century the surface effects of living within the *modern imaginary*, the strain between intellectual self-confidence and spiritual malaise, become palpable. Increasingly, Victorians felt the effects of living with reference solely to themselves, within the terms permitted by the Immanent Frame. The burdens of belief and disbelief, faith and scepticism, take on Universal proportions. Anxieties around technology and the divorce from nature collide with an agonized nostalgia for lost certainties. But Taylor's contention is that these were symptoms of a deeper yearning, a profound longing to be touched by something outside the human. The sorrowfulness exhibited by Hardy and other representative Victorian figures is a product of a barely articulable sense of estrangement from sources of innate meaning.

In Taylor's genealogy of the secular, human 'progress' has been a steady process of 'disenchantment'. The very word carries an important ambiguity, implying both disappointment with reality and freedom from illusion. On the one hand, modern anthropocentrism has granted the modern self a sense of authority and liberty, and the 'holy terror' of psychic invasion is largely a thing of the past. On the other hand, this 'achievement' is accompanied by a sense of diminishment that life in this disenchanted world is flat, stale and ultimately unreal. Security has resulted in a loss of depth, a feeling of being cut off from something vital, hiding behind defences, walled up, 'living behind a screen' (*A Secular Age* 302). Our greater 'understanding' of reality has been gained at the price of detachment *from* it. Immunity from 'holy terror' may mean insulation from so much more.

The modern 'buffered self' enjoys 'relative invulnerability to anything beyond the human world, while at the same time a sense that something may be occluded in the very closure which guarantees safety' (*A Secular Age* 303). It can withdraw into itself to the extent of giving itself autonomy over the ordering of its life, what meanings it will acknowledge. It can now virtually deny there is a world outside. Having made itself 'free' from the external threats of spiritual forces (by denying their existence as anything other than human fictions), the buffered self can feel imprisoned within itself, even to the denial of any larger reality. Hardy was alive to both the dangerous illusions of invulnerability and the equivalent experiential impoverishments of modernity. His fictional Wessex is not assailed by fairy creatures or magical spirits, but remains vulnerable to the dangerous seduction of folk belief. Hardy's characters take security from belief in something 'which lies beyond standard perception, cognition and experience' (Fisher, *The Weird and the Eerie* 12), but it is the belief itself, or rather the 'believing' it, that seems alien and eerie to the reader. What is unsettling, what presses against the Immanent Frame of our conceptions, is the lively co-existence of an equivalent 'irrational' in our midst. It is folklore and folk culture itself that haunts the *modern imaginary*. What should be dead, buried and forgotten lives on. Hardy's use of folk material does not point towards the supernatural, but towards the desire for participation in something 'other'. In doing so, folk beliefs and practices challenge that Frame by drawing attention to its existence.

Festive poetics

The suspicion that modernity has cut itself off from necessary sources of life has a long history. Romanticism expressed regret at the exclusion of the wild and unmanageable from the experience of nature. Victorian pessimism grew out of the alienation caused by the Industrial Revolution. At the turn of the twentieth century, the desire to reconnect with vital sources outside the merely societal promoted the arcane esotericism of the theosophists (W. B. Yeats) and the cult of the shamanic artist (D. H. Lawrence). This loss of immediacy may have been more dramatically and stridently expressed by Nietzsche and his heirs, but Hardy was responding to the same longing for contact with energies outside the human frame. Not that Hardy climbed back into mythic realms or dabbled in esoteric spirituality. What he cultivated was an imaginative terrain already given in childhood. He could return to it, not as an alternative scheme of belief, but as a counterweight or corrective to the dominant mentalism. For Hardy, as for Hamlet, there remained more things in heaven and earth than appeared in the philosophies of his age.

Charles Taylor sees Hardy as a major figure in the ongoing attempt to strike a compromise between Christianity and materialism, between the child's picture-book faith ('now figuring as temptation') represented by the poem 'The Oxon', and the sober austerity ('full of regret and mourning') of 'God's Funeral' (*A Secular Age* 564). Hardy remained 'enchanted' enough to wish he could believe, but enough of a 'modern' to envisage such 'magic' only within the terms permitted by the Immanent Frame. But, as Taylor says:

> These compromises arise from a deep cross-pressure, between the unacceptability of Christianity for those who have deeply internalised the immanent order (or come to see themselves totally within it), on the one hand, and a strong dissatisfaction with the flatness, emptiness of the world, and/or the inner division, atomism, ugliness or self-enclosed nature of human life in modernity.
>
> (C. Taylor, *A Secular Age* 391)

Subsequent secular generations may have come to live 'totally within it', but Hardy and the other 'great nineteenth-century prophets' had not yet fully adjusted to the purely immanent world.

Taylor sees Hardy's struggle to retain a spiritual dimension in the face of materialism, as an underappreciated response to the crisis of his age:

> At the turn of the century, we see Hardy recurring to a Primal Force underlying the universe. But this is already in a different moral space than Carlyle and Arnold. The Prime Will can be seen as blind and cruel. And although Hardy late in life puts forward the notion that it may grow and improve along with the humans whose lives it has so roughly handled, we have moved into the company of Schopenhauer (who influenced Hardy) ... And even then. this metaphysical-cosmological dimension of Hardy's thought has been largely forgotten in the reception of his novels and poetry.
>
> (C. Taylor, *A Secular Age* 390)

Taylor sees continued fascination with the 'metaphysical-cosmological dimension' as an impulse towards re-enchantment. However bleak Schopenhauer's philosophy, it revived a sense of awe, and touched upon the mystical. All was again returned to 'Spirit'. How to articulate, even register, what lies outside the culture's conceptual framework, became a major question for Victorians and Moderns alike. Is there any vantage point outside the self-determining anthropomorphic narrative? According to Taylor other opportunities to re-enchant the cosmos exist, and he identifies two that have a direct bearing on Thomas Hardy and the folk horror tradition.

The first 'opportunity' is found in Art, particularly the art exemplified by the Romantic Movement and its rebellion against the hyper-rationality of the Enlightenment. The Romantics, spurred by an Ethics of Authenticity, give us a self in search of deeper sources of meaning. The romantic self is not porous in the way of the mediaeval peasantry, but possesses a semi-porousness orientated towards what lies in indeterminacy and ambiguity outside the limits of the measurable. In its search for meanings and expressivity it finds the transcendent opened up again in aesthetic events or experiences. Taylor identifies such art as a mode to encounter meanings outside the rational. It yields moments of aesthetic communion, a re-enchantment through the poetic. Such artistic epiphanies take many forms. While a Gerard Manley Hopkins' (1844–89) celebrates the presence of God in Nature, Hardy (his near contemporary) shudders at the absence of that same God. Yet paradoxically the very confrontation with meaninglessness can open up a set of meanings which push back against the nullity, and re-enchant the world in a different key. A Universe echoing to the absence of God is a place of vertiginous oceanic depths. Abysmal Dread is no less shattering than Holy Terror. Art finds meanings resident within the event of reality itself, no matter how diminished or horrific. Even amid intimations of unrelieved mortality, existence itself can re-appear as poeticized. The poetry of the grave is still poetry.

The second 'opportunity' is the Festive. Stretching back centuries people have come together at special times to transcend their individual identity and come into a wider communion with each other and with nature. Taylor identifies these festal moments as expressions of a residual connection with the numinous, natural energy and sacred time, moments where collective enchantment can re-enter. In commemorating half-remembered festal scenes, Hardy re-enacts this exit from ordinary time. Folklore enshrined cultural memories that embody and articulate connections and relations that press beyond the limits licensed by the Immanent Frame. Something in the rough-hewn manner of rustic rites presents as compensation for the sanitized pomp of authorized ceremonial. From mediaeval Carnival to modern raves and street-parties, the festive moment has the power to disrupt the status quo and momentarily loosen the grip of 'normality'. The 1960s hippy aspiration to 'turn on, tune in and drop out' was directed against the Immanent Frame in its social political manifestation.

Folk horror can make a claim to be the union of the artistic and the festive horror texts, in all their blurring and erasure of boundaries, momentarily reawaken in the buffered identity a sense of its inescapable vulnerability to forces that can and do penetrate and invade the self's rational 'safe-space'. The mental buffer is there so that 'things beyond don't need to "get at me"' (C. Taylor, *A Secular Age* 38). In 'horror' they do. The genre represents an assault upon modernity, a breach in its collective psychological defences, not so much a return of the repressed, as a reviving of the undead.

The buffered self has been placed beyond the reach of some ancient fears, but there is a strange desire to re-experience them in artificial form. The unsettling concurrence of attraction and repulsion lies close to the core of the horror genre in general, and folk horror in particular. As Taylor says of our modern fascination with horror:

> Perhaps the clearest sign of the transformation in our world is that today many people look back to the world of the porous self with nostalgia, as if the creation of a thick emotional boundary between us and the cosmos were now lived as loss. The aim is to try to recover some measure of this lost feeling. So people go to movies about the uncanny in order to experience a frisson. Our peasant ancestors would have thought us insane. You can't get a frisson from what is really in fact terrifying you.
>
> (C. Taylor, *A Secular Age* 38)

Within the modern 'buffered' condition Taylor says:

> Our actions, goals, achievements, and the like, have a lack of weight, gravity, thickness, substance. There is a deeper resonance which they lack, which we feel should be there.
>
> (C. Taylor, *A Secular Age* 307)

Folk horror both carries the dead weight of the pre-rational and induces the double vision we might associate with the porous self: 'The boundary between agents and forces is fuzzy in the enchanted world, and the boundary between mind and world is porous, as we see in the way that charged objects can influence us' (C. Taylor, *Dilemmas and Connections: Selected Essays* 201). The primitive fear of 'possession' is simulated in the exposure to images and feelings that confuse or erase the barrier protecting the modern self from anything it cannot control or rationally subdue.

Pagan survival

Charles Taylor's broad and sweeping narrative aims to place modern secular culture in the context of a thorough anthropological survey of religious consciousness. In this he shares a great deal with his near namesake Edward Burnett Tylor (1832–1917), whose work was well known to Hardy and his circle. Hardy's interest in folklore was fed by the work of popular scholars like John Hutchins and John Brand, but it was placed on a firm intellectual foundation by the publication in 1871 of Tylor's *Primitive Culture: Researches into the Development of Mythology, Philosophy, Religion, Art and Custom* (two volumes), a massively ambitious study that gave birth to British Anthropology and aimed to reveal the surprising proximity of the ancients.

Tylor's own 'long history' bears an uncanny resemblance to Taylor's. Tylor's argument is that all societies go through a three-step process of development ('savagery', 'barbarism' and 'civilization'), but that these 'progressions' are never complete in themselves. Accordingly, the rural cultures of nineteenth-century Europe remained tangibly connected to their tribal origins, because at each level of development vestiges of more primitive customs or 'survivals' remain visible:

> Look at the modern European peasant using his hatchet and his hoe, see his food boiling or roasting over the log-fire ... hear his tale of the ghost in the nearest haunted house ... If we choose out of the way things which have altered little in a long course of centuries, we may draw a

picture where there shall be scarce a hand's breadth difference between an English ploughman and a negro of Central Africa.

(Tylor 1:6)

Tylor's theory of 'survivals' was discussed extensively in the middlebrow magazines to which Hardy faithfully subscribed, and it found its way into his work. When describing the mummers' play in *The Return of the Native*, he uses Tylor's terminology: 'A traditional pastime is to be distinguished from a mere revival in no more striking feature than this, that while in the revival all is excitement and fervour, the survival is carries on with a stolidity and absence of stir which sets one wondering why a thing that is done so perfunctorily should be kept up at all' (178). 'Revivals' are merry traditional entertainment, harkening back to bygone days. 'Survivals' require no conscious effort. They have an eerily cold and impersonal, even mindlessly mechanical, autonomy of their own. There is nothing celebratory about them, nothing Dionysian. They have the flat 'matter of fact' solemnity of something serving a purpose of its own. They have the autonomy traditionally ascribed to phantasms.

On the face of it, the atavistic within Hardy's writing, the tendency to revert to the ancient and ancestral, is at odds with what he so often explicitly professed. Auguste Comte and the other great apostles of progress who influenced so much of Hardy's thinking would not have found anything appealing in the benighted spectacle of Egdon Heath. *The Return of the Native* is a rebuke to the idea of a triumphant Enlightenment and the inevitable advance of progress. Even if Hardy had not been a born doomsayer, his vivid sense of the past as a living recalcitrant fact would have made such confidence in the future impossible. Negative forces will claw humanity backwards. The village practices recounted in Hardy's fiction carry this stubborn weight of morbidity. Tylor too shunned optimism. Part of his intellectual appeal lay in his unsentimental attitude to the subject matter. He was not bent on preserving 'traditional' values or setting up an image of the Noble Savage. Humanity may have attained a tolerable level of civilization, but it was partial and thin. He could see no intrinsic reason why 'advanced' societies should necessarily continue to 'evolve' in a positive direction, given 'how large a share stupidity and unpractical conservatism and dogged superstition have had in preserving for us traces of the history of our race' (Tylor I:150). Tylor's work stimulated a new generation of amateur antiquarians to scour the country for the mythic roots of the living past. The collective picture that emerged was of modernity resting on a heathen foundation, a sentiment without doctrine, less a matter of explicit belief than attachment to the natural features of place, springs and wells, trees and stones. A kind of ill-defined animism persisted, standing apart from the formulated creeds of Christianity. Hardy had first-hand knowledge of what went on among the common country people. Sunday observance co-existed with nocturnal practices and natural magic. A pagan substrate lay just below the surface.

Of course, Hardy was no pagan. Nevertheless, he had his own irrationalism and shared the view that rationality is not the last word in human understanding. The immemorial practices Tylor called 'survivals' represented visible cracks in the surface confidence of modernity. They represent beaches in the defences of the modern self, where primitive susceptibilities, appetites and allegiances break through. Hardy was no animist. Nevertheless, his fiction insists that animism has a place in the scheme of things. It expressed in the language of superstition what Schopenhauer offered as metaphysics. The re-animation of place and object contradicts the singular materialist narrative that says everything in the world is part of a natural order dependent on nothing but itself. It re-enchants by bringing 'things' disturbingly to life. Tylor's work aimed to replace the patchy and piecemeal investigations of amateur folklorists, by setting the new science of anthropology within a firm conceptual structure. Hardy, as artist, felt no such obligations. There is nothing systematic in his presentation or valuation of seasonal customs. At one level they serve a straightforward realist function, illustrating a colourful aspect of country life. At a quite other level they open onto a visionary space deeply and multiply layered. The cultural 'survivals' he records have the haunting resonance of things existing beyond the conventional limits of time and space. Their relation to time speaks less of continuity ('the old barn') than of things that endure for their own sake, abruptly re-asserting themselves. Then and Now are simultaneously present in vertical time. Paradox itself serves to disrupt the prevailing modern discourse, by providing 'a surplus of meaning' the Immanent Frame cannot assimilate. Virginia Woolf found intimations of this in Hardy, describing it as 'the margin of the unexpressed' and 'a surplus of undecidability'.

Surplus meaning

This 'surplus of meaning' can manifest itself as an excess of narrative possibilities. In *The Return of the Native*, the death of Eustacia Vye is an unresolved mystery. She may die from melancholy or exposure or suicide. She might be the victim of even darker forces, the primitive magic exercised by Susan Nunsuch or the diffuse malign forces emanating from the Heath. As Gillian Beer writes:

> Here, as so often, Hardy establishes contiguous routes to the overdetermined event: through coincidence and witchcraft, or at the same time, through psychological motive and independent event. Neither form of explanation

drives out the other. They appear as parallel languages rather than as opposed interpretations. Present and past belief systems coexist. They do not follow an ordered succession.

(C. Taylor, *A Secular Age* 43)

Mutually exclusive ideas cohabit. Binaries are subverted. Ambiguity reigns. No one order of reality dominates. Again, all have their place. Even if the novel succeeds with the reader *as a novel*, it fails as an intelligible *account of events*. The overdetermination of motive and action shapes *The Return of the Native* into splendid incoherence.

That readers are not dumbfounded suggests a very modern acceptance of the sort of plurality and stratification that ultimately found expression in Freud. Psychoanalysis aimed to exhume prehistoric patterns deposited in the unconscious layers of the individual psyche. Conscious or unconscious the whole of the psyche is alive. Psychoanalytic practice is the art of naming and narrating the 'survivals' that erupt onto the visible surface. Hardy's imagination is similarly archaeological, exposing the strata within the experienced moment. But Hardy would part company with Freud's in attributing some direct causal relationship between past and present. Hardy's causation is often impossible to read in any straightforward way. Readers of 'The Withered Arm' didn't need a Freudian lens to appreciate that what squats oppressively on Rhoda Brook's chest is a manifestation of her psyche. Something hideously deformed within this wronged and weary woman is outwardly projected onto the silken finery of a younger rival. However, Hardy deliberately undermines any attempt to psychologically 'normalize' the story. In terms of realist plotting, Rhoda cannot dream of Gertrude. Rhoda hasn't yet clapped eyes on her. The 'dream' falls uncomfortably between projection and premonition.

Again, we are caught between competing (mutually undermining) interpretations, which (in the manner of overdetermination) suggest yet another quite different order of explanation. Both she and Gertrude must be subject to a nameless malevolent force, working out some separate design upon their lives. A current of causation quite outside any natural or magical scheme is passing through the world of the characters, an 'enemy' to them all. And this obscure or oblique causation is itself part of the story's disconcerting effect. Furthermore, the status of the event itself recedes into unreadability: 'For the first time Gertrude Lodge visited the supplanted woman in her dreams. Rhoda Brook dreamed – since her assertion that she really saw, before falling to sleep, was not to be believed – that the young wife, in the pale silk dress and white bonnet, but with features shockingly distorted, and wrinkled as by age, was sitting upon her chest as she lay' (*Wessex Tales* 42). Her son hears a sound of something falling to the floor, which might be the incubus or Rhoda herself, further conflating dreaming and waking, the fantastic and the real: ''O, merciful heaven!'' she cried, sitting on the edge of the bed in a cold sweat; 'that was not a dream – she was here!' The 'vision' has no stability of source or purpose. Rhoda's conviction is the only fact we have. The rest of the plot is given over to logical incoherence. The dream is a premonition of what it will bring about. There is a circularity of causation, effect preceding cause. Time is ruptured, fragmented and redistributed.

Here and elsewhere, Hardy's fiction issues an epistemological challenge. Where should the reader (firmly embedded in the Immanent Frame of post-enlightenment modernity, and firmly ensconced in a fictional world of bonnet-ribbons and milk-churns) *place* such phenomena? The question arises for folklore elements more generally, and Hardy wrestled with this from his own personal perspective. In the poem 'One We Knew' (*Collected Poems* 257) he evokes his paternal grandmother, Mary Hardy, for whom 'things retold were ... as things existent', and recalls her brooding 'on such dead themes, not as one who remembers,/But rather as one who sees'. Typical of Hardy, the question is left open as to how metaphorical that last word should be. The status of memory is a vexed question for the writer whose job it is to take 'dead themes' and make the reader 'see'. It is doubly fraught for someone so closely identifying with that class of person. Hardy is not seeking to authenticate visionary experience; he is affirming its 'reality' to those who experience it. The status of these experiences was not something he could settle for himself, which may be why he was so unambiguous in stating that he invented nothing: 'I may say once for all that every superstition, custom, &c., described in my novels may be depended on as true records of the same (whatever merit in folklorists eyes they may have as such) – & not inventions of mine' (*The Collected Letters of Thomas Hardy, 7 Volumes Vol 2* 54). Nor of anyone else. The intellectual appeal of folk material in late-nineteenth-century Europe, in music as well as narrative, lay precisely its being 'unauthored', a pure product of earth or spirit, and 'innocent' of the modern culture that surrounded it. The slippage between the 'authentic' and the 'invented' (leading to the curious notion of 'genuine superstition') is another area of indeterminacy of feeling, testing the boundaries of understanding and identification. The daylight is important and in his 1896 Preface to the Wessex Tales, Hardy corrects an 'error' in his telling of 'The Withered Arm', having been subsequently informed by an authority who knew 'Rhoda Brook' that 'such a vision in the daytime is more impressive than if it had happened in a midnight dream' (5). The implication is that the story would have been more faithful to itself if the horrifying dream had entered in daylight: a trope of later folk horror. The figure of monstrosity calmly squats in the midst of the everyday. The story begins and ends in milking, but within this ordinary world a young lady's closet becomes lined with 'mystic herbs, charms, and books of necromancy' (48) and her husband is made furious by 'village beliefs ... partly because he half entertained them himself' (50–1).

Hardy was less given to constructing systems of philosophy than assembling what he famously referred to in the Preface to *Jude the Obscure* (1895) (V) as 'a series of seemings, or personal impressions'. He was an artist, and 'their consistency or their discordance' was not 'of the first moment'. Hardy deliberately entertains the odd and the incongruous, the inharmonious and incompatible. His theme is things 'out of place' and 'out of time', and the curious co-existence of the two. Furthermore, just as contradictory 'impressions' can co-exist, so too can the opposing tendencies of the interpreting mind. At times Hardy's fictional practice chimes with Mikhail Bakhtin's conception of the novel as a polyphonic discourse of discourses, modelling the plurality of perspectives embedded in language itself. Contraries are held together or overlaid creating a density of prospect that both resists the readerly impulse towards a singular meaning and deepens the fictional texture into something resembling the complexity of real life. The famous final paragraph of *Tess* perfectly illustrates Hardy's studied ambiguity:

> 'Justice' was done, and the President of the Immortals, in Aeschylean phrase, had ended his sport with Tess. And the d'Urberville knights and dames slept on in their tombs unknowing. The two speechless gazers bent themselves down to the earth, as if in prayer, and remained thus a long time, absolutely motionless: the flag continued to wave silently. As soon as they had strength they arose, joined hands again, and went on.
> (Hardy, *Tess of the d'Urbervilles* 489–90)

The first sentence is often singled out as the novel's bleak moral conclusion. The world is presided over by alien forces with little concern for homosapiens. But what follows shifts perspective. The second sentence transfers focus from myth to history, sliding from the indifference of 'the Immortals' to the indifference of the human past towards the human present. The next sentences rise from hopelessness to the dignity of mortal resolve. The final image revives hope, and points to a future shaped by human bonds of solidarity. Each sentence carries a different emphasis and points in a different direction. None is definitive. Insofar as the linear form of prose fiction allows, Hardy wants to subvert and defer finality of meaning. It is all four gestures taken together, laid across each other like accumulated strata, that mark the final state of things. The last word on the page imparts a movement that the novel won't complete. And this is the hallmark of Hardy's art. Different perspectives or impressions are set side by side or overlapped (we might say superimposed) to compose a complex inclusive vision that simply cannot be univocal or linear. The novel drives a vertical line through every level of existence.

Beyond the frame

In many ways Hardy epitomized his age. Caught in the intellectual and cultural crosscurrents, pulled by the competing claims of religious faith and rational materialism, he stood squarely on the philosophical and religious fault-lines that traumatized much of Victorian society, maximally exposed to the criss-crossing contra-flows of thought and feeling. He held these tensions in a rather unstable equilibrium, such that whichever side he cared to reveal, its opposite could still show through. He struggled to keep the disparate sides of himself together: the realistic and the romantic, the intellectual and the non-intellectual. As personal defence, he cultivated ambivalence and tolerated contradiction.

Rather than 'time-torn', we might better describe Hardy as 'many-minded' or 'Janus-faced', deliberately planting himself at the crossroads, marking the place where contraries converge: past and present, tradition and modernity, superstition and enlightenment. And it was in his writing, in the fluidity of narrative and symbol, that he could keep these contraries in play. In this he wasn't alone: 'The best and most sensitive minds, were cross-pressured, looking for a third way' (R. H. Taylor 302). For Hardy, that third way was literature. In his Apology to *Late Lyrics and Earlier* (1922) he expressed something like an Arnoldian belief that literature could replace religion as a unifier of experience: they 'modulate into each other; are indeed but different names for the same thing' (*Collected Poems* 530). He goes on:

> It may indeed be a forlorn hope, a mere dream, that of an alliance between religion, which must be retained unless the world is to perish, and complete rationality, which must come, unless also the world is to perish, by means of the interfusing effect of poetry.
>
> (Hardy, *Collected Poems* 531)

It's typical of Hardy's fatalism that he should already concede that the hope for a reconciliation of religion and reason was 'forlorn'. But the echo of Wordsworth's 'interfused' (from 'Lines Composed a Few Miles above Tintern Abbey') reflects the Romantic ideal of an alliance between imagination and intellect, heart and mind. Whether or not literature could ever satisfactorily meld these competing languages, what it provided for Hardy was the ground upon which the inherent conflict between tradition and modernity could be played out. Tensions might not be resolved, but they could be held in a troubled co-existence, so that neither side was denied. After all it is imperative that neither religion nor reason 'perishes'.

Whatever Hardy's personal investment in folklore, it served a literary purpose as a space where he could imaginatively harness the tensions that beset him. It is inevitably true that at some level his fidelity to place and people could be said to function as a nostalgic defence against time and change, but Hardy's fictional world is not concocted to escape the turbulence of modernity. Instead, it gives expression to the impact and consequences of that turbulence in terms that subsume it within an even darker mood derived from this new conception of reality. Far from cultivating a pastoral fantasy of rural existence, he made it express and communicate the psychologic disquiet of the times. But folk material also served as a fictional device for pointing beyond modernity and challenging its progressive assumptions. Arcane practices were imaginatively compelling to Hardy, not simply out of childhood attachment or antiquarian curiosity, but because they gave form and expression to a way of seeing that kept open a dimension of lived experience that secular materialism closed down. The language of animism that haunts his work gives form and force to the 'something else' that stalks the outskirts of the modern mind; it upholds the possibility of engagement with energies or presences not acknowledged within the dominant discourse.

Hardy may well have offered something like the core of his personal 'vision' when he wrote: 'I feel that Nature is played out as a Beauty, but not as a Mystery' (Millgate, *The Life and Work of Thomas Hardy* 185). It is this sense of mystery, of something not exhausted by religious pessimism or nihilistic philosophy, that Hardy gestures towards even in his most tragic and desolating work. The Universe offered little hope or comfort or coherence, but there remained still something unaccounted for, something 'out of mind'. As such the language of belief and unbelief was too rigid. The issue is not one of 'fact'. The issue is one of feeling, and whether humanity can experience a sense of 'belonging' if it is divorced from everything outside itself. Hardy's 'achievement' as an artist was to remain actively open to both reason and unreason, belief and unbelief, and in so doing to retain a space for 'the unknown', that unnamed and unnameable aspect of reality, which if unacknowledged threatens to exert a terrible vengeance on the Western mind.

The realist novel is the dominant literary mode of the modern imaginary. With its tight adherence to time and place, and its focus on self-enclosed human patterns within a material world, it reflects stable assumptions about time and space. But even while Hardy's fictional realism implicitly endorses the secular worldview, it harbours countervailing energies directed at troubling the reader's sense of the 'real'. Discordant images and disruptive patterns of plot and representation break the social surface and confound or exhaust the rational. Hardy's fictional worlds are typically 'thin places' where there exists only a narrow margin between the mundane and the mystical. Folk episodes make up pockets of alternative reality breaking out of the surrounding realist discourse, puncturing the familiar, making it strange. Hardy made the most dismal statements about the Universe. He also generated poetry and prose, drawing on the folk tradition, that reanimated that Universe. Re-enchantment begins in just such a superfluity of meaning, in the sense that there is more to express than can be expressed. By 're-enchantment' Charles Taylor does not mean romantic 'regression' into some prelapsarian bliss. It is not a falling back into dream, but a re-awakening into a fullness of being that includes recognition and acceptance of its own vulnerability. It is not a rehabilitated paganism, but a re-connection with experience that modernity increasingly disavows. Insofar as art seeks to redeem meanings other than those reflecting the dominant assumptions regarding the nature of reality, all Art Works towards re-enchantment. Art exceeds the frame. As Taylor readily accepts that 'disenchantment is irreversible' (*Dilemmas and Connections: Selected Essays* 287), and in this there is much to be grateful. Nevertheless, the process has left Western consciousness bereft of a sense of depth and immediacy. The notion that 'all that out there' is without inherent meaning, carrying only the meanings projected onto it by the human mind, has had dire consequences. If there is no 'ontic' dimension beyond the human, if all we encounter is a reflection of our own *feelings*, 'there is no further basis for a sense of awe and wonder at the universe' (*Dilemmas and Connections: Selected Essays* 302).

The prospect of re-enchantment depends upon renewed connection with something other than 'the natural order of things'. It entails an experience of touching or being touched by something 'unnatural' – something that, from within the context of the Immediate Frame, simply does not exist: 'I want to touch him for a charm, a cure of an affliction, by the advice of a man who has proved the virtue of the remedy' ('The Withered Arm' 58). The prospect of that 'touch' excites profound ambivalence, being both devoutly wished and deeply feared. Re-enchantment is not an escape from reality, but a more complete encounter with that reality, one that is prepared to receive the irrational. In certain contexts, Hardy starkly opposed religion and rationality; yet, he retained a place for the irrational.

Describing his archetypal landscape, Hardy wrote: 'To many persons this Egdon was a place which had slipped out of its century, generations ago, to intrude as an uncouth object into this. It was an obsolete thing, and few cared to study it' (*The Return of the Native* 2). Hardy of course did care a great deal, and studied this primitive 'object', this obdurate 'thing' poking out an odd angle from the world. Its jagged intrusiveness is reminiscent of Rhoda Brook's cottage: 'built of mud-walls, the surface of which had been washed by many rains into channels and depressions that left none of the original flat face visible; while here and there in the thatch above a rafter showed like a bone protruding through the skin' ('The Withered Arm' 46).

The folk elements of Hardy's fiction are not pastoral effects or social details. They are remnants, incongruously jutting out of the realist narrative frame like bone piercing flesh. In doing so they also point further out, beyond the Immanent Frame of modern Western consciousness, which regards itself immune to 'presences' which nevertheless continue to haunt it. These presences were not for Hardy, what they were for the villagers of his fiction, but they were not nothing. And that they survived and thrived in their secret way in the midst of the modern world makes them doubly disquieting. They represent a steady persistent pressure. Whatever charms, haunts or horrifies us in these images, in some measure, re-enchants the world by re-awaking us to its strangeness. As the critic John Coulson has said, 'Victorian writers kept alive in their imaginations what their reason could no longer explain or profess' (Coulson 103). Of no-one is this more true than Thomas Hardy.

5

Hardy constructed and re-constructed

Landscape is identified as a core element of folk horror in Adam Scovell's 'folk horror chain'. The creation of Wessex itself functions as an all-encompassing space, itself made uncanny by touching and intersecting with the real. Dorset is present and identifiable as a trace within the construction of a county with ancient roots. Hardy is presenting us with an alternative historical line stretching back to Alfred. What makes this yet further uncanny is that we can't see the join; the connection between the real and the fictional is blurred. Contemporary readings of Hardy cannot fail to take this into account, as further chapters will debate. This blurring of the real and the fictional is the intrusion of one state into another; 'the way in which the domestic world does not coincide with itself' (*The Weird and the Eerie* 10). Fisher argues the difference between the uncanny and the weird and the eerie. The intrusion of one state into another importantly their co-existence, is essentially the immediate effect of Hardy's construction of the space and topography of Wessex.

The manner of Hardy's delivery of narrative and the dark content of that delivery are radical features of his writing in the creation of Wessex, rooted in a simulacra where the relationship between the fiction and reality is at best blurred and, at their most unsettling, impossible to see. Terry Eagleton said of Hardy's texts that they 'refuse to stay still within their frames' and that his work 'is always on the point of breaking through its own containing forms' (Eagleton vii), the stage adaptation that Hardy wrote of his short story 'The Three Strangers' demonstrates this particularly effectively.

Hardy deploys a range of narrative perspectives in his writing and these, alongside his use of coincidence, play their part in the evocation of Wessex as a place of dark and light. Fisher suggests that any consideration of the weird should start with HP Lovecraft in which the Cthulhu mythos is a more clearly evident manifestation of the weird; there are clear tropes of this in

Hardy's work. In his discussion of Lovecraft, Fisher notes Levy, 'Lovecraft's New England ... is a world whose 'reality – physical, topographical, historical – should be emphasised' (*The Weird and the Eerie* 19). The point of contention in relation to this is the nature of the intrusion. If it is a sense of the outside breaking through in fictional terms that makes Lovecraft foundational in weird fiction, it is the same creation of this fictional world that diminishes the horror in his work in favour of the deeply unsettling and strange. The breaking through in Hardy is of a similar order, except there is a tangibility in that which breaks across from reality to text. It is in the authenticity of Dorset as perceived in the act of reading and the folklore and heritage that underpins these perceptions of the county. These are arguably far more amorphous and decentred and gain their narrative power from that. They are as fragmentary as narratives in the 'real world'.

All these factors emphasize Hardy's willingness to experiment with narrative style and to move away from the dominant mode of Victorian realism. Hardy's rejection of pastoral realism is something which has been undermined by many of the tame television and film adaptations of his work, where his work is placed firmly back in that category. Terry Wright argues that Hardy in terms of both content and form was certainly not the tame and 'good little Thomas Hardy, producer of pastoral tragedies' (Wright 2) as he was alluded to by patronizing contemporaries. Nor indeed was he limited to the writing of pastoral romance with all its 'hokum', as he is still often perceived. This is a perspective on Hardy that has emerged partly through the somewhat ineffectual manner of the screened adaptation of his work and the popularity as Paul Niemeyer suggests of 'British period dramas' and filmmakers reluctant to release him 'from his heritage trappings' (242). The non-sequential reading of a contemporary audience, where adaptation may wrestle for supremacy over the text, a revisiting of the dark and the weird and the eerie within Hardy is important. It is in this aspect of his work that an early embodiment of what will later in 2010 be identified at folk horror can be seen.

The Poor Man and the Lady and *The Hand of Ethelberta*

In 1868 Hardy completed his first novel *The Poor Man and the Lady* and, on the advice of Horace Moule, sent the completed manuscript off to the publisher Alexander Macmillan. At this point in his life Hardy had just returned to Dorset after five years working as an architectural assistant in London. Although he had used the time there profitably, hearing Dickens read, visiting the House of Commons to hear Palmerstone speak, attending concerts and recitals, it is clear from the subject matter of the novel that he had found the experience both demanding and challenging. *The Poor Man and the Lady* was never published and little remains of the manuscript but it seems one of its central intentions was to offer a critique of the upper classes and their treatment of their workers, servants and, as Claire Tomalin suggests, 'any who aspired to better themselves by getting an education' (83); years later Hardy stated that the writing was 'socialistic, not to say revolutionary' (Millgate, *Thomas Hardy: A Biography* 63). The 'poor man', Will Strong, is the son of a Dorset labourer who after showing promise at school is sponsored to become an architectural draughtsman by the local squire and his wife. All goes well until Strong falls in love with the squire's daughter 'the Lady' Geraldine Allenville, which does not meet the approval of her parents. Strong is banished to London and in his resentment adopts radical politics and by chance, whilst also in London, Lady Geraldine hears him make a socialist speech in Trafalgar Square.

Social injustice, experienced by working-class and female characters, was to become a central theme in Hardy's writing. In its focus on an intelligent man from the lower classes trying to 'better himself' and attempting upward social mobility, *The Poor Man and the Lady* anticipates the themes which would define Hardy's fiction, perhaps most fully realized in the character of Jude Fawley. Such concerns can be seen to be a response to Hardy's own experience and the perspective of his humble background; when pursuing courtship with Emma, his first wife, Hardy was to encounter her father John Gifford, a solicitor, who according to Millgate greeted his prospective son-in-law with open contempt, referring to him in a letter as a 'low-born churl who has presumed to marry into my family' (*Thomas Hardy: A Biography* 143). In the creation of the character Jude Fawley, Tomalin correctly states that 'Hardy's anger had never been extinguished' (Tomalin 254).

The Poor Man and the Lady was rejected by Alexander Macmillan, but in a letter the publisher did offer encouragement to Hardy saying that he had read the manuscript 'with care, and with much interest and admiration'; Macmillan also stated that he had some empathy with the subject matter:

> The utter heartlessness of all the conversation you give in the drawing-rooms and ballrooms about the working-classes has some ground of truth, I fear, and might justly be scourged as you aim at doing; but your chastisement would fall harmless from its very excess. Will's speech to the working men is full of wisdom [...] Much of the writing seems to me admirable. The scene in Rotten Row is full of power and insight [...] If this is your first book I think you ought to go on.
> (Millgate, *Thomas Hardy: A Biography* 60)

But he added that Hardy's treatment of the upper classes in London was far too aggressive and suggested that he should look at the writing of William Makepeace Thackeray who had treated all classes in his dealings in social satire fairly. In contrast to Thackeray, Macmillan detected that Hardy, with his vitriolic attack, 'meant mischief' (Millgate, *Thomas Hardy: A Biography* 64).

In a letter to his friend Edward Clodd in 1910, Hardy stated that *The Poor Man and the Lady* 'was the most original thing (for its date) that I ever wrote' (Purdy and Millgate 130). This originality was to be found in the form of the text, as well as its subject matter, for what also troubled Macmillan was the apparent absence of plot; the subtitle of *The Poor Man and the Lady* being: *A Story with no Plot: Containing some original verses*', its overt rejection of plot would have challenged any publisher at the time. As Rosemary Sumner comments, 'A novel without a plot in the middle of the Victorian period is clearly signalling its author's experimental intentions. Plotless and with verses, it must have been a novel in a completely new form' (Sumner 2).

Sumner's speculation is compelling when she ponders what 'experimental novels Hardy might have written if his first attempt had not been rejected' (Sumner 2). Macmillan advised Hardy that plot was an absolute necessity and that he should look at the work of Wilkie Collins and the then fashionable literary genre of the 'sensation novel', a genre which Patrica Ingham describes as comparable to

> the lurid newspaper reports of violent crimes which made popular reading, then and later. In a censorious moral climate such novels were licensed for publication and popularity by the narratorial condemnation of the shocking goings-on. As one reviewer put it, either naively or ironically: 'All the crime is done under proper reprobation and yet the writers and the readers have all the benefit of the crime'.
>
> (Ingham xiii)

This was a mode of fiction, as Louis James suggests, 'written to surprise and shock' (215). Michael Millgate and other biographers suggest that characters and episodes from *The Poor Man and the Lady* were used in other Hardy productions, most notably in the novella *An Indiscretion in the Life of an Heiress* (1878) (a moment of writerly recycling where the broader world of Wessex started to form). Hardy, eager to be published, conformed, in terms of plot and form, to market demands and produced the melodramatic and over-plotted *Desperate Remedies* in 1871. Hardy's experiments with plot therefore were mediated by the demands of publication in the same manner as the process of serialization was to curtail the subject matter of his work later in his career. 'Modernist and experimental work often strikes us a weird when we first encounter it. The sense of *wrongness* associated with the weird – the conviction that *this does not belong* – is often a sign that we are in the presence of the new. The weird here is a signal that the concepts and frameworks which we have previously employed are now obsolete' (Fisher, *The Weird and the Eerie* 13). (Arguably Hardy's work is still being censored and modified by the film and television production companies, to bring it in line with the genre of heritage drama with all its potential for financial rewards. It is this which subjugates the weirdness inherent in aspects of Hardy's fiction.)

In Hardy's fifth published novel *The Hand of Ethelberta* (1876), Peter Widdowson believes that Hardy exposes his obsession with 'acute class-consciousness' (6) and the business of being a writer and producing fiction. This novel and Widdowson's observations offer interesting perspectives on Hardy's 'realism' and 'self-reflexivity'; they also display more of the experimental, mischievous and playful approach (which might now be considered post-modern tendencies) that Hardy brought to his work. *The Hand of Ethelberta* followed on from the very successful *Far from the Madding Crowd* (1874) and was largely greeted with disappointment and dismay, in that both publishers and readers wanted more of the same, rural tales coming from the newly created domain of Wessex, but Hardy later stated that he had not 'the slightest intention of writing for ever about sheep farming, as the reading public was apparently expecting him to do' (Millgate, *Thomas Hardy: A Biography* 105). The novel tells the story of Ethelberta, a bright and intelligent woman from the lower social classes who becomes a published poet. A change of circumstances forces her to abandon poetry and become a storyteller, presenting her stories to London society as a lady, whilst concealing her lower-class upbringing.

In a later edition of the novel, 1895, Hardy wrote in the preface that it was 'a somewhat frivolous narrative' (*The Hand of Ethelberta* 31) and therefore had been given the subtitle of *A Comedy in Chapters*. This was dropped from the serial version but restored for book publication; Widdowson suggests the subtitle draws attention 'to the staged artificiality of the novel' (Widdowson 61). A typical example of what Robert Gittings referred to as a 'juvenile joke' (*The Young Thomas Hardy* 291) is in the naming one of Ethelberta's suitors Alfred Neigh, his father being a horse-knacker. Comedy or not, most critics seemed in agreement that the plot was implausible, written in an awkward farcical manner and contained unconvincing two-dimensional characterization of the gentry and the upper classes.

The whole book is concerned with social class and relations between the classes. Ethelberta and Hardy himself are both on show here as the creatures, referred to in the novel, as belonging to 'the metamorphic classes of society' (*The Hand of Ethelberta* 320). Hardy, in dealing with Ethelberta, in a self-reflexive manner displayed his own feelings, anxieties and hopes, with both heroine and author coming from lower-class parentage and trying to conceal it from their public. As Gittings observes: 'when Ethelberta's socially unmentionable relatives appear they turn out to be a fascinating amalgam of Hardy's own' (*The Young Thomas Hardy* 292). Both Hardy and his created character regard themselves as poets who have to make a living through writing fiction and yearn for financial security so that they complete their ambitions to write an epic poem, ultimately achieved by Hardy with the publication of *The Dynasts*, finally presented in one volume in 1910.

As Widdowson suggests, *The Hand of Ethelberta* 'was a strange and self-conscious novel to write at this stage of his career, if for no other reason than because of the amount of disguised autobiography it contains' (Widdowson 49). Critics have offered several accounts of Hardy's intentions in writing this text. Gittings notes that there was much gossip following the serialization of *Far from the Madding Crowd* in *Cornhill*, that the author was a woman, since Hardy's name was not printed in the magazine. Others, probably because the novel featured working people, thought that the author was a house painter, whilst *The Spectator*, of January 1874, in its review of current magazines, asserted that the author was George Eliot, the work having the same rural flavour as *Silas Marner* and *Adam Bede*. It was the *Spectator's* assertion, according to Gittings, that troubled Hardy, 'the idea that anyone writing about rustics might be mistaken for George Eliot seemed to have weighed oddly heavily with him' (*The Young Thomas Hardy* 281). Eliot was regarded as a key exponent of realism and Hardy may well have disliked the idea of being confused with her for this reason too.

Hardy at this time, having just married the very middle-class Emma Gifford, was under a great deal of pressure. The success of *Far from the Madding Crowd* and the prominence this would give him in London society meant that his humble background might soon be exposed. As the novel mainly focused on working people from whom, as Gittings suggests,

> Hardy himself was sprung. How much of this he had revealed to Emma is doubtful: but it is even more doubtful that he had told her anything like the whole truth – that his mother, for instance, had been brought up by Poor Law charity, and all the relatives in Puddletown and Stinsford had been, at one time or another, servants and labourers.
> (Gittings, *The Young Thomas Hardy* 273)

Gittings here, making a set of class-based assumptions of his own, believes that *The Hand of Ethelberta* could have been Hardy's attempt to write this problem out of his system. Certainly at the time Hardy did not want to be seen capable only of writing about the rural and so, on a superficial level, *The Hand of Ethelberta* might be read as an urban social satire in the manner of Thackeray. However, in this novel, as in the case of *The Poor Man and the Lady*, Hardy is making the same observations about the injustice of the class system in Victorian England, a class system which was reinforced and supported, as Christine Devine says:

> in part by the literary establishment – even by those middle-class novelists who were ostensibly sympathetic to the so-called 'lower' classes, and whose fiction sought to tell their story and the story of class conflict.
> (Devine, 169)

Hardy was again confronting social and political issues; he was also, through parody and pastiche, challenging the literary conventions of so-called 'realism'. The character Ethelberta is, as Widdowson states, 'seen to be solely composed by fictional discourse' (Widdowson 83). From this position, Widdowson argues, our attention is then drawn to the fact that so are all other heroines in literature, no matter how 'rounded' and 'knowable' they appear to be. The plausibility and success of characters such as Tess or Jude are reliant on their believability through, as David Lodge comments, 'the suppression of overt reference to the conventions employed [in creating them] so that the discourse seems to be a transparent window on reality'.

Towards the end of the novel Ethelberta decides to 'show herself as she really was' (*The Hand of Ethelberta* 306) to share the 'melancholy [...] thoughts of herself as a counterfeit' (205) to an audience made up of her elderly suitor, Lord Mountclere, and his guests and friends. Eventually, whilst delivering this narrative, Ethelberta breaks down, the audience are uneasy and Lord Mountclere, a 'first edition' (95) as far as original pedigree class terms is concerned, comes to her rescue. He tells the audience that they have been hearing fiction and that the first part of the story should now end: 'We have been well entertained so far. I could scarcely believe that the story I was listening to was utterly an invention, so vividly does Mrs Petherwin bring the scenes before our eyes. She must now be exhausted; we shall have the remainder tomorrow' (307).

This 'confession' of Ethelberta's true background to an audience is signalled earlier in the novel when she states, 'I have the tale of my own life – to be played as a last card' (118); its deliverance is subsequently dealt with as 'fiction'. Widdowson's conclusion is compelling and forms the basis of the argument that *The Hand of Ethelberta* is not a 'grotesque failure of fictional decorum' but that its performative and self-reflexive artifice presents both a strategic challenge to conventional realism and an exposure of the destructive 'fictions' fostered by a class society (Widdowson 7). The text is another example of Hardy's use of experimental innovations to narrative and plot, in this instance conveying subject matter concerned with issues surrounding social class, exposing his own class-based self-consciousness in the narrative form of his work.

This is then an evocation of Wessex as a three-dimensional world that is complete in its construction and exists outside the frame of the stories and then interconnects with our own. This blurring of the relationship between the fiction and the reality is beyond realism and moves swiftly to hyperrealism. The 'breaking through' that Eagleton identifies is a move from one plane of existence to another. This is the nature of the weird and the eerie as discussed by Mark Fisher.

Hardy adapting Hardy

Hardy's adventurous approach to conveying narrative can be seen in his dramatized stage version of the short story 'The Three Strangers' first performed at Terry's Theatre London under the title of 'The Three Wayfarers' in 1889. Hardy had tried adaptation before in 1882 with *Far from the Madding Crowd* which had a short run at the Globe Theatre in London but according to Carl J. Weber 'for various reasons [...] this experience had not wetted Hardy's appetite for the stage' (Weber xi). One of the most immediately striking features of Hardy's adaptation of his own work is the way that, after only three pages, he 'breaks the fourth wall' of theatre with Timothy Summers, the First Stranger, telling the audience with an aside that he is the escaped convict:

> Late it is, as you say. (Walks aside.) But
> those in chase of me will be later! ...
> God save me! ... I'd almost as soon have
> stayed to be hanged As bear the strain of
> this escape! (7)

A few pages later, with the arrival of the Second Stranger at the cottage, the audience are given a further aside with the stranger telling them who he is:

> Shepherd – Make yerself at home, master –
> make yerself at home; though you be a stranger.
>
> (Hangman removes great coat, hangs up hat.)
> Hangman – (Aside.) They'd sweat if they knew
> 'twas Jack Ketch come among 'em. (Hardy, *The Three Wayfarers* 10)

The theatrical device of the 'aside' with the actor for a time leaving the diegetic space of the stage and talking to the audience has precedents in Elizabethan and Restoration theatre. The deployment of the 'aside', another form of metafiction after all, shows Hardy in playful mode again, breaking another frame, with the actors confessing to their fictionality and acknowledging the illusion of theatre. Whilst there are clearly preemptive postmodern traits in this approach, there is in the context of viewing the potential for further weirdness. Once again Hardy's proclivities for the weird can be seen. The two states co-exist. However, Hardy was concerned about liberties which might be taken with his work in adaptations, in his own adaptation of his work he allowed himself considerable licence with the original text. When approached by music hall promoters to stage the play he had little interest in its fate, writing to his friend J. M. Barrie he said that anybody could 'play it for a guinea a night' (Millgate 194).

In the script of 'The Three Wayfarers' following the prison guns notifying that there has been an escape, Hardy has Shepherdess Fennel expressing her fear that what was to be a celebration of her daughter's christening has been over-shadowed by evil (Hardy, *The Three Wayfarers* 22):

O my poor baby! 'Tis of ill omen for her –
all this gallows work at her christening!
I wouldn't have had her if I'd known!' (Hardy, *The Three Wayfarers* 22)

Also in Hardy's adaptation the hangman, whilst singing the grim song about his occupation, pulls a rope from the bag he has brought with him. This is much to the shock of Timothy Summers and guests, although the character has already told the audience who and what he is. Hardy has the hangman, the Second Stranger, refer to himself as Jack Ketch, a famously inept and therefore exceptionally cruel seventeenth-century executioner (he died in 1686). The menace and evil of the hangman, the very agent and bridge between life and death, became a central macabre element to some of Hardy's fiction and will be discussed more fully later. The role of the executioner remains a key element of some contemporary folk horror; execution is the inevitable result for King David Hartley in *The Gallows Pole* and execution is essentially Jay's trade in Ben Wheatley's *Kill List*.

Coincidence and chance

In her discussion of Hardy's third novel *A Pair of Blue Eyes*, Laura Faulkner (92) claims that coincidence: 'If overused as a plot device draws attention to the construction of the plot and disrupts our sense of the realist frame.' Hardy's use of coincidence clearly directs us away from expectations of realism in his texts. Where the tendency towards the overt use of coincidence possibly came from and examples of the more outrageous use Hardy made of it highlights a problematic metaphysics within his work. This is a form of coincidence that plays out in some later Folk Horror texts; there is an element of this in *Robin Redbreast* in this being the village into which Norah settles. This is also true to *Starve Acre* and *Old Trash* where the suggestion is that the environment leads to action. However, the 'outrageous coincidences' give way to malevolent design in other examples, such as *The Third Day* or *The Wicker Man*. Again these are texts where the Hardyan line follows through and the presence of a guiding hand can be felt and the terror is that the hand is human, not God, a devil or any other metaphysical creature.

Hardy acting on the advice of Macmillan produced the novel *Desperate Remedies* in an attempt to comply with the high degree of melodrama of the

Victorian sensation novel genre of Wilkie Collins, Charles Reade and Charles Dickens. This type of literature was extremely popular at the time and was often produced for, and had to follow the dictates of serial publication, with the often excessive use of coincidence being a useful narrative device to compress plots. Hardy was also reared on local rural tales and folk ballads which often contained melodrama and coincidence and these narrative features were inevitably adopted in some of the writing that followed.

In reference to the novel *A Pair of Blue Eyes*, Faulkner states that 'Hardy beats us over the head with coincidence' (Faulkner 98). This novel, discussed below in the context of its status as a 'cliff hanger', tells the tale of Elfride Swancourt, a young and pretty clergyman's daughter in Cornwall who is pursued by two suitors Henry Knight and Stephen Smith. The latter is a young architect of humble background carrying out some church restoration work and his courtship echoes much of what is known about Hardy's courtship of Emma Gifford. Again Hardy presents the theme of a man from the lower classes attempting social mobility and in pursuit of a partner from a higher class.

The story begins in realistic mode, the text describing characters and actions that are plausible, and then gradually shifts towards the sensational with acts of extraordinary coincidences taking place on route. At one stage Henry Knight looks out to sea through a telescope and tells Elfride that on an incoming boat 'a slim young fellow' (*A Pair of Blue Eyes* 232) is also looking through a telescope at them, the man being Stephen Smith. Hardy created a similar situation, a 'ridiculous farce' (Widdowson 1998) in *The Hand of Ethelberta* but on this occasion three of Ethelberta's suitors all choose independently to visit her at the same time at a hotel in Rouen. Coincidences occur right to the very end in *A Pair of Blue Eyes*. By chance Knight meets Smith in London, both men are still pursuing Elfride, and a further coincidence seems to be that they are both staying in the same hotel which causes Smith to comment 'that's convenient: not to say odd' (376). Things get even odder as both men end up secretly, on 'the eve of St Valentine's – that bishop of blessed memory to youthful lovers' (390), on the same train together to Cornwall to ask Elfride for her hand in marriage – unaware that the train also carries Elfride's dead body on its final journey home. At one stage in this novel the narrator comments, apparently in defence of the coincidental occurrences: 'Strange conjunctions of phenomena, particularly those of a trivial everyday kind, are so frequent in an ordinary life that we grow used to their unaccountableness' (101). But such coincidences as these are not 'trivial conjunctions of phenomena', they are, as Faulkner suggests, 'striking coincidences' that defy our 'expectations of probability' in that they do not come from the 'naturalistic system of causation'. As she states: 'striking coincidences, while unnerving in real life, can be particularly problematic in "realist" fiction, which strives to conceal the mechanics of its production' (Faulkner 94); it is obvious that Hardy, certainly in *The Hand of Ethelberta*, is not in pursuit of realism.

Coincidental occurrences were less blatant following *The Hand of Ethelberta* when Hardy, in his major works, returned to Wessex, and plotting employed acts of 'chance' and 'accident' instead. But even 'chance' as a phenomenon, and 'chance encounters' as George Levine points out 'seem like intrusions from another mode when they occur in realistic narratives' (20) and Hardy's texts are littered with such encounters. Lawrence Jay Dessner comments on the 'moments of superhuman perception' in *The Mayor of Casterbridge* where characters, who happen to be in the right place at a certain moment, have the incredible and improbable ability to overhear the conversation of others some distance away. Dessner notes that the 'root word *hear* appears one hundred and sixty-three times in the novel' (163). Extraordinary auditory powers are not just confined to characters in *The Mayor of Casterbridge*; Tess too is able to hear Angel's brothers pass derogatory remarks about her when she is on her way to visit their father. What she hears alters her mind and Tess, with 'Tears, blinding tears' (376) running down her face, turns back: the act of overhearing a well-used trope in Hardy's fiction. This has the effect of a character becoming isolated in a crowd, becoming a stranger.

6

Hardy's range of narrative perspectives

As David Lodge identified, one of Hardy's favourite devices, used throughout his fiction, is the frequently employed 'hypothetical or unspecified observer' (81) so characteristic of his narrative style. A passer-by will notice something, or a bystander will accidently overhear a conversation, or, in the case of *A Pair of Blue Eyes*, 'had a gentleman from Scotland-yard [...] been passing at the time' (139). As Sumner points out Hardy's 'unconfident' narrator is often working on 'guesswork, assumptions, suggestions' his 'idiosyncratic way of using narrators heightens [the] sense of uncertainty. None of them is omniscient' (56). Terry Wright concurs, commenting that Hardy even when 'supposedly employing an omniscient narrator' limits the narrator's knowledge to what is observable simply from the outside (8). Wright also notes, the use Hardy makes of ellipsis, the 'gaps and discontinuities in his narrative which force the readers to supply what they cannot see' (8). This is most apparent in *Tess of the d'Urbervilles* where the reader is not explicitly given a description of the moment when Tess is raped (or controversially 'seduced'), nor when she murders Alec, not allowed to read her confession letter to Angel and not present when she makes the confession on her wedding night. All this narrative 'uncertainty' and sense of instability highlights one of the ways 'in which Hardy, ahead of most other nineteenth-century novelists, was gradually moving towards Modernist techniques' (Sumner 175). The unsettling elements of Hardy's narrative style are a combination of the traditional ballads he heard as a child, and an awareness of the writing taking place in the late 1920s. Virginia Woolf, an admirer of Hardy's writing, visited Max Gate in 1926 and recorded in her diary that when commenting on an Aldous Huxley's story 'Half-Holiday' Hardy had said: 'They've changed everything now [...] We used to think there was a beginning & a middle & end. We believed in Aristotelian theory. Now one of those stories came to an end with a woman going out of the room.

He chuckled.' Once again, the title of Claire Tomalin's biography, *Thomas Hardy The Time-Torn Man*, is apt. In Hardy's lifetime dominant literary modes shifted from traditional ballads of the early nineteenth century to the challenging literature being produced as his life was coming to its conclusion.

In *A Pair of Blue Eyes*, Hardy exhibits a broad range of narrative perspectives in the course of a few pages; the main protagonist is Henry Knight and he is left at the end of one chapter literally hanging from a cliff, whilst the woman he is romantically pursuing, Elfride, runs to get help. With Knight in this precarious state, the narrator first contemplates the height of the cliff in comparison to other cliffs on the British coast (Flamborough, Beachy Head, South Foreland) before noting that directly in front of the desperate Knight's eye

> ... was an inbedded fossil, standing forth in low relief from the rock. It was a creature with eyes. The eyes, dead and turned to stone, were even now regarding him. It was one of the early crustaceans called Trilobites. Separated by millions of years in their lives, Knight and this underling seemed to have met in their place of death.
>
> (Hardy, *A Pair of Blue Eyes* 240)

Here Hardy, fourteen years after the publication of *The Origin of the Species*, acknowledges Darwinism and the geological by taking the reader through the various stages of evolution where everything, as Levine points out, 'is detectably marked with the vestiges, scars, and incrustations of history' (xv). He is also reminding us, as Faulkner suggests, of 'the smallness of human existence on the evolutionary scale' (Faulkner 103). He interweaves this discussion, commenting that 'Knight was a fair geologist' (*A Pair of Blue Eyes* 240) with Knight's thoughts as he confronts death, demonstrating what Hardy himself referred to as 'that chaos called consciousness' (*The Mayor of Casterbridge* 121). Knight says to himself that he has been waiting for Elfride for ten minutes but the narrator contradicts this claim telling us 'she had really been gone but three' (*A Pair of Blue Eyes* 242). Knight also states that he cannot remember 'such heavy and cold rain on a summer day' and again the narrator corrects him saying that he 'was again mistaken. The rain was quite ordinary in quantity' (242). All this occurs before the narrator finally returns the reader safely back inside the 'frame' of the story, back on 'solid ground', pulling us away from Knight's musings, 'Knight gave up thoughts of life utterly and entirely, and turned to contemplate the Dark Valley and the unknown future beyond. Into the shadowy depths of these speculations we will not follow him' (243). The statement 'we will not follow him' has echoes of the cinematic, shifting the camera from Knight to a 'spot' that had appeared on the landscape, 'the head of Elfride'(243).

In *Tess of the d'Urbervilles*, an unnamed man from a cottage in Wellbridge is going out for a doctor one evening when he 'happens' to see Tess and Angel walking along in silence, just after Tess has made her confession to Angel. We are informed that he had met:

> ... two lovers in the pastures, walking very slowly, without converse, one behind the other, as in a funeral procession, and the glimpse that he obtained of their faces seemed to denote that they were anxious and sad. Returning later, he passed them again in the same field, progressing just as slowly, and as regardless of the hour and of the cheerless night as before. It was only on account of his preoccupation with his own affairs, and the illness in his house, that he did not bear in mind the curious incident, which, however, he recalled a long while after.
> (Hardy, *Tess of the d'Urbervilles* 303)

Narrative uncertainty dominates here, the passer-by locked into his own thoughts, only to remember the two sometime later.

The treatment of this particular passage in *Tess* was used in a totally different manner by Ian Sharp in the 1998 London Weekend Television production of *Tess of the D'Urbervilles*. In this production as Tess makes her confession to Angel, the two walk down a narrow street and pass an old man going the opposite way who bows and lifts his hat. As he begins his bow the voice-over declares: 'I could never forget these lovers, their faces blind to time and place, each isolated in their mutual despair.' A close-up reveals that the bowing man is an ageing Thomas Hardy both author and narrator. The contrast between the depiction of the scene in the novel and its presentation on the screen, with its attempt at authorial authority, completely reverses the usual state of affairs, in which, as Seymour Chatman states, fiction asserts and film, where 'the dominant mode is presentational' (132), simply presents.

One of the hypothetical observers in *The Return of the Native* is Egdon Heath itself, the location where most of the story is set. On a landscape populated with individuals seemingly occupied in viewing, spying and often 'over-looking' each other, the narrator tells us that 'on the evening under consideration it would have been noticed that [...] the white surface of the road remained almost as clear as ever' (57); as Jacquelin Dillion and Phillip Mallett point out: 'it would have been noticed, that is, had there been need of further witnesses than the heath itself' (Dillion 91). When the narrator treats Egdon with the same respect as a character, 'A Face on Which Time Makes But Little Impression', the reader should not be surprised that it is also capable of watching events. Egdon is presented as a character and with this becomes ever watchful, part of the controlling landscape which is such a key feature of folk horror. This is beyond the isolation that the landscape provides and is much more central in being a character who is omnipresent and yet had no clear narrative voice. This is, in itself, unsettling. The location of the reader in a place is clearly evoked by Hardy and his conception of Wessex furthers this. As readers we are set in a location that is within the text and at the same time exists beyond and between texts. We are plunged into a landscape which can start as threatening, in which odd behaviour is seen as strange. The horror is in part invoked by the oddity of the place becoming normalized by our immersion and isolation alongside the character. This trope can be seen as recurrent in the representation of place in later folk horror, for example, the rural spaces of *Robin Redbreast* (1970) or *Starve Acre* (2020). In both of these examples there is nothing intrinsically wrong with behaviours; rather, it is more that there is a slightly perceptual difference between recognized urban norms and the people of the village. What might be initially perceived to be subtle differences becomes confirmed to be rooted in a different belief system.

Hardy and the visual arts

One of the ways that Hardy experimented with his narrative style was to look towards the then recent developments in the visual arts rather than what was current in literature. Hardy always had an interest in this area and in 1898 he proved his competency as a visual artist by publishing an anthology of poetry entitled *Wessex Poems and Other Verses* accompanied by thirty of his drawings linked to the poems. The public were somewhat surprised by this publication since Hardy was not known at that stage for his poetry and even less for his interest and abilities in the visual arts. Sarah Hook suggests that by this venture Hardy was placing his 'first book of poems within the tradition of Victorian book illustration' (Hook 71). She further notes that in the same way as Hermann Lea was to photograph the fictional places in *Thomas Hardy's Wessex* (1913) for tourists, Hardy's choice of title for *Wessex Poems* 'suggests his at least partial awareness of self-marketing his poetic venture by way of the topography of the novels that made him famous' (86). Several of the drawings in the collection depict local places, for example, Stinsford Church and an inn in Dorchester, interestingly with a figure standing outside playing a fiddle. However, others, as will be further debated, relate more to his imagination; these include amongst others: drawings of an open book, a broken key and wilted flowers in a jug.

As early as 1865 when Hardy was twenty-five and still vaguely considering going to Cambridge and becoming a curate in a country village, he was already aware of the restrictions and limitations of what was commonly perceived as realism, or 'the mannered artifice of fiction' as Widdowson calls it (82). In a jotting of that time he acknowledged: 'The poetry of a scene varies with the minds of the perceivers. Indeed, it does not lie in the scene at all' (Millgate, *Thomas Hardy: A Biography* 84). Hardy, whilst living in London, was a keen gallery visitor and became particularly impressed by the work and techniques of the Impressionists and the paintings of William Turner, who, Roger Webster notes, had abandoned a fixed 'one-point perspective for a shifting, multiple representation' (Webster 27). Hardy likened Turner to Wagner, whose music he thought offered a 'spectacle of the inside of a brain at work like the inside of a hive' (Millgate, *Thomas Hardy: A Biography* 354). Hardy's narrative viewpoint is rarely fixed and can be on occasions, as we shall see, that of a passing bird. Writing in January 1887 on the compositions of various landscape paintings Hardy stated his dissatisfaction with some of them, feeling that nature

> is played out as Beauty, but not as a Mystery. I don't want to see landscapes, i.e., scenic paintings of them, because I don't want to see the original realities – as optical effects, that is. I want to see the deeper reality underlying the scenic, the expression of what are called abstract imaginings […] The 'simply natural' is interesting no longer.
> (Millgate, *The Life and Work of Thomas Hardy* 192)

Hardy's expressed desire in wanting to go beyond the superficial in order to see the 'deeper reality' is key here and explains his attraction to 'the mad, late-Turner [whose] rendering is now necessary to create my interest' (192).

According to Webster the influence of Turner and the Impressionists accounted for 'the intensely visual' aspects which sets Hardy's novels 'apart from the conventions of nineteenth-century classic realism' (20). This influence, Robert Gittings suggests, can be seen actually shaping the form of a piece of Hardy's writing in *Tess of the d'Urbervilles*. Hardy attended an exhibition at the Royal Academy in January 1869 and was much impressed by Turner's work and one painting, the *Snowstorm*, in particular, a depiction of a steam boat caught in the vortex of a severe storm. Turner was fascinated by the effects of extreme weather, mist and light on an image and anecdotally had himself strapped to the mast of a ship for four hours during a storm. Hardy used the 'Snowstorm', Gittings notes, as the basis for the 'weird impressionistic passage about the Arctic birds in the Dorset uplands' (*The Older Hardy* 88) in *Tess of the d'Urbervilles*. The chapter 'The Woman Pays' starts off with Tess and Marion working on the bleak winter landscape of Flintcomb-Ash farm, defined by Marian as a 'starve-acre place' (a phrase later used by Andrew Michael Hurley as the title of his 2020 novel, directly inspired by Hardy). Labouring hour after hour stoically in the rain of the swede-field the two recall: 'the time when they lived and loved together at Talbothays Dairy, that happy green tract of land where summer had been liberal in her gifts' (*Tess of the d'Urbervilles* 361). At this point the text remains focused on the moment it seeks to describe; we understand and empathize with the two women in terms of their present predicament and past reminiscences; but we are about to be disturbed, for way above the two, 'Turner's' storm is brewing and, yet again, Hardy's cinematic narrative takes us up there to view it:

> After this season of congealed dampness came a spell of dry frost, when strange birds from behind the North Pole began to arrive silently on the upland of Flintcomb-Ash; gaunt spectral creatures with tragical eyes – eyes which had witnessed scenes of cataclysmal horror in inaccessible polar regions of a magnitude such as no human being had ever conceived, in curdling temperatures that no man could endure; which had beheld the crash of icebergs and the slide of snow-hills by the shooting light of the Aurora; been half blinded by the whirl of colossal storms and terraqueous distortions; and retained the expression of features that such scenes had engendered.
>
> (Hardy, *Tess of the d'Urbervilles* 363–4)

The narrator goes on to say that these birds flew just above Tess and Marion but brought 'no account' of what they had witnessed on their travels, sights 'which humanity would never see' (363–4). Once again Hardy is reminding us of the insignificance of the human experience, 'the trivia' of the two women, in this case, set against the vastness of the universe.

Hardy makes the most straightforward and identifiable appropriation from a painting in *Jude the Obscure*, where Jude, returning to Christminster, finds Arabella working in a tavern. Arabella is alongside another barmaid behind the bar and the narrator informs us that at the back of them there were

> rose bevel-edged mirrors, with glass shelves running along their front, on which stood precious liquids that Jude did not know the name of, in bottles of topaz, sapphire, ruby and amethyst [...] The barmaid attending to [customers in the next] compartment was invisible to Jude's direct glance, through a reflection of her back in the glass behind her occasionally caught his eyes. He had observed this listlessly, when she turned her face for a moment to the glass to set her hair tidy. Then he was amazed to discover that the face was Arabella's.
>
> (Hardy, *Jude the Obscure* 187)

The whole scene that the narrative creates resembles Edouard Manet's 1881 painting 'A Bar at the Folies-Bergere' (Courtauld Gallery, London) which Hardy had seen on a trip to Paris. It is worth noting that the journey from painting to text, accomplished by Hardy in using Manet's painting, was to go one stage further in Winterbottom's (1996) film, where it was again appropriated. As Webster notes, in the film, the 'dislocating mirrors' mean that 'the unitary perspective of the viewer is fragmented and problematised' and this

> innovative uses of perspective and narrative point of view reveal that Arabella's reflection is in a sense her true self, though her true self is multiple and fractured – arguably more equipped to survive in a modern and mobile environment than Jude is.
>
> (Webster, 33)

The fragmented view of Arabella, plus noise from the till and banter between her and customers in the next cubicle, adds to Jude's confusion.

Finally, Hardy's indebtedness to Turner can be seen in another three-stage set of intertextuality: that of the use as a setting of Stonehenge, the 'heathen temple' (26) as Tess calls it. The monument had been the subject of an engraving by Turner in 1832 and the original watercolour was on display in the Royal Academy in 1889, which, Webster informs us, Hardy would have seen. Hardy's narrative description of Stonehenge just before Tess is arrested is, to say the least, 'painterly' echoing elements of Turner's work and this process was continued by Roman Polanski's in his film *Tess* in 1979. (At this point in the film, Polanski attempts to replicate Hardy's light sensitive narrative with an atmospheric mist which swirls around, just as the sun is beginning to rise.) As Webster states: 'Turner's paintings in particular offered Hardy a visual aesthetic which served his desire to move beyond realism' (26).

Hardy, surrealism and psychology

In her study *A Route to Modernism* (2000), Rosemary Sumner has noted many aspects of Hardy's writing and narrative style that anticipated the concerns of the Surrealist movement in the twentieth century. After the collapse of the nihilistic Dada movement in 1922 and interest generated by Sigmund Freud, the French doctor and poet Andre Breton (1896–1966) gathered like-minded individuals who wished to explore areas of the subconscious, 'the true process of thought' not governed by reason. The Surrealist movement developed in many directions and signalled its dislocation from logic and reason; it inspired the literature of Andre Breton and Philippe Soupault and the paintings of Rene Magritte, Max Ernst, Salvador Dali and others, and in film, Luis Bunuel's *Un Chein Andalou* of 1928 with its eye-slicing scene being probably the most notorious. The odd and fantastic juxtapositions of objects that have no obvious relationship with each other were one feature of surrealism which was taken up by the visual artists; the rallying cry of the movement being as Lautreamont stated was 'as beautiful as the chance meeting on a dissecting table of a sewing machine and an umbrella' (Murray 402) written by Isidore Ducasse (1846–70) better known by the pseudonym, the Comte de Lautreamont. Hardy, in *Tess of the d'Urbervilles*, sets up a similar surrealist scene when Tess's family settle down for the night on a four-poster bed outside a church, 'coincidently' one having a d'Urberville window; the narrator commenting on the very odd out of context juxtaposition of 'indoor articles abandoned to the vicissitudes of a roofless exposure for which they were never made' (447) is startling. The situation is forced on the Durbeyfields when they are on the move to new lodgings and are let down in their arrangements; although anxiety levels are high because of their plight the family seem relatively relaxed, as if what they are experiencing is an everyday occurrence. The bed outside the church represents a form of 'montage', the form, as Fisher tells us, that is 'most appropriate to the weird [...] the conjoining of *two or more things which do not belong together*' (*The Weird and the Eerie* 11).

An even more striking example of Hardy's surrealism, this one expressed visually, can be seen in his publication *Wessex Poems and Other Verses*, referred to above. The most reproduced image from the collection was drawn to accompany his poem 'In a Eweleaze Near Weatherbury'. This is a sketch of a landscape dotted with sheep, onto which is superimposed a pair of spectacles which stretch right across the picture. The poem is all about the passing of time and the ageing process and, as Hook suggests, the inclusion of the 'gratuitous spectacles, the lenses of which leave the landscape curiously undistorted, alludes to visual modernism' (Hook 84). Hardy, like the surrealists to follow, wanted 'to see the deeper reality underlying the scenic' (Millgate, *Thomas Hardy: A Biography* 192) and to him the deeper reality lay in the mind of the perceiver, in 'abstract imaginings', the subconscious. The drawing, as Hook comments, 'eludes definitive interpretation' (84) and seems to foretell movements in the visual arts of the twentieth century and particularly surrealism and in this case, as Hook suggests, the work of the Belgian painter Reni Magritte.

A process followed by the literary wing of the movement, in the attempt to provide access to the unconscious, was automatic writing, automatism. Andre Breton engaged in this as did the poet Kurt Schwitters (1887–1948); they would cut up newspapers at random, picking out words and sentences and combining them to see what was hinted at, suggested, what, as they saw it, they unlocked from the subconscious. Hardy also used a similar technique when looking for inspiration; Millgate informs us that Hardy would look

> through a passage from the Old Testament or the Book of Common Prayer, picking up particular words and using them in modified grammatical forms and totally different contexts, evidently with the objective of developing and exercising a literary vocabulary of his own, generating

new expressive phrases from the impulsion of great models of the past or even evolving the outline of a possible poem.

(*Thomas Hardy: A Biography* 88)

Though Hardy did not engage directly with sleep deprivation and drug use as Breton and Schwitters did, his methods in trying to reach the same goal are remarkably close.

A final instance on Hardy as prototype Surrealist is the wild and uninhibited dancing of the musically hypnotized Car'line in the 'The Fiddler of the Reels'. Sumner suggests, paraphrasing Breton, that surrealism was interested in 'dreams, erotic experiences' and 'moments when normality is shaken by something *other*, as in the loss of control in panic [...] a disturbance which overwhelms reason' (Sumner 43). Certainly Car'line, who at the start of the story is a 'pretty, invocating, weak-mouthed' (288) eighteen year old engaged to the good and steady Ned, is victim of such phenomena; for following her encounter with Mop Ollamoor she rejects Ned because 'he could not play the fiddle so as to draw your soul out of your body like a spider's thread' (290). The description of Car'line's wild dancing in response to Mop's music is, as Sumner states, full of 'orgasmic suggestiveness' (Sumner 117) and can be interpreted by either supernatural forces or psychological ones; Hardy comments that to understand Car'line's behaviour 'would require a neurologist to fully explain' (289). Hardy frequently uses music and dance as the forceful agents in acts of sensory disturbance and loss of control; a good example of this being the illicit meeting of Eustacia and Wildeve in *The Return of the Native* where at a dance 'paganism was revised in their hearts' (321) as 'Eustacia floated round and round on Wildeve's arm, her face rapt and statuesque; her soul had passed away from and forgotten her features, which were left empty and quiescent, as they always are when feeling goes beyond their register. How near she was to Wildeve!' (322–3). Eustacia here, with emotions 'beyond their register', is approaching the early stages of the state that Car'line reaches in 'The Fiddler of the Reels'.

When Car'line first meets Mop by the bridge, he is playing his 'fiddle for the benefit of passers-by and laughing as the tears rolled down the cheeks of the little children hanging round him' (289). A little later Mop's fiddle playing is described as 'capable of drawing tears from a statue' (301). Hardy himself who was

> of ecstatic temperament, extraordinarily sensitive to music, and among the endless jigs, hornpipes, reels, waltzes, and country-dances that his father played of an evening in his early married years, and to which the boy danced a pas seul in the middle of the room, there were three or four that always moved the child to tears, though he strenuously tried to hide them [...] This peculiarity in himself troubled the mind of 'Tommy'

as he was called, and set him wondering at a phenomenon to which he ventured not to confess.

(Millgate, *Thomas Hardy: A Biography* 19)

One of the reels the young Hardy responded to emotionally was 'My Fancy Lad', the same tune with all of its 'seductive strains' that Car'line 'was least able to resist – the one he had played when she was leaning over the bridge at the date of their first acquaintance' (The Fiddler of the Reels 300). Hardy therefore, at least as a child, and like his character Car'line was also susceptible to experiencing 'disturbance which overwhelms reason' one of the principal interests of the Surrealists. This total emotional disturbance of the senses forms a powerful ingredient in 'The Fiddler of the Reels'.

Hardy's experiments with form and narrative in his writing are wide ranging: from offering a critique of other writer's 'realism', in creating characters lacking credibility, as in *The Hand of Ethelberta* and thereby drawing attention to the implausibility of all fictional characters; to his narrative style with its sudden switches of mode, its uncertainty, its gaps and employment of the hypothetical observer. From the start of his career with the unpublished *The Poor Man and the Lady*, a novel without plot and with verses, onwards, where he was to eventually pre-empt some of the concerns and the interests of Surrealism, all confirm, as Widdowson argues, that

> Hardy is not trying and failing to write realist fiction [...] he is strategically experimenting with forms and practices which themselves crack open the discourse of realism.
>
> (Widdowson, 54)

If Hardy questioned the discourse of realism by the narrative form that his writing often took, he also questioned it by the frequent inclusion of supernatural and irrational elements. This form of experimentation may seem a long way from the Folk Horror of the first wave in the late 1960s. However the interest in the unconscious and the deeper workings of the psyche were being played out in many fields, from the musings of RD Laing to the counter cultural interest in LSD. The audience for this was relatively localized and largely middle class (Sklower). This 'alternative' tradition drew on the renewed interest in a folk tradition broke out into popular culture as can be seen in Paul Simon's interest in traditional folk music and his use of *Scarborough Fair* (as taught to him by Martin Carthy in 1965) and used on their 1965 Simon and Garfunkel Parsley, Sage, Rosemary and Thyme LP and later on the 1968 soundtrack of *The Graduate*. This broader interest in a darker side to a 'folk tradition' can be seen on the Traffic's 1970 release of *John Barleycorn Must Die*, and *The Sergeant Pepper's Lonely Hearts Club Band* LP cover infamously features 'the beast' Aleister

Crowley amongst the throng. This counterculture LSD-inspired trend draws out the inner workings of the psyche in the same manner that Hardy was attempting in his experiments. However, as Hardy drew on new ideas and started looking forward to the analysis of the mind, he located the effects of that investigation in a traditional context. This is more evidence of the process of looking backwards and forwards at the same time. This too is evident in the second wave of folk horror, perhaps most notably in the work of Ben Wheatley and Amy Jump. The effects of inhabiting an inner world are keenly felt in *A Field in England* and *In the Earth*. In each of these the presentation of the world becomes a bad trip. Even in his adaptation of *Rebecca* he inserts contemporary musical artist Jason Williamson of the band *Sleaford Mods* as a folk singer, preceding a nightmare like vision of the party for the second Mrs de Winter as she is surrounded by guests wearing 'Wicker Man-esque' animal heads. The gothic classic is given a momentary folk horror twist for the twenty-first century.

Hardy's Wessex and Egdon Heath

As we have seen in a letter to his friend Edward, Clodd Hardy stressed that the supernatural elements on display in his writing were not invented but existed as 'real folklore' – folklore, believed in and practised by a section of the rural population in Dorset and recorded by writers such as John Symonds Udal (1848–1925) and the 'Dorset Poet' William Barnes (1801–86). In a letter written to John Pasco in 1901, again concerning folklore, Hardy was to confirm the reliability of his source material:

> To your other question, if the legendary matter & folk-lore in my books is traditionary, & not invented, I can answer yes, in, every case; this being a point on which I was careful not to falsify local beliefs & customs.
> (Millgate, *The Life and Work of Thomas Hardy* 94)

Hardy was very aware that the demographics of the area around him were rapidly changing and that age-old Dorset customs, superstitions and traditions were disappearing quickly, as Keith Selby points out:

> Throughout the last half of the nineteenth century, and even into the first decade of the twentieth, Dorset was experiencing that social phenomenon now euphemistically referred to as the 'depopulation of the English village'. During the fifty years of the period 1860–1910, about 350,000 agricultural workers simply disappeared from the land.
> (Selby, 100)

Against this backdrop of rapid change, Hardy sought to preserve the folklore, customs and traditional culture of Dorset, an important element of which was the supernatural. In his writing and particularly in his short stories there is a wide range of this on display: from the downright horrific, like a corpse having a six-foot stake hammered into it, as in 'The Grave by the Handpost' and the somewhat subtler, but nevertheless disturbing depiction of a musician who could 'well-nigh have drawn an ache from the heart of a gate-post' as in Mop Ollamoor in 'The Fiddler of the Reels' (287). They are also unified by the fact that they all occur at a particular location: Egdon Heath in Hardy's Wessex.

Hardy's first major success came with the publication of *Far from the Madding Crowd* (1874) and it was at this stage that he decided to set his novels in the landscape of a mythical 'Wessex'. This was a region which, as Hardy stated in a preface written twenty years later, was 'partly real, partly dream-country' (*Far from the Madding Crowd* 48) and the insertion of some of the folklore of Dorset can be seen to sit somewhere between the two states, believed as fact by some, dismissed as rustic nonsense by others. Initially Wessex was based on the area of Dorset in which Hardy grew up, but by the time of his last novel *Jude the Obscure* (1896) it had enlarged to include Oxford, which became that novel's Christminster. Hardy seems to have used this solid base of Wessex, adopted 'from the pages of early English history' (*Far from the Madding Crowd* 47), as a conceptual space onto which he might graft his tales, a surface, on which, as Michael Irwin and Ian Gregor have suggested, he could 'shift his narrative stance slightly [...] so that he was freed from a manner of narration which suggested the inventor of tales, to a manner which suggested he was their chronicler' (110).

It was in the landscapes of Wessex (amongst his fourteen novels and over fifty short stories, and some of his poetry) that Hardy explored his passion for the dark folkloric tales, imported as they were, from his childhood in Dorset; many of the tales the 'chronicler' (to use Irwin and Gregor's term again) told concerned the 'Mephistophelian Visitants', first mentioned in *The Return of the Native* (131), that seemed attracted to the area, and Egdon Heath in particular. Mark Fisher when describing the notion of the 'eerie' says that it 'clings to certain kinds of physical spaces and landscapes' (*The Weird and the Eerie* 61); Egdon Heath, Wessex is just such a landscape. Egdon Heath is at the very centre of the dark proceedings in *The Return of the Native*. In this novel Hardy allocates the first chapter 'A Face on Which Time Makes but Little Impression', exclusively to the location, and treats its timelessness in as much detail as a main character, stating that 'civilization was its enemy; and ever since the beginning of vegetation its soil had worn the same antique brown dress, the natural and invariable garment of the particular formation' (*The Return of the Native* 56).

It is clear that any feeble attempts by humankind to tame the heath, to control it, will be destined to fail. No plough 'had ever disturbed a grain of that stubborn soil. In the heath's barrenness to the farmer lay its fertility to the historian' (66). The landscape and the setting play a major role in the novel governing the lives of characters that inhabit it.

Egdon is the location of the supernatural and is regarded by Christian Cantle, a local to the heath, as a place to be avoided 'after dark' unless one wants to be 'pixy-led','Tis very lonesome for 'ee in the heth tonight, mis'ess [...] Mind you don't get lost. Egdon Heath is a bad place to get lost in, and the winds do huffle queerer tonight than ever I heard 'em afore. Them that know Egdon best have been pixy-led here at times' (*The Return of the Native* 84). The phrase seems to sum up aspects of Egdon which as Ruth A Firor notes was believed by some to be 'full of pixies' who simply loved to 'lead travellers away, over moors and into bogs, laughing heartily' (Firor 56). Pixies, synonymous with elves and sprites, were generally regarded in folklore as mischievous, but under the cover of darkness seem happy to join the menace of Egdon, where even a thorn bush had 'a ghastly habit [...] of putting on the shapes of jumping madmen, sprawling giants, and hideous cripples' (*The Return of the Native* 125).

Most of the action in *The Return of the Native* takes place on the Rainbarrow, itself one of three prehistoric burial mounds on Egdon Heath, whose people engage in activities and seasonal rituals which seek to celebrate an ancient pre-Christian past. The Rainbarrow, as Kroll suggests, draws the heathfolk to it because it has been 'a site of human significance in the past' (342) and in their engagement with it the present heath dwellers become part of its evolving history. Eustacia and Wildeve meet at the country dance where 'paganism was revised in their hearts' (321); on another occasion when people are gathered dressing the maypole in preparation for a celebration, the narrator tells us

> the impulses of all such outlandish hamlets are pagan still: in these spots homage to nature, self adoration, frantic gaieties, fragments of Teutonic rites to divinities whose names are forgotten, seem in some way or other to have survived mediaeval doctrine.
> (Hardy, *The Return of the Native* 452)

As in much of folk horror the landscape, as Scovell comments, is 'essentially the first link, where elements within its topography have adverse effects on the social and moral identity of its inhabitants' (*Folk Horror: Hours Dreadful and Things Strange* 17). There are many examples such as this in the text: Chapter 3 opens on the Rainbarrow with what Ruth Firor describes as 'a scene of pagan revelry' depicting the Guy Fawkes bonfires 'the whole heath alive with suns of fire, some pale and distant, some red, like dreadful wounds'

(147). According to Firor the Guy Fawkes celebration 'took over pre-existing customs and transferred them to a fixed date' (148), which became, as depicted in *The Return of the Native*, a date of great significance to the locals.

Andrew Norman notes that the 'real' Egdon Heath lay behind Hardy's childhood home in Higher Bockhampton: 'Behind the house extends a huge area of heathland, which in Thomas III's time [...] was dotted with isolated cottages' (Norman 20). Egdon Heath, the blend of fact and fantasy, became a key ingredient in Hardy's fiction in which supernatural forces were suspected of imposing themselves on the everyday lives of mere mortals, and, as George Levine suggests, such matters do not belong in 'realistic fiction' where 'mystery is merely a temporary gap in knowledge' (Levine 19). Throughout Hardy's work, 'mystery is the effect of a spiritual and inexplicable intrusion or initiation from outside of nature' (19).

Egdon Heath's Mephistophelian visitants

Hardy first used the term 'Mephistophelian visitants' in connection with his character Diggory Venn in *The Return of the Native* (131); the term is used here as it neatly describes some of the inhabitants of the Heath and their particular supernatural practices. The story of 'The Withered Arm' makes reference, amongst its other macabre elements, to the process of 'overlooking' or being given the 'evil-eye', and the custom of consulting white witches or 'Conjurors'. The nineteenth-century Dorset poet William Barnes defined the conjuror as 'cunnen man, or wizard; a low kind of seer' (Barnes 17), a 'white witch' with supernatural expertise and one to consult, as Udal states, whenever an individual fears that 'either himself or his property to be under the malefic influence of the evil eye' (Udal 1970). The conjuror figure, of central importance in 'The Withered Arm', runs throughout Hardy's oeuvre; indeed, even in the light and jovial *Under the Greenwood Tree*, one of Hardy's early novels (1872) he engaged with witch folklore for his character Elizabeth Endorsfield, the name being reminiscent of the biblical Witch of Endor. We are told Elizabeth's house

> stood in a lonely place; she never went to church; she wore a red cloak; she always retained her bonnet indoors; she had a pointed chin. Thus far all her attributes were distinctly Satanic; and those who looked no further called her in plain terms, a witch.
>
> (Hardy, *Under the Greenwood Tree* 125)

The witch in 'The Withered Arm' is Conjuror Trendle and in a letter to Hermann Lea in July 1907 Hardy explained that although the name was an invention in the story, the conjuror as a character was not. Hardy states that he does not remember

> what his real name was, or rather, he is a composite figure of two or three who used to be heard of... Conjuror Minterne, or Mynterne, who lived out Blackmoor way, you have of course heard of: he was one of the most celebrated.
>
> (Purdy and Millgate, *The Collected Letters of Thomas Hardy, 7 Volumes* 264)

The custom of consulting white witches or conjurors is mentioned in *Tess of the d'Urbervilles*; Dairyman Crick, when the cream will not turn to butter, suspects that 'somebody in the house is in love' (189), another local superstition. He adds that if the situation does not improve he will have to seek the help of Conjuror Trendle, although he 'don't believe in en':

> Tis years since I went to Conjuror Trendle's son in Egdon – years!" said the dairyman bitterly. "And he was nothing to what his father had been. I have said fifty times, if I have said once, that I don't believe in en. But I shall have to go to 'n if he's still alive. O yes, I shall have to go to 'n, if this sort of thing continnys!
>
> (Hardy, *Tess of the d'Urbervilles* 189)

Jonathan Kail who is in the dairy at the time says that he always preferred Conjuror Fall 't'other side of Casterbridge [...] But he's rotten as touchwood now' (189). Conjuror Fall also appears in *The Mayor of Casterbridge* when Henchard, a corn merchant, consults him for a weather forecast in connection with the harvest. Henchard does not take Fall's advice and when things go wrong he questions whether 'some power was working against him', 'I wonder if it can be that somebody has been roasting a waxen image of me, or stirring an unholy brew to confound me! I don't believe in such power; and yet – what if they should ha' been doing it!' (191).

Although Henchard has lifted himself above such rustic beliefs as witchcraft, he is not totally confident in dismissing its presence. The 'Mephistophelian visitants' and their particular supernatural practices are well represented in Wessex and, as Jacquline Dillion correctly points out, 'no single version of reality or agreed belief exists' (Dillion 23). John Symonds Udal in *Dorsetshire Folk-lore* lists a number of instances of supposed witchcraft, evidenced by reports from local newspapers in nineteenth- and early twentieth-century Dorset, particularly in connection with being 'overlooked', the term usually referring to being given the 'evil eye' by a witch and the victim then suffering as a result. Hermann Lea, Hardy's friend and photographer, writing in 1907 suggested that 'the immediate effect on a person who has been overlooked, ill-wished, or hagrod [...] as it is variously called consists as a rule of some sort of indisposition. This gradually increases to severe sickness, and finally death supervenes' and Udal states that 'the most effectual way of neutralizing, or of removing, the baneful influence exerted by the witch, or other person who was supposed to be overlooking the sufferer, was to draw blood from the "overlooker"' (Udal 207). This 'belief' is referenced in Shakespeare's play *Henry VI*, in Act I, Scene V, when Talbot tells Joan la Pucelle: 'Devil or devil's dam, I'll conjure thee: Blood will I draw on thee, thou art a witch' (Shakespeare 463). As Udal suggests, the mention of the 'cure' in a Shakespearian text gives the practice the 'imprint of some antiquity' (Udal 207).

In *The Return of the Native* Hardy offers an example of the drawing of blood from the 'overlooker' when Susan Nunsuch attacks Eustacia Vye in church one morning 'with a long stocking-needle' (235): Susan wrongly believing that Eustacia is bewitching her son. Christian Cantle reports that 'Sue pricked her that deep that the maid fainted away' (235). Udal comments that an 'additional interest is afforded in this case from the fact that'

> this gross outrage took place in church, the deluded woman, no doubt, believing that a fuller success would attend her 'charm' if the supposed witch could be met with attending divine service.
>
> (Udal 210)

Susan Nunsuch is deluded because although Eustacia appears at times both exotic and 'unworldly' her 'Pagan eyes, full of nocturnal mysteries' (118) she is not a witch, but her end in drowning is one suffered by many that were. Later in the novel, just before her death when Eustacia is 'standing on Rainbarrow, her soul in an abyss of desolation seldom plumbed by one so young' (424), Susan busies herself by making a wax effigy of Eustacia, in which she then sticks pins, before finally melting it on the fire. This process is accompanied by the 'murmur of words', Susan slowly reciting the Lord's Prayer backwards three times. The narrator notes that this was 'a practice well known on Egdon at that date, and one that is not quite extinct at the present day' (422). The emphasis on 'not quite extinct' is telling in furthering the sense of the co-existence of two time frames, the mythical past with its perceived longevity and the future, which is on the horizon but never quite reached. The reality is that the extinction of this belief is forever deferred, a further chilling effect of the 'hauntings' of the recent past. As with Richard Littler's *Discovering Scarfolk*, we are in a perpetual loop where nothing ever progresses and develops. This can be seen in *Water Shall Refuse Them* (L. M. Hardy) where the belief in a form of witchcraft that is actually defined in the 1970s infects the present through its evocation in a contemporary novel.

Diggory Venn, Mop Ollamoor and the Freudian uncanny

As noted, Hardy first used the term 'Mephistophelian visitants' in connection with the appearance of Venn the 'reddleman' whose job it was to mark sheep in preparation for them to go to market. This character, covered from head to foot in bright red pigment, is a good example of Hardy trying to capture and retain an image of the vanishing life of rural Dorset, explaining that 'reddlemen of the old school are now but seldom seen. Since the introduction of railways, Wessex farmers have managed to do without these Mephistophelian visitants' (131). Because of his appearance and the red pigment that 'permeated him' (58), the reddleman was often the cause of fear in children. The narrator describes how a

> child's first sight of a reddleman was an epoch in his life. That blood-covered figure was a sublimation of all the horrid dreams which had afflicted the juvenile spirit since imagination began. 'The reddleman is coming for you!' had been the formulated threat of Wessex mothers for many generations.
>
> (Hardy, *The Return of the Native* 131)

It is not just children in *The Return of the Native* who are frightened by the appearance of the reddleman, Timothy Fairway is also startled:

> No slight to your looks reddleman, for ye bain't bad-looking in the groundwork, though the finish is queer. My meaning is just to say how curious I felt. I half thought it 'twas the devil or the red ghost the boy told of.
>
> (Hardy, *Return of the Native* 82)

Venn leads a Gypsy-like lifestyle on the heath sleeping in his van and visiting farms when necessary; he is a solitary, mysterious, ghostly figure living on the very edge of the Egdon Heath community in every sense.

In her discussions on Diggory Venn, Tracy Hayes recalls Freud's 1919 essay *Das Unheiml ich*, or *The Uncanny*, noting that Venn is 'unknowable' ('The Red Ghost and the No-Moon Man: Masculinity as Other in the Return of the Native' 52) and therefore an example of 'Otherness' occupying a 'position outside the *status quo*' (51) with an appearance and a manner that causes fear. Freud stated that the term 'uncanny' applies to everything 'that was intended to remain secret, hidden away, and has come into the open' (Freud 132). It is something that we have some familiarity with and yet is foreign to us, leaving us feeling uncomfortably disturbed. Yet, as

Hayes points out it is Venn who is of key importance in the text, he 'steers the course of the plot' and even 'though he remains *unheimlich,* Other to all he interacts with', Venn 'remains vital to the progression of the society he watches over' ('The Red Ghost and the No-Moon Man: Masculinity As Other In the Return of the Native' 53). Ironically it is when Diggory Venn leaves his role as reddleman and becomes 'white' that he alarms his future wife Thomasin: 'O, how you frightened me!' she said to someone who had just entered 'I thought you were the ghost of yourself' (450). Later she tells Yeobright that she was so 'alarmed' when she had first seen him and 'couldn't believe that he had got white of his own accord! It seemed supernatural' (450).

For all the strangeness of both his appearance and the working role he occupies on the Wessex landscape, Diggory Venn is not an agent of the supernatural, Mop Ollamoor in 'The Fiddler of the Reels', however, certainly is. He occupies a place of 'Otherness' outside the 'status quo' identified by Hayes. The term 'Otherness' was originally associated with Michel Foucault as a critique of Enlightenment thought that was used, as an 'ethnocentric construct that implicitly naturalises a white, masculine perspective' (L. McNay 5). Although Hardy never refers directly to Mop as a Gypsy, the fact that the narrator states that he first appeared in the area as a 'fiddle-player at Greenhill Fair' has 'rather un-English' looks; his 'complexion being a rich olive' (287) would suggest that at least functionally he is playing that role in the story; therefore, in a structural sense Mop is the 'Other' in Foucault's terms, part of a marginalized group and, in some ways, he is also 'Other' in the supernatural sense. No one knows where Mop comes from and he also has the ability to disappear without trace; we are told early on in the story that he has a power, especially over women, which 'seemed sometimes to have a touch of the weird and wizardly in it' (287). If Diggory Venn, because of the red pigment colour, has something of Satan surrounding him, Mop's power lies in his fiddle playing. Venn is the bogey man to children in the area, but Mop can reduce them to tears by playing his fiddle. Mop's fiddle playing is described as able to

> claim for itself a most peculiar and personal quality, like that of a moving preacher. There were tones in it which bred the immediate conviction that indolence and averseness to systematic application were all that lay between 'Mop' and the career of a second Paganini.
>
> (Hardy the Fiddler of the Reels 287)

The significance of the reference to 'a second Paginini' is important here. It is very likely that Hardy had heard of the exploits of the Italian violinist Niccolo Paginini (1782–1840) who he referred to above and based his character Mop Ollamoor on him. Paginini was popularly believed to have sold his soul to the devil: his performances frequently causing fainting amongst the females in the audience. By connecting the fictional character Mop with this well-known musician, Hardy makes an implicit connection between satanic possession and the power of music to influence and bewitch. He also draws on a familiar cultural myth. Like Robert Johnson in decades to come the Paganini myth draws on Faust and brings the devil to bear on the lives of ordinary mortals. This is in itself an example of Christian doctrine being applied to the everyday interaction of ordinary people. This is not to suggest that Paganini or Johnson were ordinary but their lives as translated into folk narratives gave rise to the use, reuse and embedding of this myth.

The notion of 'evil' and the weird surrounds Mop, the weird being 'constituted by a presence – *the presence of that which does not belong*' (Fisher, *The Weird and the Eerie* 61). The first sighting of him in the story is when he's standing on a doorstep playing his fiddle and 'laughing as the tears rolled down the cheeks of the little children hanging round him' (289). Again, Fisher makes the point that 'doors, thresholds and portals [...] *the between* is crucial to the weird' (28). Mop's appearance in rural Sticklefield stands out and disturbs, Mop coming from a much darker place, as the narrator notes 'nobody knew where' (287).

In later folk horror texts this trope is seemingly reversed and the stranger who comes into town is brought there precisely because they are ordinary. This is clearly evident in Sergeant Howie's arrival on Summerisle but as a device is much more commonly evident in folk horror than might otherwise be noted. In respect of what might be considered to be the first wave of folk horror the 'spectral western', *High Plains Drifter* features a stranger who comes into an isolated community ostensibly to save them in conventional Western format. However the 'stranger', in echoes of the reddleman, covers the town in red paint and affixes a sign welcoming visitors 'to hell'. To save the town it has to be destroyed. The mid-west might seem a long way from Wessex but the narrative devices are remarkable in their similarity. This trope evolves in much contemporary fiction where the stranger appears to be an innocent and we learn it at the centre of the darkness; for examples with the revelation of Nif as the perpetrator and 'witch' in *Water Shall Refuse Them* (L. M. Hardy) or Sam's lineage to the isolated Osea Island in *The Third Day*. In this latter example it is clearly the character who returns to a place where they 'belong', even if they themselves don't yet know or believe that they do. This is the essence of *The Third Day*; Sam comes to believe this is the place from which he originates and where his son is located, even when it is clear the child presented as his is false.

Skimmington-rides, ghostly coaches and other superstitions

One of the uncanniest moments in the major novels of Hardy occurs in *The Mayor of Casterbridge* when Michael Henchard is suicidal and ready to jump in a pool 'where the water was at its deepest' (296). He is about to do this when something becomes visible in the water, a shape emerges, that of a human body:

> lying stiff and stark upon the surface of the stream. In the circular current imparted by the central flow the form was brought forward, till it passed under his eyes; and then he perceived with a sense of horror that it was himself. Not a man somewhat resembling him, but one in all respect his counterpart, his actual double, was floating as if dead in Ten Hatches Hole. The sense of the supernatural was strong in this unhappy man, and he turned away as one might have done in the actual presence of an appalling miracle.
>
> (Hardy, *The Mayor of Casterbridge* 297)

This situation occurs because of another folkloric practice that Hardy brings into this text, the practice of 'skimmington' or 'skimmington riding'. Skimmington rides involved the parading through the streets of effigies of those deemed to have been engaging in illicit behaviour: in this instance, Lucetta and Henchard, who had a prior relationship before Lucetta married Farfrae. The parading was often accompanied by locals noisily banging pots and pans. Udal, quoting from George Robert's *History of Lyme Regis* published in 1834, states that skimmington riding 'checks those instances of openly profligate and licentious conduct, which else might become too prevalent among the lower orders'. He goes on to suggest that it 'brands with infamy all gross instances of licentiousness, and exposes to lasting ridicule those couples who by their dissensions disturb the quiet and order of the neighbourhood, and so set[s] a bad example' (Udal 193).

Both Henchard and his former lover Lucetta are deemed to be in disgrace and their two effigies are led through Casterbridge back to back on a donkey; the narrator comments that 'it was impossible to mistake the pair for other than the intended victims' (279). Lucetta from her open window sees and hears the crowd in the street below: ''Tis me!' she said, with a face as pale as death. 'A procession – a scandal – an effigy of me, and him!' (279). The shock of witnessing the 'spectacle of the uncanny revel' (279) of the skimmington procession, and the thought of her husband seeing it too, causes Lucetta to have an epileptic seizure. She is pregnant at this time and miscarries before dying.

Skimmington riding, although only a moderately uncanny practice, being more of a moral warning to the lower classes about licentious behaviour, becomes deeply unsettling when Hardy uses the effigies in this way, both Lucetta and Henchard are confronted with their doubles. Lucetta is shocked by shame and subsequently dies and Henchard believes that he has been part of some sort of divine intervention, questioning the whereabouts of the effigy of Lucetta, Henchard asks: 'But where is the other? Why that one only? [...] That performance of theirs killed her, but kept me alive!' (298).

As Andrew Hewitt states, Henchard seems to take the effigy as some sort of 'bizarre compliment' recognizing that 'ritual mockery can be read as a tribute' (Hewitt 90) to one who had been used to power.

Skimmington riding, hang-fairs and pre-Christian festivities on Egdon Heath were staged events involving a number of people and regarded as entertainment; Hardy also makes use of local folklore and superstition in relation to certain places. In 'The Fiddler of the Reels', Ned, Car'line and Carry, after returning from London, arrange to meet up at 'The Quiet Woman' inn. On their way there Car'line and Carry pass 'Heedless William's Pool'. As in the case of 'The Quiet Woman' inn, the pool did exist and was close to the cottage where Hardy grew up in Higher Bockhampton, it was also, as Fran and Geoff Doel point out, 'supposed to be the site of a coaching disaster, where the driver William and his passengers perished. The pool is also said to have been dug out by fairy shovels and to be bottomless' (Doel 19). Disappearing and ghostly coaches feature frequently in Dorset folklore: Edward Waring in *Ghosts and Legends of the Dorset Countryside* gives a useful account of these and says of the 'Heedless (vulgo Headless) William's Pool', 'Disappearing into a pool is a familiar trick of ghostly coaches. If they are denizens of the underworld, what better exit from the world could they find than a deep or "bottomless" pool?' (Waring 19).

Hardy refers to one of these legends in *Tess of the d'Urbervilles*. After their wedding service, Tess (whose ancestors were from the noble d'Urberville family) and Angel are about to get on a coach to take them on their doomed honeymoon. Tess admits to feeling troubled and having a notion that she has seen the coach somewhere before, at this point Angel begins to explain the myth:

> Well – I would rather not tell it in detail just now. A certain d'Urberville of the sixteenth or seventeenth century committed a dreadful crime in his family coach; and since that time members of the family see or hear the old coach whenever – But I'll tell you another day – it is rather gloomy. Evidently some dim knowledge of it has been brought back to your mind by the sight of this venerable caravan.
> (Hardy, *Tess of the d'Urbervilles* 280)

Hardy gives no more detail about the legend till later in the novel when the story is recounted to Tess by Alec, who is not of course 'a genuine d'Urberville':

> 'If you are a genuine d'Urberville I ought not to tell you either, I suppose. As for me, I'm a sham one, so it doesn't matter. It is rather dismal. It is that this sound of a non-existent coach can only be heard by one of d'Urberville blood, and it is held to be of ill-omen to the one who hears it. It has to do with a murder, committed by one of the family, centuries ago.'

'Now you have begun it, finish it.'

'Very well. One of the family is said to have abducted some beautiful woman, who tried to escape from the coach in which he was carrying her off, and in the struggle he killed her – or she killed him – I forget which.'

(Hardy, *Tess of the d'Urbervilles* 437)

In a letter written from Dorchester in 1903, to someone questioning him about the legend of the phantom coach, Hardy responded by stating that the story of the coach was well known in the area and made itself manifest in 'two properties formerly owned by branches of the same family – the Turbervilles. The cause of the appearances is said to be some family murder' (Millgate, *The Life and Work of Thomas Hardy* 93). This is a further case of Hardy using local folklore from his particular area of Dorset and transposing it to his created Wessex. This is a aspect of a great deal of contemporary folk horror which does as Hardy did; it delves back into a past which is, from the perspective of the novelist, within living memory. In *The Apparition Phase* Will McLean takes us back to a 1970s childhood and draws directly on the image of a spectral hooded monk so familiar from the *Usborne World of the Unknown: Ghosts* (Maynard). This book was reissued in 2019 by Usborne editor Anna Howarth and featured a new introduction by writer and actor Reece Shearsmith, who himself notes the foundational place of this book in inspiring a generation of writers. What McLean (and Shearsmith et al.) do was initiated by Hardy. In a blurring of the line between fact and fiction, the provenance of the image as real is due to its location in a source which is validated by its first effect being made in childhood. This is a foundation of contemporary folklore that has its foundations in the same approach as made by Hardy in his visceral evocation of Skimmington Rides and other forms of folk tale: recounting and creation of myth collapse into each other. This is not simply an effect of time, as Bob Fischer notes:

> The book is an extraordinary feat of research, and I was intrigued to note that folklorist Eric Maple had been credited as "Special Consultant". Maple, born in 1916 in Essex, was the son of a spiritualist medium and a voracious collector of folk and occult tales; his magnificently-titled works *The Dark World of Witches, The Realm of Ghosts* and *The Domain of Devils* forming a quintessentially 1960s triumvirate of books, published – entirely appropriately – by Pan.
>
> (Fischer, 'Where Ghosts Gather')

The effect of someone of 'Turberville blood' seeing the coach is explained by Wilkinson Sherran in his book *The Wessex of Romance* (1908) and quoted in Udal:

> An anecdote is told of a gentleman who, passing across the old Elizabethan bridge on his way to dine with a friend, saw the ghostly coach [...] On

arriving at his destination he spoke of it [...] Much to his astonishment he was told it was the Turberville coach [...] the sight [...] is said to forebode disaster to the descendant to whom it appears.

(Udal 175)

The ill-fated wedding of Tess is also predicted by the omen of a cock crowing in the afternoon, as she and Angel are about to leave the farm; everyone gathered in the yard to wish them well is aware of the bad luck associated with this, as is Tess herself: 'I don't like to hear him!' said Tess to her husband 'tell the man to drive on.' After the coach has gone Crick the farmer comments to his wife: 'Now, to think o' that just to-day! I've not heard his crow of an afternoon all the year afore' (282). Mrs Crick tries to play down the importance of the cock's behaviour by placing another folkloric interpretation on it: 'It only means a change in the weather,' said she, 'not what you think 'tis impossible!' (282). Udal confirms that the crowing of a cock in the afternoon was a widely held superstition in Dorset at the time, an old woman in Symondsbury stating: 'If the cock crows after twelve o'clock noon her is doing it to bring I bad news, or John may be bad again. I can't a-bear to hear 'en' (Udal 180). The same phenomena can then have two possible interpretations; yet, the text makes clear which one applies to Tess.

Hardy: Death, the grave, faith and the Church

A sweet face is a page of sadness to a man over thirty – the raw material of a corpse (29). This quotation is taken from *Thomas Hardy's Notebooks* edited by Evelyn Hardy and was written a month before his thirtieth birthday. Hardy's writings are littered with such comments and totally enforce James F. Scott's claim that Hardy had a 'preoccupation with graves and corpses' (373). Throughout his fiction there is a noticeable recurrence of situations where characters express particular wishes to be buried in certain places, but often end up interred elsewhere. When Michael Henchard's death is imminent in *The Mayor of Casterbridge*, one of his instructions 'written in the anguish of dying' (333) is that 'I not be bury'd in consecrated ground' (333) and the narrator explains that his wishes were 'respected as far as practicable' (333). It is not coincidence that throughout his writing Hardy flagged the idea of the horrors of an individual being buried in a place or a way they would not have chosen. In the short story 'The Grave by the Handpost', neither Sergeant Holway nor his son Luke end up being buried where they wished to be; Luke's written wishes to be buried with his father by the handpost being blown away by the wind and the Church not allowing the Sergeant in consecrated ground as he has committed the act of 'felo-de-se', suicide. In an entry in his notebook of 1882 Hardy recorded: 'Burial of suicides at cross roads abolished c1830. (Stake driven through it: between 9 & 12. Times)' (R. H. Taylor 24). John Fowles and Joe Draper discuss one particular cross-road Warmwell Cross, near Owermoigne, where such burials took place, noting that 'they have a long association with bad luck, perhaps because they were where suicides and witches were always buried, and certainly they were where the gibbets stood' (Draper 99). This is also the backdrop to *Old Trash*, *The Third Day* and *The Loney*, amongst other works. They are set in places where 'events' have occurred and rituals are known to have happened. Unlike the Jamesian lineage of folk horror, where there is an object which is proven to be connected to something 'outside', there is a belief that these places have some form of connection to an event or person and therefore impact directly on how people behave.

Cross-roads, like pools that devour passing coaches, are places infused with dark deeds and dark history, folkloric narrative that Hardy brings to our notice. Sergeant Holway of course is not the first Hardy character to be denied a Christian burial; Tess was not allowed to bury her baby Sorrow within the churchyard because the child had not been 'officially' baptized, so the baby was to be placed at night, 'in that shabby corner of God's allotment where He lets the nettles grow, and where all unbaptized infants, notorious drunkards, suicides, and others of the conjecturally damned are laid' (*Tess of the d'Urbervilles* 148). (There are also eerie echoes of Sergent Holway in Anthony Shaffer's creation of Sergent Howie in *The Wicker Man*, who himself is denied a Christian burial. It is perhaps no accident that Shaffer reworked David Pinner's Inspector Hanlin from his 1967 novel *Ritual* into this Hardyesque character.)

Places of burial make frequent appearances in Hardy's writing; in his poem 'Something Tapped' Hardy imagines Emma calling him:

> 'O I am tired of waiting,' she said,
> 'Night, morn, noon, afternoon;
> So cold it is in my lonely bed,
> And I thought you would join me soon!'

'Something Tapped', included in the *Selected Poems* collection written in 1913 a year after Emma's death, is one of the series of elegies where Hardy expresses his remorse at his wife's death, even though, as we have seen, all biographical sources suggest that their marriage at the time of her death had broken down completely, with both living separate lives at Max Gate.

At the point of writing the poem Hardy believed that he would be buried alongside Emma and the rest of his family in Stinsford, having left space on the tombstone for his own name and stated these instructions in his will. It is therefore ironic that the reality of Hardy's death and own funeral(s) in January 1928 far outstripped that of any of his fictional creations. When Hardy died, Sir Sydney Cockerell and J. M. Barrie (both friends of

Hardy) completely took over the funeral arrangements, asserting 'their male authority' over what Cockerell had already referred to as 'the houseful of women' (Millgate, *Thomas Hardy: A Biography* 574). The two were to totally disregard Hardy's wishes, believing that he should be the first novelist since Dickens in 1870 and the first poet since Tennyson in 1892, to be buried in Poets' Corner at Westminster Abbey. They quickly made moves to arrange this and despite objections from both Hardy's family and some in the Church, on Monday 16th of January the burial at Poets' Corner took place.

Hardy's family also objected to and were horrified by two other features of his funeral arrangements: before his remains were interred at Westminster he was to be cremated and before the cremation took place Hardy's heart was to be removed. The cremation took place at Brookwood near Woking on the 13th of January and the heart was buried at Stinsford at the same time 2.00 pm on the 16th of January as the ashes were interred in London. The removal of the heart was at the suggestion of the local vicar the Reverend Cowley who had possibly estimated the future value of having the writer's organ deposited in his churchyard, because ninety-odd years later its resting place is still a big attraction, almost a site of pilgrimage for interested literary tourists. Despite protestations from all of Hardy's family these somewhat macabre acts of 'medieval butchery' as Hardy's friend Edmund Gosse called it went ahead as planned (Tomalin 372).

Another equally bizarre occurrence was said to have happened concerning Hardy's heart which was believed (by some) to have been eaten by a cat. Whose cat and where the incident took place vary: Martin Seymour-Smith (1995) suggests that a surgeon came to Max Gate to remove the heart, which he placed in a biscuit tin, a cat then gained entry to where the heart was being stored, knocked off the lid and started devouring the contents. Subsequently the undertaker arrived killed the cat and gathered the remaining morsels of unconsumed heart and both were then buried in a casket at the service in Stinsford. The other version blames the doctor's cat, the heart being taken back to his home following its removal. Tomalin states that the story 'may have originated in the pubs of Dorchester, where macabre jokes were no doubt appreciated' (Seymour-Smith 372). Hardy had served as a Justice of the Peace in Dorchester, sitting on thirty-eight occasions between 1884 and1919 and that he was unpopular with some in the town. Seymour-Smith's suggestion that this tale, which has become folkloric, 'would have hugely amused Tom' (863) is as compelling as it is fitting. It is an exemplar of the nature of folklore and suggestive of how it develops.

Although Hardy did not end up in 'a shabby corner of God's allotment' (*Tess of the d'Urbervilles* 148), his relationship with the Church and Christianity in general was deeply troubled. In 1913 when Hardy was about to receive an honorary fellowship from Magdalen College Cambridge, he was described in the *Cambridge Magazine* as a 'celebrated Atheist' and bearing in mind that the vice-chancellor at the time was the Reverend Alexander Donaldson one would have imagined some tension, but according to Tomalin (330) the event passed smoothly. The speculation that there might be problems followed on from the hostile reception to *Tess of the d'Urbervilles* and *Jude the Obscure* where, in connection with the latter, the then Bishop of Wakefield, Walsham How, famously burnt a copy and wrote to the *Yorkshire Post* labelling it indecent and persuaded W. H. Smith to withdraw it from their circulating library. Writing about this in the preface to *Jude the Obscure* in 1912 Hardy commented: 'So much for the unhappy beginning of *Jude*'s career as a book. After these verdicts from the press its next misfortune was to be burnt by a bishop – probably in his despair at not being able to burn me' (vi).

Hardy also stated that the negative reaction he had received to the book had completely cured him 'of any future interest in novel writing' (vii); *Jude* was to be Hardy's last major novel. There is an account in *Jude the Obscure* which has been consistently omitted from screen adaptations and may have added to the Church's unease with the narrative. When Jude and Sue are working as stone masons on the lettering of the Ten Commandments, the churchwarden tells them a story told to him as a child. Whilst workmen were engaged in the same activity in a nearby church, when the 'Commandments wanted doing up' (312), the workers had to labour on long into a Saturday night, where they got drunk and eventually 'fell down senseless, one and all'. When they sobered up, 'there was a terrible thunderstorm a-raging, and they seemed to see in the gloom a dark figure with very thin legs and a curious voot, a-standing on the ladder, and finishing their work' (312–13).

The next morning as the congregation gathered for the Sunday service, they all witnessed the devil's work, 'all saw that the Ten Commandments wez painted with the "Nots" left out' (313). Was Hardy in this tale simply being mischievous about the Commandments and the Church, or did this tale come from some form of folkloric legend? Certainly Jo Draper (90) feels that *Jude the Obscure* 'expressed the most anti-Christian views' out of all Hardy's work and recalls Sue's statement when Jude asks her whether she'd like to go and sit in the cathedral: 'Cathedral? Yes. Though I think I'd rather sit in the railway station [...] That's the centre of the town life now. The Cathedral has had its day!' (141). Hardy is displaying Sue's modernity and her atheistic views here, but were those views also his own?

As has previously been referred to, the confusion between science and the irrational is echoed in the issue of Hardy's religious beliefs. The Rt Revd Stephen Platten, a former Bishop of Wakefield, addressed Hardy devotees and scholars at the *Thomas Hardy Society London Lecture, 2013* and suggested that Hardy's 'entire life and work are interwoven with musing on faith and doubt' (Platten 14). Certainly, as a child in his rural environment Hardy and his family were very involved in local church matters at Stinsford and this is depicted in the Mellstock choir in *Under the Greenwood Tree*.

The vicar at the time, the Reverend Shirley, noted that the young Hardy 'was bright' and encouraged him 'to join his own sons as a teacher in the Sunday School' (Tomalin 39). Indeed, Hardy 'even practised sermon writing in the late 1850s' (Platten 16) and at one stage considered going into the church as a county curate, but as was the case of his character Jude, this plan would have involved study at university and so was eventually rejected.

It is generally agreed, from all biographical sources, that Hardy's move from Dorset to London in 1862, as an architectural draftsman, marked a watershed in his religious belief. In London he encountered all that was current in intellectual thought and he himself stated in 1882 that 'as a young man he had been among the earliest acclaimers of *The Origin of Species*' (Millgate, *Thomas Hardy: A Biography* 158). He attended Darwin's funeral at Westminster Abbey in 1882 and was in agreement as Sven Backman states with the 'rationalist views of men such as J. S. Mill [...] Herbert Spencer [and] Auguste Comte' (10). These claims may be accurate but it is also true, as Backman goes on to say, that he never lost his fascination with 'the mysterious forces that he felt were at work behind the veil of reality' (Backman 10). Hardy, through his writing, made sure that these 'mysterious forces' were never totally neglected.

On his deathbed on Boxing Day 1927 he asked his wife Florence to read him the Gospel account of the birth of Christ and the massacre of the innocents, remarking when she had finished 'that there was not a grain of evidence that the Gospel was true' (Tomalin, 367). Yet Platten notes that even as a very old man, 'Hardy would cycle the two miles or so from Max Gate to Stinsford to attend Evening Prayer. His Bible and his Book of Common Prayer were annotated with extraordinary care' (Platten 22).

Outwardly, post-Darwin Hardy would not admit to any religious involvement, which might have seemed unfashionable; for as Platten states 'his self-education, impressive as it was, did not reinforce a proper intellectual security' (20). Hardy's class-based anxiety mirrored his reluctance explicitly to state that stories of the supernatural had been passed down to him by his family. Tomalin makes a convincing point that Hardy 'atheistic or agnostic as he was – he was not sure which [...] could never quite get away from the Christian God' (Tomalin 223). Neither could he ever get away from the supernatural and the folkloric narratives that he grew up with in Dorset, which he then transported with his pen to Wessex. The narrator's description of Egdon Heath in *The Return of the Native* sets out a vision of how

> the storm was its lover, and the wind its friend. Then it became the home of strange phantoms; and it was found to be the hitherto unrecognised original of those wild regions of obscurity which are vaguely felt to be compassing us about in midnight dreams of flight and disaster, and are never thought of after the dream till revived by scenes like this.
>
> (Hardy, *The Return of the Native* 55)

It was the landscape that Jacqueline Dillion and Phillip Mallett and others have likened to Freud's 'concept of the *Abseits*, a space off-side or to the edge which leaves room for the uncanny' (Dillion 100). It was the landscape lying just behind Hardy's childhood home in Higher Bockhampton that fed the writer's imagination and lies behind his literary inventions, Egdon Heath and Wessex. From this, as Angelique Richardson states, Hardy opened 'windows into the supernatural; onto magical worlds in which powers of the mind, of dreams and fantasies overpower reason' (Mallett 168).

All of this highlights both Hardy's adventures with narrative and his passion for Dorset folklore both of the actual 'reality' of characters like Diggory Venn, carrying out their completely rational everyday tasks, to the irrational beliefs and superstitions held by many in the power of witches and demons. This passion has been consistently ignored by the majority of screen adaptations of his work. Hardy wished to record the folklore as the rural world vanished into the twentieth century, as we shall see the 'horror' of the 'folk' is still very much alive in the twenty-first century with the genre of folk horror; Hardy, with his focus on the isolated landscape of Egdon Heath, was one of the first to lay down its foundations.

7

Wessex on page and screen

Hardy wrote over fifty short stories most of which are collected in five published anthologies: *Wessex Tales*, *Life's Little Ironies*, *A Few Crusted Characters*, *A Group of Noble Dames* and *A Changed Man*. The collection of stories in *Wessex Tales*, first published in 1888, provides a perfect example of what has been referred to as Hardy's telescopic vision: whereby he looks at the broader aspects of a landscape, in this case Wessex, and then focuses in on the personal circumstances of people within that landscape. Wessex provides the site and space for the presentation of individual vignettes which are frequently eerie in nature.

The anthology contains seven separate stories: 'The Three Strangers', 'A Tradition of Eighteen Hundred and Four', 'The Melancholy Hussar of the German Legion', 'The Withered Arm', 'Fellow- Townsmen', 'Interlopers at the Knap' and 'The Distracted Preacher'. As has been previously mentioned in the preface to the collection, Hardy apologizes for 'the neglect of contrast which is shown by presenting two stories of hangmen […] in such a small collection' (*Wessex Tales* x) and then explains that in the 'neighbourhood of county-towns hanging matters used to form a large proportion of the local tradition' – the executions being a form of popular entertainment, attracting large crowds of people to the 'hang-fair'. Even though they are evident throughout his writing, the short story is an ideal format for Hardy to deliver such dark narratives and focus totally on the macabre. For as Ailsa Cox states: 'A short story distils or condenses. It captures the essence of an experience' (2) and if that experience is of the weird, uncanny or eerie its presence will be all-encompassing in the short story form and, because the narrative is compressed, it will be all the more powerful. Narrative compression is obviously a feature of short stories along with the fact that they are totally self-contained. This 'self-containment' functions as a little world that in Hardy's case, the reader is invited into.

Paraphrasing the Argentinian writer Julio Cortazar (1914–84), Charles May refers to the intensity of the short story stating that it 'is a paradoxical form which cuts off a fragment of reality in such a way that the fragment acts like an explosion that opens up a more ample reality' (xvii). The 'reality' of Hardy's Wessex is very dark indeed especially when he is often recycling narrative told to him as a child, for as May states: 'In their very shortness, short stories have remained close to the original source of narrative in myth, folklore, fable, and fairy tale' (xxvii).

The evil of the hangman

In his teenage years Hardy witnessed two hangings in Dorchester, one in attendance at a 'fair' standing near to the gallows, the other viewed through a telescope from a slope high on the heath. In the case of the latter:

> the sun behind his back shone straight on the white stone façade of the gaol, the gallows upon it, and the form of the murderer in white fustian, the executioner and officials in dark clothing, and the crowd below, being invisible at this distance of three miles. At the moment of placing the glass to his eye the white figure dropped downwards, and the faint note of the town clock struck eight.
>
> The whole thing had been so sudden that the glass nearly fell down from Hardy's hands. He seemed alone on the heath with the hanged man; and he crept homeward wishing he had not been so curious.
>
> (Millgate, *Thomas Hardy: A Biography* 33)

Hardy used this location in the short story 'The Withered Arm' for similar purposes when Gertrude rides over Egdon Heath to seek the cure for her arm and halts 'before a pool called Rushy Pond' (64). From there she looks over towards the county jail and sees men on the roof erecting the gallows; we are told that at the sight of this 'her flesh crept' (64). The actual location of Rushy Pond existed near Hardy's home and Michael Millgate tells us that 'the Hardy children heard at an early age that Rushy Pond on the heath had been dug by fairy shovels' (*Thomas Hardy: A Biography* 30) obviously a happier place in former times.

Although from all accounts Hardy was shocked on the second hanging he witnessed, it was the former event that stayed in the sixteen-year-old Hardy's mind. As has been referred to earlier the person being executed on that day was Elizabeth Martha Brown (usually referred to as Martha Brown), Brown having murdered her husband after suffering years of abuse. Hardy, an architectural apprentice at the time, attended the execution on a Saturday morning along with three to four thousand other people. Robert Gittings, in *Young Thomas Hardy*, notes the effect the hanging had on the young man and refers to a newspaper article that Hardy had cut out and pasted in a scrapbook. The article, written by a well-respected journalist called Neil Munro and dated the 2nd of November 1904, appeared in the *Sketch* and claimed that the hanging had haunted Hardy and had subsequently inspired him in his creation of Tess. It is significant that in the scrapbook that Hardy had marked 'Personal' he had crossed out certain details in the article and written 'Corrected' by the side, but the suggestion that Martha Brown had inspired Tess remained unaltered.

The hanging of Martha Brown would seem, as Gittings suggests, to have 'supplied at least part of the emotional power of [Hardy's] best-known novel' (*The Young Thomas Hardy* 60). The executioner on that day was William Calcraft Britain's principal executioner from 1829 to 1874. Calcraft was born in 1800 and it is estimated that during his long career he hung between 400 and 450 people. In the 'Foreword' section of Geoffrey Abbott's book *William Calcraft: Executioner Extra-Ordinaire* (2004), Muriel Brooke (nee Calcraft) and Thomas Calcraft, William's great grandchildren, comment that amongst executioners: 'William may have had the longest reign, but he used the shortest rope, three foot or less in length, the vast majority of his victims thereby dying slowly by strangulation' (x). In the early years of his hanging career Calcraft, prior to an execution, was asked by a man with a cyst on his neck if he could have contact with the corpse following the hanging, in the belief that this would offer a 'cure' for his disfigurement. When the victim had stopped struggling Calcraft:

> beckoned the man up on to the scaffold and, lifting one of the corpse's limp hands, rubbed it on the man's neck. On seeing that, the crowd, superstitious or not, went wild, causing the sheriffs to step in quickly and terminate the "curative" performance.
>
> (Abbott, 24)

The belief that the blood could be 'turned' by such an act was then a very real one, and a dark procedure referenced by Hardy in 'The Withered Arm'.

'The Withered Arm'

It is generally agreed that 'The Withered Arm' is one of Hardy's most sensational stories and is the one most often cited in contemporary folk horror collections (Wells) (Flint). In this story Hardy displays not just one element of the supernatural but three: being 'hag-rid', the process of 'overlooking' or being given the 'evil-eye', and the custom of consulting white witches or 'Conjurors'. Nooral Hasan described this story as an example of 'Hardy's ability to domesticate the occult' (118) since amongst the local characters involved, the manifestation of witchcraft and the supernatural are almost regarded as ordinary everyday experiences. 'The Withered Arm' principally involves Rhoda Brook who dreams one night that she is being 'hag-rid' by her former lover's new wife Gertrude Lodge. Hardy uses the term 'hagrode' or 'hag-rid' in its literal sense as defined by the nineteenth-century Dorset poet William Barnes, that is: 'the nightmare attributed to the supernatural presence of a witch or *hag* by whom one is *ridden* in sleep' (Barnes 20).

The phenomena of hag-riding is also referred to in *Tess of the d'Urbervilles*, as Tess gets down from the threshing machine looking exhausted her fellow worker Marion remarks that Tess's face looks as if she has 'been hagrode!' (407). In *The Mayor of Casterbridge* when Elizabeth-Jane, who is trying to 'improve' herself and speak in a more genteel way, suffers a sleepless night, we are told 'she did not quaintly tell the servants next morning that she had been "hag-rid," but that she had suffered from indigestion' (131). Hardy also uses the term in the fifth verse of the poem 'The Ruined Maid' which in style, as Mark Ford points out, bears a strong 'relationship to mid-Victorian music hall' (Ford 89) with its 'fallen woman' theme:

You used to call home-life a hag-ridden dream,
And you'd sigh, and you'd sock; but at present you seem
To know not of megrims or melancho-ly! -
'True. One's pretty lively when ruined', said she.

(Hardy, *Selected Poems* 113)

Over time in 'The Withered Arm' the condition of Gertrude's arm, which was seized by Rhoda Brook in her 'dream', deteriorates and gossip has it that Gertrude is being 'overlooked' or given the 'evil eye' by Rhoda – Rhoda being viewed as a witch by some, primarily because she had a child out of wedlock. Gertrude after trying all manner of medications reluctantly consults Conjuror Trendle.

Most of the action in 'The Withered Arm' is again centred round Egdon; Rhoda and her son live in a 'lonely spot' near 'the border of Egdon Heath, whose dark countenance was visible in the distance as they drew nigh to their home' (46). Conjuror Trendle also lives 'in the heart of Egdon' (56); he is, as Romey T. Keys states, 'a creature of the heath' which is a 'space belonging to the supernatural, to magic' (118). As Gertrude, with her terribly disfigured arm, makes her way over Egdon to visit Trendle, the narrator informs us that 'thick clouds made the atmosphere dark, though it was as yet only early afternoon' and adds that the landscape she was walking on was probably 'the same heath which had witnessed the agony of the Wessex King Ina, presented to after-ages as Lear' (57). Here Hardy draws attention to the history that lurks just below the surface, the way in which, as Fisher comments, 'particular terrains are stained by traumatic events' (*The Weird and the Eerie* 97). For Hardy the connect is temporal as well as geographical. The recent past, that which is within living memory, becomes 'stained'. There are echoes of this in contemporary folk horror where the actions of the recent past are hidden beneath the surface. This is literal in the case of a text like Andrew Michael Hurley's *Starve Acre* where the traces of the gibbet are slowly uncovered next to the house.

Trendle, after looking at Gertrude's arm, tells her she has an enemy, and the divination process which follows in the story matches the practice noted by Hardy in an entry in his notebook dated December 1872. Hardy recorded that another 'man of the sort was called a conjuror; he lived in Blackmoor Vale. He would cause your enemy to rise in a glass of water. He did not know your enemy's name, but the bewitched person did, of course' (R. H. Taylor 12). After a few years, and a temporal gap in Hardy's narrative, a desperate Gertrude goes to visit Conjuror Trendle again and he informs her that the only cure, the only counterspell, would be to have her 'blood turned' by the affected arm coming into contact with the neck of a corpse following a hanging. In the preface to *Wessex Tales*, Hardy refers to 'the facts out of which the tale grew':

> In those days, too, there was still living an old woman who, for the cure of some eating disease, had been taken in her youth to have her 'blood turned' by a convict's corpse, in the manner described in 'The Withered Arm'.
>
> (*Wessex Tales* xxi)

Hardy goes on to say that he had been told the story by 'an aged friend' who in all likelihood had been his mother Jemima – an example of him trying to conceal what he considered to be his humble background and the class of people who believed in such things. Certainly, it is amongst the less educated in Hardy's stories that the belief in witchcraft is strongest. But Hardy, as Dillion rightly states, throughout his work, 'undermines the assumption that rational, standardized knowledge is wholly superior to "imbibed" knowledge. He was in a unique position to understand both of these worlds' (121). Hardy's character Gertrude, who comes from an urbanized middle-class background, is reluctant at first to seek help in supernatural form from a white witch but eventually accepts the 'fact' that she needs to have her 'blood turned'. Rejecting both the thoughts of her husband who hated these 'smouldering village beliefs' ('The Withered Arm' 62) and the church who 'strongly condemned' (62) activities which involved witchcraft, this formerly rational woman is so influenced by Egdon and its macabre nature that she prays that a corpse will soon become available and does not particularly care where it comes from or the manner in which it finds itself there: 'O Lord, hang some guilty or innocent person soon!' (62). She also goes on to express, when a hanging is imminent, the hope that the condemned man is not granted a reprieve. Following an execution and the bribing of the hangman 'for a trifling fee' (67), Gertrude eventually is given the opportunity to place her 'poor curst arm' (69) on the still warm neck, 'the colour of an unripe blackberry' (69) of a young man, that, as events transpire, is that of Rhoda's son.

'The Three Strangers'

In echoes of contemporary writers' increasing interest in recounting the folkloric roots of their own childhood, most of the stories in *The Wessex Tales* are set thirty-five years before the time of its publication, in the case of the other story featuring the hangman, 'The Three Strangers' the narrator supplies us with a rough date: 'the night of the twenty eighth of March 182-' (4). The story opens in a typical Hardyesque manner with a broad view of an 'agricultural' (3) English landscape on a wild and stormy night, the narration then zooming in on a 'lonely cottage' both 'detached and undefended' (3). The subsequent events within the cottage, a party celebrating the christening of the Fennel's little girl and the three subsequent uninvited visitors form the content of the story.

The first stranger to arrive at the cottage on the stormy wet evening looking for shelter is the escaped convict Timothy Summers; somewhat damp and bedraggled, he quietly avails himself of the Fennel's hospitality. Although the invited 'nineteen persons' present (4) have no knowledge who the first stranger is, they are aware that there is to be a hanging the next morning in Casterbridge. The person to be executed, a poor clock-maker from Shottsford, for having stolen a sheep because his 'family were a starving' (14).

The second stranger's arrival is more theatrical and self-assured 'hanging his hat on a nail in one of the ceiling-beams as if he had been specifically invited to put it there' (10). Mrs Fennel in particular takes a dislike to him 'a stranger unbeknown to any of us. For my part, I don't like the look of the man at all' (15). The 'stranger in cinder-grey' (14) is loud and, with the large quantities of the strong mead he asks for and consumes during his stay, much to the annoyance of Mrs Fennel, gets even louder. Seated next to Timothy Summers in the corner of the room, the second stranger announces that he's on his way to Casterbridge and must be there by eight the next morning 'het or wet, blow or snow, famine or sword, my day's work tomorrow must be done' (11). This raises the question as to what his occupation is, and the hedge-carpenter, one of the invited guests, suggests that you can usually tell what someone does by the state of 'his claws' (12) to which the second stranger replies that 'the oddity of my trade is that, instead of setting a mark upon me, it sets a mark on my customers' (13).

The guests start to feel uneasy in the presence of the second stranger and when he thrusts 'one thumb into the arm-hole of his waistcoat' (13) and begins to sing, their unease is added to:

O my trade it is the rarest one,
Simple shepherds all,
My trade is a sight to see;
For my customers I tie, and take them up on high,
And waft 'em to a far countree.

(Hardy, *The Three Strangers* 13)

Following this the room is silent except for Timothy Summers who joins in when the second stranger shouts 'Chorus': 'And waft 'em to a far countree' (13) – Summers feigning ease and joviality in an effect to disguise the fact that he is supposed to be the man to be hanged.

The second stranger sings two more verses connected to his trade, one specifically about the execution the next morning:

For the farmer's sheep is slain, and the lad who did it ta'en,
And on his soul may God ha' merc-y!'

(Hardy, *The Three Strangers* 15)

Whilst he is singing, a third stranger arrives at the door asking for directions and looks round the room noting the first stranger in the corner and the second stranger singing; after what he sees and hears, he is, as the narrator tells us, a trembling 'picture of abject terror' (15). Obviously fearful of what is occurring in the room he quickly flees, adding doubt and uncertainty to the already-bemused guests.

The unease that guests feel about the presence of the second stranger increases as they realize who he is and the act he is to perform the next morning; moving 'instinctively' away they form a 'remote circle' around the 'grim gentleman in their midst' (15), some seeming to take him for the 'Prince of Darkness', the narrator using the phrase: 'circulus, cujus centrum diabolus' (15). In the notes at the end of *Wessex Tales*, Michael Irwin suggests that this means 'a circle, at whose centre was the devil' (193). A distant gunshot breaks the silence in the room and it is suggested that the firing only occurs when a prisoner has escaped from the gaol at Casterbridge. All suspect that it is the third stranger that fled away from the cottage when he'd seen the hangman. The gun goes off at intervals and the 'King's man', the second stranger, sends all the men out to search for the escaped prisoner. The search party arrest the third stranger out on the heath only to find that he is Timothy Summer's brother who was on his way to see him before the hanging. Summer manages to escape, and we are told that he was never captured, and it is inferred by the narrator that he was never pursued with too much rigour for he had a lot of sympathy from local people, the 'intended punishment was cruelly disproportioned to the transgression' ('The Three Strangers' 21).

Dorset at this time, and for a considerable period in the nineteenth century, was suffering a severe agricultural depression, extremely low wages being paid to farm labourers resulting in rural poverty, further contributing to the 'traumatic stain' on the land Hardy's character Rhoda from 'The Withered Arm' being an example of this, living in a 'mud hovel' whose rafters show through the thatch 'like bone protruding through the skin' (46). Remembering the poverty of agricultural labourers in Dorset years later Hardy commented: 'down to 1850 or 1855 their condition was in general one of great hardship' and shared a memory from his childhood of a 'sheep-keeping boy who to my horror shortly afterwards died of want – the contents of his stomach at the autopsy being raw turnip only. His father's wages were six shillings a week' (Millgate, *Thomas Hardy: A Biography* 33).

The poverty of the 1830s led to rural unrest and riots led by the mythical 'Captain Swing', and in 1834 the six 'martyrs' from Tolpuddle, only a few miles from the Hardy's home, were sentenced to transportation for trying to organize a union. Timothy Summers was a victim of these times, a local man trying to feed his family, just as Rhoda's son in *The Withered Arm* was a victim, found to be near a rick-burning, which was an act of protest at the time where hay or corn stacks were burnt. In the case of Rhoda's son even the hangman, whilst still 'as a matter of business' (66) wanting the hanging to take place, has some sympathy with the condemned man 'just turned eighteen, and only present by chance when the rick was fired' (66). This type of execution which followed the burning of a rick was common; Millgate notes that Hardy's father recalled seeing, the 'hanging on little more than suspicion of a youth so light through hunger that weights were attached to his feet to ensure that strangulation would occur' (*Thomas Hardy: A Biography* 32).

Hardy was then very aware of the brutality of the troubled 1830s and the hardship of the peasant class. In respect of 'The Three Strangers' the hangman is not a Jack Ketch, who Hardy alluded to in his stage adaptation of this story, and nor is he a William Calcraft, but he is still evil: clearly enjoying his work and exercising the King's justice on a poor impoverished local man. In 1868 public hangings were abolished and this must have been a time of great sadness for Calcraft et al. 'The Three Strangers' ends with the narrator reminding us of the brevity of human existence: 'The grass has long been green on the graves of Shepherd Fennel and his frugal wife; the guests who made up the christening-party have mainly followed their entertainers to the tomb' (22). But he tells us, at the time of writing, the story is 'as well known as ever in the country about Higher Crowstairs' (22). Although Hardy stated in the preface to the *Wessex Tales* anthology that 'the stories are but dreams and not records' (XX11), so much of his writing recalls stories told to him, haunting tales, unlike the fate of the Fennels and the rest of us, that live on.

Hardy reinvented: Heritage and screens

Hardy's presence within the literary canon is hotly contested. The variations in his work are perhaps responsible for this; the movement from Victorian Realist to experimental writer makes a single identifiable positioning of his work difficult. His work has been in and out of popular favour and therefore not as fully represented as some other novelists. There is an argument to be made that his work is known through its adaptation and its extratextual existence in 'Hardy Country' in the south of England. There is a facet of his writing and its focus on nature which makes it ideal for cinematic adaptation; however, it is the world of heritage drama that has suppressed aspects of content whilst drawing on the rich visual aspects of his work.

Neil Sinyard once stated that Hardy is 'so intimidatingly visual as to make the camera seem almost redundant: the director can only duplicate, not enhance' (Sinyard 48) and this would be a belief shared by a variety of commentators on his work. Hardy's narratives often comprise elements of the cinematic particularly in his use of point of view or focalization, but these are used in the manner of a filmmaker rather than a novelist. David Lodge has listed the differences between verbal and film narrative:

> Apart from dialogue and monologue (which are available to both) and the use of music for emotive suggestion, film is obliged to tell its story purely in terms of the visible – behaviour, physical appearance, setting – whereas the verbal medium of the novel can describe anything, visible or invisible (notably the thoughts passing through a character's head), and can do so as abstractly as it pleases.
>
> (Lodge, 80)

Lodge goes on to state that he believes Hardy to be a 'cinematic novelist' because he deliberately 'renounces some of the freedom of representation and report afforded by the verbal medium' (80), often choosing to present his material in a purely visual way 'presenting' rather than 'asserting'.

As noted previously the main narrative element that Lodge identifies in Hardy's work is the use the writer makes of the hypothetical or 'unspecified observer'; Lodge uses *The Return of the Native* to illustrate this. After the opening chapter 'A Face on Which Time Makes but Little Impression' which introduces the reader to the moody character of Egdon Heath 'a near relation of night' (53), Hardy then 'zooms in' onto the landscape, showing us 'a little speck of human life in a vast expanse of nature' (Lodge 82). He does this, as Lodge points out, by 'restricting himself voluntarily to a limitation that is binding on the film-maker' (82) drawing our attention to an old man, who 'one would have said' (*The Return of the Native* 58) had the appearance of a naval officer 'of some sort' making his way across the heath. The old man, whom we later discover, is Captain Vye, acts as the focalizer as he gazes over towards 'the tract that he had yet to traverse' and discerns: 'a long distance in front of him, a moving spot, which appeared to be a vehicle, and it proved to be going the same way as that in which he was journeying' (58). Captain Vye catches up with the 'lurid red' van that belongs to the reddleman Diggory Venn, who then takes his turn in becoming the focalizer seeing the 'pantomime of silhouettes' (63) of a woman's figure on the barrow outlined against the sky. As Terry Wright suggests, the 'narrative technique here resembles a shooting script even before it indulges in a close-up of Eustace Vye's face' (11). This is a facet of Hardy's work that endures; Andrew Michael Hurley discusses the visual dimension of his own work as directly drawn from Hardy, 'It feels like a cinematic opening but Hurley learned the technique from Thomas Hardy. "I go back to Hardy a lot," says Hurley when I ask about his influences. "The landscape in his novels has the facets of a character"' (Liu). From panoramic views to the focus on the individual, Hardy is equally capable of 'close-ups'. Clym, a character in *The Return of the Native*, is gradually losing his sight and is increasingly restricted visually 'to a circuit of a few feet from his person. His familiars were creeping and winged things' (312). Hardy then proceeds to describe the bees, the butterflies and grasshoppers 'which Egdon produced' (312) that have become Clym's 'whole world' (312). Similarly, Gilmartin and Mengham note that in his poem 'Afterwards' published in 1917 Hardy acknowledges his 'telescopic vision' (1) by being able to record both: 'where the hedgehog travels furtively over the lawn' and comment on 'the full-starred heavens that winter sees' for he was 'a man who used to notice such things' (304).

On a purely visual level Hardy is the 'cinematic novelist' that Lodge claims, and photographically his work has transferred successfully to the medium of film. Joss Marsh and Kamilla Elliot (460) suggest that early in the development of film the medium might have 'derived scopic (that is, highly visual narration)', from a writer such as Hardy and also cites the opening to *The Return of the Native* as an example of this. Hardy had been influenced by painters such as Turner and the Impressionists and these aspects of his work are obviously attractive to the filmmaker, especially when they can be used in conjunction with the 'ready-made' rurally idyllic Wessex on display in heritage productions. There are however other aspects of Hardy's writing that make it decidedly un-cinematic; these would include: the uncertainty and irregularity of his narrative ellipses, where he leaves the reader to fill in the blanks and the cacophony of voices, evident throughout his work, recalling Mikhail Bakhtin's term 'polyphony'. Paul Niemeyer believes that

Hardy's novels 'are multifaceted and generally unstable. Film, by contrast, is a relatively *stable* medium that depends on a more unified point of view' (2003). In agreement with this, Roger Webster points out that in Hardy's novels 'visualised scenes are followed by dense and sometimes awkward passages' (2005). Certainly, Hardy's irregular narrative patterns are the void that most adaptations have been unable to cross.

Early cinematic adaptations

The first screen adaptation of Hardy's work *Tess of the d'Urbervilles* was produced in America in 1913 by Adolph Zukor's 'Famous Players Film Co.,' later to become Paramount. Apparently, after agreeing and signing the rights to this company, Hardy began to have doubts about the venture and wrote to his publisher Sir Frederick Macmillan, expressing his anxiety about the filming and questioning whether it would harm the novel; he was concerned that they might alter the content; he didn't want them to have the 'power to tamper with the story to an extent, such as might injure its circulation e.g. changing if from a tragedy to a story in which everything ends happily' (Niemeyer 302).

Hardy saw the film in the autumn of 1913 and wrote to his friend Edward Clodd telling him how he 'would be amused to see an Americanised Wessex Dairy' (*The Collected Letters of Thomas Hardy, 7 Volumes* 291). This is suggestive of the attitude to adapting Hardy in the early part of the twentieth century. The implied respect given by the veneer of fidelity to the source material is not in evidence. Eight years later the Progress Film Company of Shoreham, Sussex began production on *The Mayor of Casterbridge* shot mostly in Sussex and Dorset. Hardy was invited to visit the set and talk to the actors when filming was taking place in Dorchester. In a letter to a friend following the visit, he expressed how odd he had found the experience:

> The film-makers are here doing scenes for 'The Mayor of C.' & they asked us to come & see the process. The result is that I have been talking to The Mayor, Mrs. Henchard, Eliz(abeth) Jane, & the rest, in the flesh ... It is a strange business to be engaged in.
> (Purdy and Millgate, *The Collected Letters of Thomas Hardy, Volume 7* 93)

It wasn't really surprising that an eighty-one-year-old Hardy was somewhat bemused by the new medium of film although he had already had some experience and been consulted about a production of *Far From the Madding Crowd* by another UK film company, Turner Films UK in 1915. Indeed, he had contributed to a booklet available at the launch of the film. But with the production of the *Mayor of Casterbridge*, he was again to express concern to his publisher, who was negotiating the sale. Hardy thought that the contract should state that

> in order to run no risk of injuring the sale of the book ... No alteration or adaptation such as to burlesque or otherwise misinterpret the general character of the novel.
>
> (Purdy and Millgate, *The Collected Letters of Thomas Hardy*, Volume 7 140)

One can see from Hardy's remarks and concerns that the plea for 'fidelity' in the adaptation from the literary to the filmic has a long history. Of course, in saying this it must be remembered that Hardy, like other writers from that period, frequently had to change the ending of their works on the demands of their publishers. *The Return of the Native*, for example, didn't originally have the reddleman Diggory Venn and Thomasin marrying, but Hardy 'caught up in the Victorian literary treadmill of serialisation' (Woodcock 17) bowed to the demands of his publisher Belgravia for a slightly happier ending. Hardy being a very shrewd businessman acquiesced, be it reluctantly, to his editor's demands. Letters show that in the end Hardy's main interest was in his book sales. This presents a rather contemporary picture of a novelist who became engaged and embroiled in a medium which still dominates. His work, like many other writers since, was created in and amongst his writing.

The first two decades of the twentieth century were busy ones in terms of Hardy's work being appropriated to other mediums and not simply film; in 1909 an operatic version of *Tess* had been produced at Covent Garden after opening in Naples in 1906. Hardy had also had discussions with Elgar about the possibility of musical adaptations, he considered *A Pair of Blue Eyes* (1873) as being particularly suitable, but nothing came of this. There had also been several amateur dramatizations of Hardy's work produced locally.

The last silent adaptation of Hardy's work and the last film to be made whilst he was still alive was a 1924 American production of *Tess of the D'Urbervilles* by Metro-Goldwyn Pictures. Interestingly the production

> removed the novel from its 1880s setting and placed it squarely in the 1920s, with the characters driving cars and using telephones .... MGM apparently blanched at Hardy's tragic ending. Two endings were shot: one with Tess being hanged, the other with Tess and Angel happily reunited. Exhibitors were given the choice of which ending to show, but in subsequent re-releases only the tragic ending was issued.
>
> (Niemeyer 253)

Parts of the film were shot in Dorset and Hardy would have certainly been pleased that the tragic ending had been retained in the production and that 'the President of the Immortals, in Aeschylean phrase' had still had 'his sport with Tess' (*Tess of the d'Urbervilles* 489).

Heritage drama

Writing on *The Guardian* website in 2015 Robert MacFarlane argued that in all manner of the arts there is renewed interest in the 'English eerie', an 'eerie counterculture fascinated in particular with the English landscape in terms of its anomalies rather than its continuities, a movement, that is sceptical of comfortable notions of "dwelling" and "belonging", and of the packagings of the past as "heritage", and that locates itself within a spectred rather than a sceptred isle.' This particular focus continues to the present day but has yet to translate to big screen adaptations of Hardy's written narratives – film productions persisting to ignore the isolated landscape of Egdon Heath and the feared and fearful folk wandering on its bleak menacing soil.

Egdon heath becomes a space where arcane pre-Christian folkloric beliefs not only survived but often dominated. The action to tame Hardy's narrative has been a common phenomenon in screen adaptations of his work as productions have consistently pointed themselves towards 'heritage'. The haunted space behind the writer's childhood home which became the menacing landscape of Egdon Heath being robbed of its dark character. Because of the attention and the power Hardy invests in this landscape, the 1994 TV film of *The Return of the Native* was therefore noticeable by its absence. In this adaptation directed by Jack Gold and produced by the American greeting card company Hallmark, Egdon is changed, as Rosemary Morgan suggests, 'to suit a modern audience's idea of old England. Rugged Egdon, its characterisation as a unique entity, becomes an idealised rural landscape' (118), here with echoes of the earliest of the adaptations. The 'prettification of the past' (118) is much in evidence in this production as it is in many other adaptations of Hardy; the television audience offered pastoral romance but denied the force and power of his dark narrative. As Niemeyer rightly states, in this one-hundred-minute production, 'locations, period details, and atmosphere are played up to the expense of the story' (218). This production and others have added to the popular misconception of Hardy's stories, when adapted to the screen, as being 'safe' and written by, as Wright suggests, 'the good, little Thomas Hardy, producer of pastoral tragedies' (2).

Heritage or costume drama is identifiable in its focus on the past and the genre is noticeable for its attention to detail in terms of period costume, its use of magnificent country houses, its big budget and the casting of well-regarded actors. The work of Jane Austen has proved to be particularly suitable for this type of treatment; Lez Cooke offers the example of the BBC's 1995 *Pride and Prejudice* by way of illustration, commenting that the series drew a 'huge audience of 10 million viewers' and that its '£6 million budget guaranteed high production values' (168). Deborah Cartmell and Imelda Whelehan note that the adaptation of the Austen novel by Andrew Davies was 'phenomenally successful' and 'was saturated with the norms of the genre' (189). Following this production, Davies, who had 'intensified every convention and exaggerated every code' (190) of the genre in *Pride and Prejudice*, was then to turn his attention to two more adaptations: *The Fortunes and Misfortunes of Moll Flanders* (1996) and *Vanity Fair* (1998) both of which moved away from overt heritage indulgence, being much more reflexive in style. Although this might have been interpreted as heralding a new stage in the evolution of form, in regard to heritage drama, subsequent productions do not indicate that reflexivity is the new dominant mode in this genre.

The 'pastness' of heritage, merging as it does with all the industries that surround it, has continued to please both television and film audiences. The repackaged heritage authors, including Hardy, have been accorded a central position in this industry, as Linda Troost comments, the genre of heritage drama has made such writers as 'Jane Austen a household name even in non-bookish households' (84). This type of drama often equates to what James Chapman terms 'heritage export' (135) and can bring in very lucrative finance, particularly from the United States. As Andrew Higson states, films about the English past have played 'a key role in establishing and reproducing the brand image of England as a historical place, and American capital has ensured that this brand image circulates globally' (191).

The positive elements of the English brand and all that goes with it were heralded politically by Prime Minister John Major in 1993 when he addressed the Conservative Group for Europe at a conference in Manchester, twenty years after the UK had joined the European Union. The content, somewhat ironic now considering what happened in the vote to leave in 2016, was one of reassurance to his audience. The speech was an assertion of the quality of Englishness and a statement that the country with all its distinctive and unique properties would never be damaged by membership of the European Union:

> Fifty years from now Britain will still be the country of long shadows on county grounds, warm beer, invincible green suburbs, dog lovers and pool fillers and – as George Orwell said – 'old maids bicycling to Holy Communion through the morning mist' […] Britain will survive unamenable in all essentials.
>
> (Major)

The ITV series *Downton Abbey* has done much globally to reinforce and strengthen that image, sending out the correct message should anyone be in any doubt. The series which cost over 1 million pound per episode to make was a joint venture between Carnival Films, a UK production company and WGBH-TV Boston. Although not adapted from the work of a canonized author from the nineteenth century, the success of *Downton Abbey*, written and created by Julian Fellows, epitomizes 'heritage' and the global interest in the British aristocracy and British culture. As Chapman suggests, 'the costume drama distances itself from the problems of the present through recourse to cultural nostalgia for the "past"', it being 'a safe alternative to the more agitational style of social realist plays and serials' (132). Chapman states that *Downton* is reckoned to be one of the 'most-watched television series in the world with an estimated global audience of over 120 million' (135). It has won numerous international awards and is regarded as the best British costume drama since ITV's 1981 series *Brideshead Revisited*, an adaptation of Evelyn Waugh's 1945 novel.

Downton Abbey was first aired in the UK in 2010 and 2011 in the United States where it was broadcast by the *Masterpiece* strand on PBS (Public Broadcast Service) associated with presenting 'quality drama', and ran for six series. *Downton Abbey*, like the earlier production *Upstairs, Downstairs* (ITV 1971–5), also featured the lives of the serving classes as well as the aristocracy and contained what Lez Cooke describes as a 'flexi-narrative structure deriving in part from soap opera where multiple interwoven narrative strands have always been a convention of the genre' (176). In *Downton* the various 'narrative strands' were all conducted against the backdrop of 'real life' occurrences in the period the series covered 1912–26 and included, amongst other events, the sinking of the Titanic, the Suffragist movement, the First World War and the Battle of the Somme.

The Director Alan Parker once described the heritage genre as the 'Laura Ashley school of filmmaking' (2005, cited in Voigts-Virchow, 2007, p. 128) and it has attracted many critics. Steve Rose writing in the *Guardian Guide* about film biopics of nineteenth-century authors comments dryly that they also offer 'another excuse to revisit historic Britain at its most jolly decent and imperially mighty' (21). In agreement with Rose it is also worth noting the compelling argument that John Caughie makes when he states that heritage drama 'has avoided its historical appointment either with modernism, with naturalism, or with critical realism' (216). Talking to Leigh Holmwood, for an article on *The Guardian* website, Andrew Davies stated that he felt 'fairly optimistic for the future of period drama because it's just such a popular thing. People like bonnets. I don't think you can underestimate that'. Davies is of course quite correct, over the years the viewing public have responded enthusiastically to such drama and his adaptations in particular, right up to his well-rated 2015 serial *War and Peace*. Linda Troost notes that the summer after Davies's 1995 BBC serial *Pride and Prejudice* was aired 'Lyme Park, the National Trust property that served as Pemberley was jammed with hundreds of paying visitors' (84) mostly those eager to see the pond where Darcy (portrayed by Colin Firth) had taken off his clothes and dived in. This 'invented scene' as Troost refers to it, which gave birth to 'Darcymania', has now become iconic in the history of classic-novel adaptation and exemplifies viewers' attraction to the genre. Although considered somewhat racy for this type of drama at the time, with scenes which show 'Darcy's smouldering passion for Elizabeth' (Troost 84), the series was absorbed into the heritage genre and marked another stage in its evolution and contemporization.

The heritage industries that are built around canonical writers are huge, screened adaptations of a writer's work often redirect the viewers' attention back to the original text and there are obvious benefits to this process. What is objectionable and reiterated here is the tameness with which filmed adaptations of Hardy's work have been reduced in order to comply with the heritage aesthetic of charm and rural nostalgia; the eerie has sadly been replaced by the dreary. The quest for global appeal and corresponding financial success has silenced both Hardy's experiments with narrative and his admiration and fascination for the supernatural. Hardy's work is riddled with the folkloric elements that he grew up with in nineteenth-century Dorset. These elements, his 'haunted heritage', passed down orally through the ages, were deeply threatened by the rapid approach of urbanization and industrialization in the last half of the nineteenth century. Hardy was wishing to preserve the dark practices and beliefs he had grown up with but aware of the speed of change.

Hardy was largely ignored between the 1930s and the 1960s in all forms of visual adaptation and he was not an attractive prospect for the BBC in their 'literary classics' Sunday tea-time slot; as Roy Pierce-Jones says: 'Whilst Dickens's *Oliver Twist* could be softened and made more palatable for these audiences, Hardy's work could not' (64). Hardy's time on television and in cinema had to wait for the new permissiveness of the 1960s, but the freedom gained since that time, in terms of what can be screened, has not, apart from Polanski's *Tess* and Winterbottom's *Jude*, been accompanied by markedly innovative productions. The television series *Wessex Tales* is still the only screen production to acknowledge Hardy's interest in the supernatural. It is the heritage tag associated with Hardy and the accompanying finance, which has contributed to the present state of affairs; unfortunately, Chapman is correct when he states that 'the American market represents a sort of Holy Grail for British film and television producers' (135).

Far From the Madding Crowd 1967 and 2015

Far From the Madding Crowd (1874) was Hardy's first major success and the novel in which Hardy first used the setting of Wessex as a specific location; alongside *Under the Greenwood Tree* (1872) it was the work that placed Hardy in the popular imagination as the writer of the rustic. It would generally be regarded as one of Hardy's lighter tales indeed as Elizabeth Drew observes: 'For Hardy, a story with only three deaths in it, one life sentence and a final marriage between the two chief characters can almost claim to be a comedy' (Drew 143). Comedy, *Far From the Madding Crowd*, is certainly not, but it remains as one of Hardy's most popular novels.

John Schlesinger's 1967 adaptation of the novel with cinematography by Nicholas Roeg and a screenplay by Frederic Raphael was the first screening of a Hardy novel to use colour, wide-screen technology and aerial shots. The film starred Julie Christie, Alan Bates, Terence Stamp and Peter Finch who collectively placed Hardy in the 1960s; indeed, the cast, as Keith Selby comments, all looked as if they had 'arrived on the set after a shopping-spree in Carnaby Street' (97) (Carnaby Street being a then fashionable boutique area of London and an emblem of the 'Swinging Sixties'). All the principal actors playing Bathsheba and her three suitors – Gabriel Oak, Sergeant Troy and the gentleman farmer William Boldwood – enjoyed 'pop star status' at the time. As Peter Widdowson observes, the 'instantly recognisable face of Christie with her Mick Jagger mouth to Stamp with his arrogant George Best features' these very sixties characters contrasted somewhat with the 'gormless faces of the yokels' (109). The 'yokels', including the character Joseph Poorgrass, a worker at Bathsheba's farm, join others in one scene in the ample swilling of ale, adding the typical ingredient of Hardean hokum – 'hokum' being a term first used by Keith Selby in relation to screen adaptations of Hardy's work, denoting the simplified, idealized world that they frequently present. The rural poor on the screen always able to raise a glass and raise laughter, unlike the reality of the impoverished peasants in Dorset in the nineteenth century.

Schlesinger's production filmed in Dorset and Wiltshire was lavish, full of Victorian period detail, and showed great fidelity to Hardy's novel and with the quality of the cinematography obviously aimed to reproduce pastoral bliss; rural scenes of splendour accompanied throughout by rustic folk music. There is a degree of intertextuality to other Hardy novels in the film; at one stage a reddleman's wagon is briefly on show, alluding to *The Return of the Native*; when Fanny turns up to marry Troy at the wrong church, she finds a band practising bringing to mind the Mellstock Quire from *Under the Greenwood Tree* and there is also the scene with the workers in the field and Boldwood's threshing machine which invites us to remember *Tess of the d'Urbervilles*. There is a recognition that Wessex exists beyond the edges of the cinema screen. As in the 1998 London Weekend Television production of *Tess*, Hardy makes an appearance as a character, this time at William Boldwood's Christmas party. This act of course, and the then 'modernity' of the production, placed Hardy 'as a participant in the swinging decade' and is a good 'example of the process by which a "great writer" is reproduced and reconstituted by the period in which s/he is being consumed' (Widdowson 112). As stated, despite its then very modern appearance the film follows the narrative of the novel faithfully with no disruption to the main, in Roland Barthes terms, *cardinal functions* or 'hinge-points' of the plot. Schlesinger takes no major risks in the adaptation and as one critic pointed out the film 'plods' on quite pleasantly. Selby suggests that a lot of the film is similar to, and worthy of, the 'Sunday tea-time dramatisations which rattled off the ... assembly-line at the BBC during the late 1960s and 1970s' (97) and this isn't surprising as Schlesinger had worked for the BBC from 1956 to 1961 mostly in documentary filmmaking; having directed the film *A Kind of Loving* in 1962 he was seen as having involvement with the social realist movement in British cinema.

Nicholas Roeg's photography in the production often stresses the enormity of the landscape in relation to the smallness of the individual, a frequently used trope of Hardy, calling to mind the solitary figure of Tess as she stands on an 'expanse of verdant flatness, like a fly on a billiard table' (*Tess of the d'Urbervilles* 159). But as Webster suggests, the camera tends to dwell too much on the 'picturesque and pastoral to the point of cliché' (28). This is a common criticism of Hardy's adaptations and Polanski's *Tess* attracted similar comments; but as has been suggested whilst discussing the power Hardy invests in Egdon Heath, he himself was so enthused about the landscape he was writing about, that it is an issue for film makers trying to achieve some sort of balance between reflecting this and it becoming Webster's 'visual cliché'. In *Tess of the d'Urbervilles* Hardy, describing the landscape in which Angel is falling in love with Tess, states, 'Amid the oozing fatness and warm ferments of the Var Vale, at a season when the rush of juices could almost be heard below the hiss of fertilization, it was impossible that the most fanciful love should not grow passionate. The ready bosoms existing there were impregnated by their surroundings' (207). In Hardy the landscape is seldom passive and never 'just' a backcloth: here, indeed, it is almost promiscuous.

The production was full of Hardean charm but many at the time agreed with Widdowson that it appeared too 'modern' – the principal actors all being so well known and key 1960 'faces'. Widdowson offers examples of this comparing the film with BBC's 1978 production of *The Mayor of Casterbridge*, a serial in seven parts adapted by Dennis Potter: Alan Bates played in both productions but in *Far from the Madding Crowd*, playing the character Gabriel Oak, he 'looks like a modern man in a costume', in the other a '"true" man of the period' (109). Likewise, Widdowson believes that the TV production sought to portray the 'real' past of nineteenth-century Wessex, whilst *Far from the Madding Crowd* is 'constantly modern in attitude and appearance. If it is a form of pastoral, it is 1960s pastoral: a bright, exuberant ... colourful piece of filmic display' (109). But in terms of subject matter, it could be about a bright young businesswoman in the 1960s who experiences issues in relationships before finally settling down happily in the end. Hardy's adapted narrative is delivered safely as a pleasant pastoral tale.

Forty-eight years later in 2015 *Far from the Madding Crowd* was to emerge again on to the screen with a film by the Danish Director Thomas Vinterberg and a screenplay by David Nicholls 'based on a novel by Thomas Hardy'. The film, with Carey Mulligan playing Bathsheba, was generally well received but the *Guardian* in April of that year wrote a quite scathing review;

headed *A hygienic Bathsheba* Lucasta Miller stated that in comparison to the 'classic' 1967 production the 2015 version tended to flatten and 'normalize' elements of the story labelling it as a 'George Eliot – version of Hardy' (17). Writing in the *Hardy Society Journal* Tony Finchman was in agreement with this saying that the film had shortened, abbreviated and excluded events from the source narrative which represented 'an immense dumbing down of Hardy's novel compared with the 1967 version' (112).

Vinterberg's film is thirty-nine minutes shorter than the 1967 offering and Finchman suggests that this is probably because a 2015 audience would not tolerate a film of a hundred and fifty-six minutes. Keith Wilson is in agreement with this saying that the 1967 version was a flop in America because of its length and that audiences found it 'tediously slow-paced' (102). Could this be the reason then for the 'dumbing down' in Finchman's terms, to make it sharper and more accessible? Certainly that market is sought for in the title sequence the audience is given an immediate reminder of where Dorset is: following a viewing of a distant Hollywood sign on the hills, we see the date of 1870 and are told that Dorset, England is '200 miles outside London'. As in the 1967 version the cinematography is stunning, providing a visual echo of Hardy's narrative description of the Dorset landscape. But how that landscape is used at times does seem, as Finchman observes, a 'little bizarre' – a good example being the 'Hollywood film set of two hundred people at work in a cornfield', Finchman adding that he 'expected them to burst into a rousing musical chorus at any moment' (113). Miller regrets the loss of the scene in which Sergeant Troy, at this point in the story presumed dead, plays Dick Turpin in a circus act at a country fair. His act is watched by Bathsheba unaware of her husband's presence and in its 'theatricality – and implicit commentary on the novel as an entertainment;' this scene, Miller tells us, 'could have come directly from sensation fiction, where masquerade is a frequent theme' (17). The 'surreal absurdity' of the scene, as portrayed in both Schlesinger's adaptation and the novel, was probably too much for Vinterberg in his quest for realism. As would be the cacophony of narrative voices Hardy uses in the novel where he confuses his readers, not only with which suitor Bathsheba would choose, but with which literary style, which 'hybrid voice,' he would adopt – varying it in mode between 'pastoral, social realism, melodrama, gothic and sensation' (Miller 17).

When discussing the 2015 screening Scott Foundas writes on the *Variety* website, referred to the 'Downton Abbey set' when reviewing its release saying they will 'find much to enjoy' in the production with its 'solid cast and impeccable production values' but adding that for him it represented 'a perfectly respectable, but never particularly stirring, night at the movies'. This was a production that focuses more on heritage than Hardy and one, as he notes, that 'should generate pleasing returns for this May 1 Fox Searchlight release'. He also points out that Hardy's irony in the choice of the title of the novel, taken from Thomas Gray's poem of 1750 'Elegy

Written in a Country Churchyard', an idealization of the peace of country life onto which Hardy grafts his sensational plot, is totally removed so that 'you could almost mistake Hardy for a literalist on the basis of this calm, stately new film version'. Overall the production was a rather tame pastoral romance, one very much aimed at English heritage brand status.

Roman Polanski's *Tess* (1979)

In the introduction to *Thomas Hardy on Screen* Terry Wright suggests that Hardy's radicalism, both in his experimentation with form and his moral and political challenges to the norms and conventions of his day, has not always made him acceptable to the 'classic serial' slot on television. Indeed, as we have seen between 1930 and the late 1960s no one was particularly in a hurry to screen Hardy for the cinema either. This situation mirrored Hardy's experience in trying to publish his work in his lifetime where he became increasingly frustrated and oppositional to the demands made on him – frustration culminating in his refusal to write prose following the publication of *Jude the Obscure* (1895) and its hostile reception, 'the experience completely curing me of further interest in novel-writing' (vii) he wrote in 1912. To Wright, Hardy was a radical and to him this explains, 'Why similarly radical film-makers such as Roman Polanski and Michael Winterbottom, also prepared to shock audiences out of their complacencies, make the most powerful interpreters of his work' (2). In agreement with Wright the films of these directors certainly stand out as brave attempts to lift Hardy away from the humdrum of the hokum that had surrounded him and in the case of Winterbottom's *Jude* represented a direct and deliberate assault on the genre of heritage.

Any discussion about Roman Polanski's *Tess* has to be accompanied by a description of the personal circumstances of the director both before and during the filming, as these circumstances had a direct impact on the film. The film had to be shot in Normandy because at the time Polanski had been charged with the statutory rape of a thirteen-year-old girl in America and would have risked extradition in the UK. Further to this it was rumoured that the actress he chose to play Tess, Nastassia Kinski, a German by nationality, had been sexually involved with Polanski whilst being a minor at the time of their relationship. A further personal link is that Polanski dedicated the film (the dedication on the opening credits) to his late wife and actress Sharon Tate who was murdered in a ritualistic killing by the Charlie Manson's 'family' in Los Angeles in August 1969. It is believed that Tate had given Polanski a copy of the novel before she died, suggesting it would make a good film.

If Polanski arrived at *Tess* with a certain personal notoriety, he was also in possession of established status in the world of film. His previous works included *Rosemary's Baby* (1968) and *Chinatown* (1974), and he was, as Paul Niemeyer observes, 'labelled an auteur, a director whose personality is stamped on every aspect of the film' (106) and since he engaged in producing, screenwriting (he co-wrote *Tess* with Gerard Brach and John Brownjohn) and even acting, as he had in the 1976 psychological thriller *The Tenant*, it is easy to see why he was regarded as such. *Tess* ended up having a running time of 186 minutes and cost just under £5 million to make and at that time was the most expensive film ever made in France; it was very well received and nominated for six Academy Awards and the winner of three.

The light plays its part in whether Tess was raped or seduced by Alec in the sequence in *The Chase* (of course the irony of the 'was it rape or seduction' question was well commented on given the director's circumstances). It's night-time and Alec kisses Tess, who at first seems asleep and then struggles, but as Niemeyer comments the 'scene is draped in artificiality' and it's difficult to tell 'if she's fighting or enjoying what is happening' (145), the fog rolls in and the couple are enveloped; as with the novel the audience are left unsure. Polanski also uses fog or mist in other scenes usually signifying grimness; low light is present all the time after Tess and Angel's parting when she works with her friend Marion in the swede-field or 'starve-acre place' as Marion called it. Atmospheric mist also swirls around as Tess is arrested at Stonehenge, the sun only beginning to rise as she is taken away by the police. At one point in the novel the narrator tells us that Tess 'was in a dream wherein familiar objects appeared as having light and shade and position, but no particular outline' (232). Frequently in both Hardy's and Polanski's texts, as Webster observes, 'form is only present in the background' (30).

Tess herself remains somewhat of an enigma throughout the film; she is remote and very different to the other more robust country girls, her speech is delicate and at times almost infant like. This could of course be simply due to the fact that Nastassia Kinski is a German playing the role of someone English or it could be a deliberate strategy by Polanski, no one can be sure, but John Paul Riquelme comments: 'Her spoken performance is a brilliantly dissonant feature, one that makes it impossible for the spectator to mistake *Tess* for realism' (160). Even in the novel she remains as a character difficult to 'pin-down' and as Niemeyer suggests 'largely constructed by how she is read and perceived by others' (107). Angel's views on her being a good example of this, likening her to characters from pastoral myth:

> She was no longer the milkmaid, but a visionary essence of woman a whole sex condensed into one typical form. He called her Artemis, Demeter, and other fanciful names half teasingly, which she did not like because she did not understand them.
>
> 'Call me Tess,' she would askance; and he did.
>
> (Hardy, *Tess of the d'Urbervilles* 187)

Widdowson suggests that Tess in the Polanski film 'is a late twentieth-century existential heroine' (119) and sees the similarities between her and the character Sarah Woodruff in John Fowles's novel *The French Lieutenant's Woman* (1967, the film version appeared in 1981). Fowles was a great admirer of Hardy whose 'very relevant shadow' (262), he stated, he was under (Fowles also lived in Dorset). No one is sure whether Polanski had read Fowles's novel but one can see some similarities. The 'fallen woman' theme was much used in literature in the nineteenth century and Fowles wrote that he always visualized his character Sarah: 'In the same shot, with her back turned, she represented a reproach to the Victorian age. An outcast' (13).

In the film Polanski utilizes the uncertainty of Hardy's narrative ellipses, adding in the process some of his own and the viewer is frequently left to fill in the details. We're not present when Tess conducts the candlelit baptism for her baby 'Sorrow' (who is not named in the film); indeed, the fact that Tess has had a baby in the first place is only revealed months after its birth. After four months of working for Alec at the poultry farm, she leaves her 'cousin' and the next we see of Tess is when she's gathering hay in a field. As the workers take a break to eat, Tess's sister arrives with Tess's baby which Tess duly breast feeds. A fellow worker looks over from his lunch commenting that the baby 'don't look long for this world'. The baby dies of course, and Tess buries the body with the rest of the 'conjecturally damned', 'in the shabby corner of God's allotment where he lets the nettles grow' (148). This scene is accompanied by the haunting music of the lullaby *Bye Baby Bunting* which then becomes a refrain throughout the film. A further gap and Tess arrives at the dairy where she meets Angel and so on. Niemeyer is right that it is in these ambiguous or even 'blank spaces where the reader can both participate in the narrative and seemingly uncover the "true" Hardy – that actual convergence between the novel and the film takes place' (107).

Polanski emitted quite a few of the cardinal functions of Hardy's text; in the film Tess is not responsible for the death of 'Prince', the Durbeyfield family horse, that starts the whole chain of events off: Tess's family needing money and sending her to seek out what they believed were rich relations. This removal takes away the sense of fate (possibly because of her ancestry), playing its part by Tess's actions in her own downfall, for as the narrator tells us, people in those parts never tired of saying 'in their fatalistic way: it was to be. There lay the pity of it' (119). Polanski doesn't include Angel's sleep walking scene where he carries Tess to a church ruin and places her in a stone coffin, merging, as Jeremy Strong suggests, 'melodramatic action and a high gothic setting' (197); there are also no references to the curse on the d'Urberville family and the ghostly legend of the d'Urberville coach. These may have been removed to aid Polanski in his pursuit of realism, but the finished product, the film, is realism on Polanski's terms; the narrative ellipses, the manner in which colour and light are used and the beautiful, stately dissonance Tess achieves from the other characters in the production, are in confluence with many of Hardy's intentions, that of showing the brutalized treatment of a society on what he called a 'pure woman'.

Kamilla Elliott, refuting the claims by some critics that in adaptation, film is incapable of conveying the figurative and connotative elements of the source text, uses Polanski's *Tess* to demonstrate how it can be achieved. Early in the novel Hardy offers a description of Tess saying that she was 'a fine and handsome girl – not handsomer than some others, possibly – but her mobile peony mouth and large innocent eyes added eloquence to colour and shape' (51). The reader of this would recognize that the phrase 'mobile peony mouth' was a metaphor and not take it literally. But in a film governed by the conventions of realism, Elliott points out the challenges to a director in trying to present an equivalent 'filmic metaphor'. She suggests that this is achieved by Polanski when he has Alec placing a strawberry in Tess's open mouth which 'enhances and modifies Tess's lips visually' in much the same way that the metaphoric 'peony' does in Hardy's text; the strawberry is eaten in the film, just as the 'figurative verbal peony fades' (235) in the text. The use of the strawberry satisfies the diegetic world of the film as well as drawing attention, as Hardy's metaphor wished, to the shape of Tess's mouth and lips. Of course, the action of Alec inserting the strawberry in Tess's mouth also signals later events when Tess is sexually violated by him.

Elliot gives further examples from *Tess* to show how the film whilst presenting the literal can also suggest the figurative. She describes the scene where Tess is attempting to whistle to Mrs d'Urberville's birds; as she walks along the row of cages the camera movement and angle shows her alternatively caught between being caged and being free, pulling 'the viewer back and forth between the literal and the figurative dimensions of the Tess-in-the-cages metaphor' (236). This perfectly represents Tess' figurative plight at that particular time. A similar technique was used in a 1998 ITV version of *Tess of the D'Urbervilles* when Tess visits the d'Urberville's house, 'The Slopes', for the first time; on her arrival we see a workman sharpening his scythe and a camera shot shows Tess positioned under the blade. This serial, delivered in two ninety-minute parts, was seen by many to be a reaction against Polanski's *Tess*, which some considered too detached in its approach. But with an overtly signposted narrative pathway and numerous voice-over intrusions the television production seemed clumsy by comparison to a film, as Niemeyer commented in 2003, that was 'still studied for its filmcraft' (235). Polanski is the only director who seems content to acknowledge the narrative gaps of silence that Hardy uses in his work.

Michael Winterbottom's *Jude* 1996

In Michael Winterbottom's *Jude* he has his character Sue Bridehead going into a political meeting in Christminster, followed by Jude Fawley, unaware at that time that she is his cousin. The speaker at the meeting, in which Sue is the only female, is attacking the social divisions and inequity of nineteenth-century society:

> Then there's your back-to-back houses, your grubby children hanging off scaffolding. It's the same city; maybe a five-minute walk from Church Street to Scum Street. Why don't we go over? Why don't we go over and knock on their doors? Because they've convinced us that this is the way it is. No change. Why change? They've won their argument. They educate their kind to win that argument.

This production firmly locates us in Scum rather than Church Street, the latter being the usual destination for heritage or costume drama; it also perfectly describes Jude's position he is not of the Church Street 'kind' and will not receive the education he so badly seeks.

In his study of Michael Winterbottom's films Bruce Bennett states that the screenwriter of *Jude*, British-Iranian writer Hossein Amini, recounted that the intention behind the film was 'destroying the heritage film from within', a statement clearly indicating 'a dissatisfaction with the politics of heritage drama' (113). The production can be also seen as a firm expression of dissatisfaction with the politics of the time, belonging to a stable of films that Niemeyer and others identified as the 'Post-Thatcher' era. During this period writers and directors expressed the alienation and dislocation felt by the working classes and the disenfranchised in the 'cold materialistic society' of the 1990s, all trying to function 'in a landscape that often resembled a wasteland' (Niemeyer 168). Directors such as Danny Boyle and his 1994 *Shallow Grave* and *Trainspotting* in 1996, the work of Mike Leigh and Ken Loach, all made films that can be seen as critiques of a society where the poor were marginalized and left to drift aimlessly. Winterbottom's *Jude* clearly fits into this category of genre. Margaret Thatcher and other Conservative politicians from their period of power (1979–97) had frequently referred to the Victorian era and advocated, as Niemeyer states, a return to 'Victorian family values' (167). Winterbottom in *Jude* drew on and exploited the themes already evident in the text to show that class-based inequality, injustice and cruelty were rife in the Victorian era and were supported and encouraged by the ruling social elite, and thereby tacitly calling attention to the continuation of such themes in contemporary society. The focus of all this, in this story, is Christminster, the thinly disguised Oxford, where privilege is seen to be enshrined as it remained in 1996.

Michael Winterbottom started his career in television working on some of the first episodes of *Cracker*, an ITV series created by Jimmy McGovern and starring Robbie Coltrane as a forensic psychologist who, despite being a heavy drinker and gambler, had the ability to get into the minds of the criminally disturbed. The series, set in Manchester, was very popular and ran for three years from 1993 to 1996. Christopher Ecclestone, who was cast as Jude Fawley, in Winterbottom's film had appeared in *Cracker*, as well as having a film role in Danny Boyle's *Shallow Grave* (1994). Ecclestone's other television appearances had been in *Hearts and Minds* (1995) created by Jimmy McGovern and *Our Friends in the North* (1996). He was, at this time, associated with narratives, as Strong puts it, which had 'a largely negative view of society' (201). This is an interesting precursor to the second wave of politicized folk horror in the new millennium. This is a film of direct rebellion where the 'folk' are those who have been ignored under a unified and oppressive political system. The 'realignment' of traditional class politics twenty years later after the Blair/Brown governments would lead to a reconsideration of the role of the 'folk' and with it traditional political binarisms.

In contrast to Polanski's *Tess* colour is largely subdued in this production in its quest for 'gritty realism'. The film begins in monochrome signalling immediately its difference to the usual rich visual splendour of heritage cinema. The tone of the film is further established in the opening scene where the young Jude is at work scaring crows in a recently ploughed field, noticing the carcases of a group of dead crows hanging on a gibbet he decides rather than scaring them he will offer them food. Jude is seen by the farmer doing this and subsequently beaten. The film foregrounds, as Bennett comments: 'the working-class labouring bodies and lives that normally remain in the background of heritage films' (114). Strong points out similarities, inter-filmic dialogue, between this particular scene in *Jude* and some of the films directed by the social realist Ken Loach; the beating of the young, thin and vulnerable Jude by the farmer brings to mind the treatment of the boy (Billy) by his P. E. teacher in *Kes* (adapted from Barry Hines's *A Kestrel for a Knave* in 1969); likewise, the shot of the gibbet of dead crows recalls the outcome of the kestrel that belonged to Billy in that novel. Strong also suggests the opening of Ken Loach's *Poor Cow* (1967), where the female lead is filmed during childbirth, seems to provide a likely source of inspiration for the very graphic and gory childbirth scene in *Jude*. Deborah Allison notes that this particular scene in *Jude* and some of the films explicit sexual content were noted by some reviewers as an 'exceptionally radical move in the context of the heritage film' (31), which is the generic convention that *Jude* was expected to join. It is interesting that the discussion of the sexual content of the film runs parallel to the discussion on the novel's arrival in 1895 when it scandalized Victorian readers who considered it an attack on marriage, religion and class. In an act of parody, it was retitled *Jude the Obscene* by at least one reviewer.

Jude was shot in the north of England and Scotland, well away from the much used television backdrop of an idyllic Oxford (used in *Brideshead Revisited* and *Inspector Morse* for example) with its famous spires and the domed roof of the Bodleian library. Winterbottom, ironically a graduate of Balliol College Oxford, wanted a landscape that reflected Jude's dejection and hopelessness, and as Strong states the 'shared northern texture' (2006, p. 201) of the film extends to its 'feel' and its then recent past, the north of England having suffered particularly badly from the outcome of Thatcherite policies during the 1980s and 1990s. Winterbottom's production nudges the film towards the genre of social realism, as exemplified by Boyle, Lee and Loach – a definite move away from, as Christine Etherington-Wright and Ruth Doughty state, the American model of 'commercial filmmaking that is typically reliant on spectacle and high production values' (115). *Jude*, as Strong claims, 'consistently reverses the heritage aesthetic and the reassuring view of Britain that heritage film perpetuates and exports' (202).

The film is divided up by Jude's train journeys functioning as scene transitions between Christminster and his aunt's house in Marygreen: shots of the wheels spinning, and Jude's dejected face pressed hopelessly against the window. There is no notion of romance related to the train; rather, it acts as a symbol of modernity, again making the link between impoverishment in Victorian society and that in the post-Thatcher era; in both a depressed and dejected individual looks out, his hopes shattered. The film shows what Sinyard describes as 'fidelity not to the letter of the source but to the spirit' (135) and is representative of a good portion of Hardy's polemic concerns and convictions that go back to 1868 and the unpublished *The Poor Man and the Lady*. Striving for uncompromising realism and aligning itself with the genre of certain British television and film in the 1990s did not help *Jude* achieve success in the United States. Allison states that box office figures 'fell far short of those achieved by *Sense and Sensibility* (1995) and *Emma* (1996)'; the former 'had played in 1,054 US cinemas (...) and *Emma* in 848, *Jude* never played in more than twenty cinemas per week' (39). Allison adds that *Jude* was not too successful in the UK either and comments that its failure 'left little doubt that the majority of costume drama fans preferred pictures of a more conservative ilk' (39). Winterbottom went on to make two further Hardy adaptations: *The Claim* (2000) with a script by Frank Cotrell Boyce, a reworking of the *Mayor of Casterbridge*, relocated to the time following the Californian gold rush of 1849, and *Trishna* (2011) based on *Tess of the d'Urbervilles* set in contemporary Rajasthan. Winterbottom's take on the 'classic' is therefore one of inspiration rather than attention to 'fidelity'. Whilst he uses the class dimension of Hardy's work to great effect, this still does not take into account the folkloric and horrific elements inherent in the prose. It is why certain elements have disappeared in adaptation or why a text such as *Return of the Native* had never found its way on to the big screen, although it was of course present on UK television in 1994.

Wessex Tales BBC2 1973

Apart from a 1969 BBC production of 'The Distracted Preacher' and two productions aimed for children based on 'Our Exploits at West Poley' (1953 and 1985), the only televisual attention given to Hardy's shorter works remains the 1973 BBC2's *Wessex Tales* series. Produced at the same time as *The Wicker Man* and shortly following *Robin Redbreast*, *The Witchfinder General* and *The Blood on Satan's Claw*, these adaptations seem to have slipped into relative obscurity compared to their contemporaries. Whether this is a result of the pervasive quality of the heritage tag is debateable. The adaptations represent the only screening on television or film to show Hardy's obsessive interest in the irrational. In this series of six fifty-minute episodes there was, as Wright notes, a 'deliberate attempt to reproduce on screen the authentic Wessex of the tales' (2). In the series, the picturesque had to make way for both dark clouds and a corresponding mood. According to Roy Pierce-Jones, the producer of the series, Irene Shubik demanded that each episode 'began with a long shot of Wessex and any human character would be seen from afar, dwarfed by the landscape' (67), and at the end, the camera would pull away from the individual and return to the vastness of that landscape. Small, insignificant individuals with their burden of anxieties and concerns, big indifferent landscape, are all familiar tropes in Hardy's writing. For an example of this one only needs to think of Hardy's apparent indifference in his description of Tess on the landscape of Wessex, when he compares her to 'a fly on a billiard-table of indefinite length, and no more consequence to the surrounding than that fly' (159). The opening credits, as Pierce-Jones points out, 'combine both literary motifs and suggestions of dark forebodings, synonymous with Hardy' (68): old photographs, handwritten letters, a lock of hair, hands entwined in stone, falling flowers and dark cloudy skies.

As a BBC producer Shubik emerged from the background of the so-called 'permissive' society of the 1960s where television, with drama production like the *Wednesday Play*, began to loosen the tight grip of John Reith its first Director General. During the 1960s, in literature as in film and television, there was a move towards social realism and issues surrounding sex, class and race were being approached and aired for the first time and this trend was to continue in challenging dramatic form in the *Play for Today* series which began in 1970, in which year *Robin Redbreast* was first screened. *Wessex Tales* was first aired on BBC2, which was now directing itself to be a slightly more sophisticated channel than BBC1, involved as it was in the contest for ratings with the very popular ITV. Shubik chose both, which stories to adapt and which writer would be responsible for the individual screenplays; to her Hardy's stories appeared relevant to the times, and Shubik stated that Hardy presented them

> in many dimensions, viewing them with a profoundly ironic and very modern eye. His attitudes to women, religion and class could be those of now. Even in those melodramatic tales of witchcraft and horror, 'The Withered Arm' and 'Barbara of the House of Glebe', no characters behave other than believably in terms of modern psychology.
>
> (Pierce-Jones 66)

The series comprised 'The Withered Arm', 'Fellow Townsmen', 'A Tragedy of Two Ambitions', 'An Imaginative Woman', 'The Melancholy Hussar of the German Legion' and 'Barbara of the House of Glebe'. The six episodes were further and effectively bound together by the musical score of Joseph Horovitz and this featured both at moments in the individual stories and in the credit sequences.

The first story shown was 'The Withered Arm', Rhys Adrian's script keeping fairly close to Hardy's story; Billie Whitelaw gave a strong performance as Rhoda Brook, her presence throughout displaying the burden which Hardy places on this character's shoulders. One of the key moments in Hardy's story occurs when Rhoda believes that she is being 'hag-rid' by a wrinkled and 'shockingly distorted' ('The Withered Arm' 50) Gertrude, who is sitting across her chest and flaunting her wedding ring in her face. In the attempt to free herself Rhoda grabs Gertrude's left arm and flings the 'incubus' (Hardy's term) to the floor. This scene is echoed later in the story when a distraught and aged Gertrude discovers that the corpse that she is about to touch with her damaged arm is Rhoda's son ('Jamie' in this production, unnamed in Hardy) and collapses on the floor. Rhoda's – 'This is the meaning of what Satan showed me in the vision! You are like her at last!' (69).

In another episode from the *Wessex Tales* series 'A Tragedy of Two Ambitions', scripted by Dennis Potter, the tone is much lighter and at times verges on the comical. John Hurt plays the older of two brothers who are both emotionally cold, strictly disciplined clergy in contrast to their father who is amoral, usually drunk, and the source of embarrassment and resentment to the two sons. One day in his drunken meanderings, the father falls into a weir and is drowned. The two sons witness the event and do nothing to try and save him and afterwards feel guilt and although they carry on with their church roles, their faith has been broken. As Pierce-Jones comments: 'Such a dark comedy clearly fitted in with contemporary tastes that mistrusted the moral certainties of the more edifying Victorian texts' (70). The viewer of this story, like the reader of the original text, is positioned to dislike the brothers for their cold calculating way of seeking personal and family advancement through the Church. In complete contrast to them, joy is to be taken at the freedom of their father, whose movements in the screened story are accompanied by the music of the oboe, which, as Pierce-Jones suggests, signals 'mischief' (70).

In the story 'The Melancholy Hussar of the German Legion' the narrator recalls a conversation with a Phyllis Grove, an old lady of seventy-five, about a thwarted love affair she'd once had with a German soldier Mâtthaus Tina who'd been serving in an English regiment and based for a time in Wessex. Eighteen-year-old Phyllis had led a very solitary life confined to her house and garden by her father and it is at the boundary of the garden wall where she had first met the soldier. Over subsequent meetings the two had fallen in love and planned to elope. In readiness of this he'd deserted from his regiment and was subsequently arrested along with a comrade. The two soldiers are shot and unceremoniously buried, Phyllis witnessing the event. Whilst Phyllis was alive, the narrator tells us, she had kept his unmarked grave tidy, but following her death the area had become overgrown, with Phyllis herself buried nearby. All Hardy tells us is that the burial took place 'at the back of the little church' ('The Melancholoy Hussar of the German Legion' 44). The story is a good example of Hardy using facts relating to Dorset and placing them in his Wessex, for near the end of the tale the narrator offers proof of the soldiers' existence by showing the actual register of burials.

In the adaptation, whether indicated in Ken Taylor's script or following a decision made by director Mike Newell, we first see the 'fresh' mound of the two graves and then see them overgrown. The mounds are at the side of the wall, very much 'outside' the church, and this is reminiscent (again) of the passage from *Tess of the d'Urbervilles*:

> in that shabby corner of God's allotment where He lets the nettles grow, and where all unbaptized infants, notorious drunkards, suicides, and others of the conjecturally damned are laid.
> (Hardy, *Tess of the d'Urbervilles* 148)

The camera pans upwards and away from 'the conjecturally damned' to just inside the churchyard where we see the grave of Phyllis Grove whose tombstone tells us that she lived till she was eighty-seven and remained a spinster. This story was made into an unconvincing film *The Scarlet Tunic* in 1998 but flopped both in Britain and the United States.

'Barbara of the House of Grebe', which came from *A Group of Noble Dames*, a collection of short stories published in 1891, is probably the weakest episode in the series and a poor adaptation of one of Hardy's most Gothic tales. The production, which featured Ben Kingsley, is somewhat sterile; the characters are overtly melodramatic and rather wooden. Unlike the other stories, most of the filming takes place indoors with little or no contact with the moody and timeless backdrop of the Wessex landscape that had been established in the series. Barbara Grebe from a privileged aristocratic family falls in love and elopes with Edmond Willowes, a handsome young man from a humble background. When the couple visit Sir John and Lady Grebe asking for forgiveness for their rash act, Sir John suggests that Edmond should spend a year on the Continent with a tutor to raise the standard of education expected of an heiress's husband. The couple agree to this, and Edmond goes off. At the meeting Lady Grebe is impressed by Edmond's good looks: 'How handsome he is!' she said to herself. 'I don't wonder at Barbara's craze for him' (52).

The trip to the Continent extends to fourteen months and then news comes that Edmond had been badly burnt in a fire at a theatre in Venice, where he was heroically trying to rescue other members of the audience. The worst of the wounds from the fire had apparently occurred to his head and face: 'that handsome face which had won her heart' (55). Edmond eventually recovers his health and although highly disfigured returns to England to meet Barbara. The meeting occurs at Barbara's new home at Yewsholt Lodge, a gift from her father which is described as a building which

> stood on a slope so solitary, and surrounded by trees so dense, that the birds who inhabited boughs sang at strange hours, as if they hardly could distinguish night from day.
>
> (Hardy, *Barbara of the House of Grebe* 54)

Near midnight in this isolated abode Edmond arrives wearing a mask and on eventually revealing his mutilated face sends Barbara into a state of shock and panic, feeling the 'same sense of dismay and fearfulness that she would have had in the presence of an apparition' (61). Barbara goes off terrified and spends the night in the greenhouse, needing time to gather her senses. When daylight comes, she feels sufficiently emboldened to be with him again, and to 'accustom herself to the spectacle' (62). But when she looks in the house, she only finds a letter, Edmond has gone.

Time passes and Lord Uplandtowers, who had romantically pursued Barbara before she eloped with Edmond, revives his interest in her and when news comes that Edmond is dead, the couple marry. Sometime after this, when they are living at Knollingwood Hall, Lord Uplandtowers' residence, a package arrives containing a full-length figure in marble depicting Edmond in 'all his original beauty' (67); the sculpture completed in Pisa before the accident. On seeing the statue Barbara enters a trance-like state much to the annoyance of her husband and her fascination with the figure intensifies. She starts visiting the statue in the night and on one occasion Lord Uplandtowers follows her and sees his wife:

> Standing with her arms clasped tightly round the neck of Edmond, and her mouth on his. The shawl which she had thrown round her nightclothes had slipped from her shoulders, and her long white robe and pale face lent her the blanched appearance of a second statue embracing the first.
>
> (Hardy, *Barbara of the House of Grebe* 69)

Having rejected Edmond when he was alive, Barbara now worships the full-size marble statue. As Gilmartin and Mengham suggest the sculpture not only becomes a sexual object to Barbara, a site of admiration for her former husband with his good looks, but also in the absence of a grave, it 'provides her with a site for her mourning' (64). Lord Uplandtowers, having witnessed Barbara expressing her desires and emotions in this manner, decides that 'a statue should represent a man as he appeared in life' (70) and has the sculpture mutilated to match Edmond's features following the accident in which he was burnt. On seeing the damaged statue, Barbara faints and Uplandtowers carries her back to the bedroom saying:

> Frightened, dear one hey? What a baby 'tis! Only a joke, sure, Barbara – a splendid joke! But a baby should not go to closets at midnight to look for the ghost of the dear departed! If it do it must expect to be terrified at his aspect – ho – ho – ho!
>
> (Hardy, *Barbara of the House of Grebe* 71)

The destruction of the statue also destroys Barbara; she adopts a 'fictitious love' for her husband 'wrung from her by terror' (74) and dies 'completely worn out in mind and body' (75) after producing eleven children, only one of which survived. If the musical use of the oboe suggests mischief in a *Tragedy of Two Ambitions*, a sombre and mournful clarinet accompanies Barbara in this adaptation. The two other episodes in the series 'The Fellow Townsman' from *Wessex Tales* and 'An Imaginative Woman' from *Life's Little Ironies* were well presented, and illustrated, in case anyone needed reminding, Hardy's interests with twists of fate and coincidence that always nudge towards the uncanny.

As the 1970s moved on and the first phase off folk horror slipped away, adaptations of Hardy slipped into heritage mode waiting until its revival some forty years later. His security as icon of national standing is conferred when *Tess of the d'Urbervilles* becomes a set text for British school children. In the popular consciousness the heritage drama of the late 1980s and 1990s sweeps up canonical figures, even if they are on the margins of the canon. The dark folkloric elements that Hardy exemplifies find an audience predominantly in children's fiction and in television adaptation of same. This form of folk horror finds its way back into the popular consciousness in the 1990s initially through gentle parody in television such as *The League of Gentlemen* – the deep politicization of the genre in earlier forms perhaps giving way to a less oppositional and friendlier use of the tropes. As the new millennia wears on, the political scene changes, darkens and the conditions in which Hardy was writing resurface. This does not result in a whole renewed examination of Hardy as a writer in prose or in screen. Rather a new generation of writers draw on similar ideas and techniques to express a view of the world as dark and unstable.

Conclusion: 'Teach me to live that I may dread the grave as little as my bed'

At the end of the nineteenth century, the nation had an identity crisis. The slow movement that had occurred with industrialization had moved great swathes of the population from rural communities to large urban centres and distanced the population at large from their recent forbears. The rural felt isolated and for many poverty-stricken urban dwellers it was physically remote as well. This underlined what can be seen as a defining characteristic of a line of Hardyan folk horror, the separation of rural and urban. But this is not separation into two opposites; rather in the urban there remains a trace of the rural, of the past – of the 'folk' and the traditions that they embody. Hardy represents this change in topography and in class and this manifests itself in the writer and his writing.

Hardy firmly belongs in the context of the cultural trauma of nineteenth-century 'belief'. This process of disenchantment has a complex history and is explored by Charles Taylor's *A Secular Age*. Taylor charts a process that took centuries, but had its greatest surface effects during Hardy's lifetime. A collision of forces (religious, philosophical, scientific and social) contributed to the delegitimization of local practices that dealt with certain existential needs (association with the land, communal identity, protection from perceived dangers, contact with the ancestral past). The refusal to acknowledge these practices having inherent meaning is a specific instance of the Western worldview that insists there are no higher meanings being expressed in the Universe, that Mankind is the measure of all things. Taylor brings out the tension in modern consciousness, between 'belief' (explicit objectivity) and 'belonging' (embedded interaction). Hardy's working through of folk material engages with that tension, but makes no attempt to 'resolve' it. The Old and New live awkwardly, often frighteningly, cheek by jowl together.

At this point of the 'old world' splitting from the 'new', there were questions regarding who or what determined its character and whether it was still the property of an aristocratic landholding class. Was it defined by the pronouncements of philosophers, churchmen and poets, a few well-educated, well-connected intellectuals who claimed responsibility for its continuing traditions and values? The idea that it would be handed over to the democratic will of the masses seemed like an aspiration for a hopeful future. The cultural despair expressed by Arnold et al. was the shadow side of the immense positivity that accompanied the unprecedented technological progress and imperial grandeur of the era. It is then perhaps no wonder that the first wave of folk horror occurs in that great swell of counterculture in the late 1960s where there is seemingly a similar challenging of dominant authority, and in Britain this remained rooted firmly in class. The challenge to dominant ideology came in attempts to return, metaphorically as well as physically, to the rural. This nostalgic evocation of Britain's rural past, as represented by a back to nature existence and folk music, presented itself as an ideological challenge to the mainstream. However the strength of the cultural industries swiftly sanitized this and the terror of *Robin Redbreast* gave way to the charming depiction of an alternative way of life in Tom and Barbara Good's Surbiton based rural experiment in getting 'back to nature' in the 1970s BBC series *The Good Life*. The urbanization that Hardy reflects on became the norm in the twentieth century and the Urban Wyrd marks the movement of the folk into urban spaces that, with the passage of time, take on the character of the rural in Hardy's work. These are the tower blocks and council estates darkened by political discourse and years of financial and social neglect.

It would seem logical that as the socio-political strife of 1970s Britain gave way to the social upheavals of the 1980s would have been a time ripe for the rise of the 'folk'. However the omnipresence of a neo-liberal political system sanitized and softened these darker edges. The countryside and the past had become playparks. This can be seen in the heritage treatment of Hardy's work on screen, with only Winterbottom notable in drawing attention to aspects of radical thought therein. It can also be seen when driving into Dorset and being welcomed to 'Hardy Country', the real and the fictional morphing into one unified whole – a simulacra. Not even the supposed apocalyptic threat of the millennium could shake this creation of Britain. When 'the folk' return, it is first as parody with television such as *The League of Gentlemen*. What resurrects their malevolence is the post-banking sector crisis and with it a collapse in the belief in neo-liberal social progression. The rise of the right and other forms of extremism evokes the 1970s. The rise of a second wave of folk horror can be mapped against the impending Brexit vote and the rise of political parties who conjure a view of the past as nostalgia. As with Hardy, writers, filmmakers and artists of today know that this view of the past hides a dark reality. Britain is increasingly haunted by its past and this can be seen politically in the evocation of a history in the Second World War that is now too distant to touch and therefore is easily evoked and weaponized. Folk horror takes us to a different past, one of memories of childhood. This is a haunting – a past within living memory. The effect of this is to establish contemporary 'folk tales' as they are forged in the mind of the young and exist in the memory of the adult. The revelations of Operation Yewtree have succeeded in corrupting a past which, at distance, was dark enough already.

The Hardyan line of folk horror is one where there are no demons or ghosts made manifest. There is then a distinction to be made between those authors who find an uneasy charm in the rural past and with the evocation of 'folk': from Zoe Gilbert to Mackenzie Crook's *The Detectorists* and those writers who produce work where the past and the present, progress and regression, rationality and irrationality are locked in perpetual conflict. The Hardyan strand of folk horror is one of hangmen, folk belief and the ability to tap in to a set of beliefs which are, most horrifyingly, within us all. Hardy is not then a simple precursor to folk horror writers, although there are a number who note his influence. Hardy represents something about our fractured society which has contemporary resonance.

In April 2022 musician and poet P. J. Harvey produced *Orlam*, 'It is a poem with a steadiness about death that would not have shamed Dorset's greatest poet, Thomas Hardy' (Kellaway). It is perhaps no surprise that a long narrative poem written in Dorset dialect would draw comparison with Hardy; however, Harvey has long been associated with the second wave of folk horror, in particular in her ruminations on the country's recent past on *Let England Shake*, a text which contributes the revival of folk horror. Given Harvey's roots in Bridport it would be very easy to identify her as a 'descendant' of Hardy, and her work echoes the themes and the form that Hardy worked in. There is undoubtedly a connection to place and she cites William Barnes as a significant influence in her use of Dorset dialect in the poetry. There is also a visceral connection to the countryside, as Harvey states: 'Dorset is light and dark, ecstasy and melancholy. If you stand at the top of Eggardon Hill, you feel your heart come open with beauty. But if you're in a valley that doesn't get much light, you feel this beautiful melancholy' (Kellaway).

The narrative poem takes us on a journey through the protagonist, Ira's, life. In hauntological fashion we are plunged into a childhood of the 1970s and 1980s:

> Yet when Harvey brings Ira's world back to the details of her late-70s, early-80s girlhood we feel the book spark again, catching and surprising us: Ira and her brother Kane-Jude hanging around and getting into

trouble on a loose 'Black Saturday'; Ira standing in Gore Woods 'in the violet half-light ... by a car battery / a jerry can / the electric fence.

(Berry)

The description of place blends and melds different references to the past and the present. This is not however post-modern bricolage, rather a present blurring of representations; 'Wyman-Elvis' sit alongside references to a First World War soldier alongside folklore which is both constructed and real. It is in this conscious alignment of references that the work holds its power and through which an uneasy authenticity is conferred on the text as a whole. This is book which follows the Hardyan line in that there is an uneasy co-existence of many elements:

> Her poetry mixes paganism with Christianity. 'I like to see the possibility of everything: no God – lots of Gods,' ... 'I don't dismiss anything as ridiculous or unbelievable. As a child, I thought of God as the land itself. I'd imagine a large hill was the tiny, moley bump on God's leg ...' ... She is also an authority on ancient superstition ... But she is not superstitious herself except, as she concedes with a laugh, about the bad luck of breaking mirrors: 'I suppose we're afraid of it because a mirror is the thing we look at our image in and if it smashes.'
>
> (Kellaway)

Harvey uses paratext alongside Dorset dialect to confer a sense of the authentic on *Orlam*; in the lineage of *The Withered Arm*, she tells us, 'want – mole if you rub a wart with the blood of a small animal such as mole, mouse or a cat, the wart will disappear' (59). At the same time as this 'ancient' remedy is recounted, the 'modern' world is evoked. In a discussion of sexuality 'Randy in Ecstasy', Harvey reminds us of the corruption of the 1970s with a reference to Jimmy Savile:

> He yearned to hook
> anything that moved.
> I think it gave him
> Jim'll-fix-its. (Harvey, 240)

The conclusion of Harvey's narrative is the end of the year and the culmination of Ira's journey. At this moment and with all the symbolism that the new year holds, Harvey concludes by eschewing narrative conclusion. To do otherwise would be to provide some form of satisfaction. *Orlam* leaves us, as does the writing of Thomas Hardy, with the perpetual co-existence of states, of folklore and rational belief, of the recent past and the present, of the sacred and profane and of the pagan and the Christian.

Elms unveiled in secret places
a thousand sooner-children's faces

and drisk enshrouded in its cloak
holway, river, brook and oak,

and all souls under Orlam's reign
made passage for the born again.

So look before and look behind
at life and death all intertwined

and teake towards your dark-haired Lord
forever bleeding with The Word. (Harvey, 281)

WORKS CITED

A Field in England. Dir. Ben Wheatley. 2013.
A History of Horror. Dir. John Das & Rachel Jardine. 2010.
Abbot, Geoffrey. *William Calcraft: Executioner Extra-ordinaire.* Kent: Eric Dobby Publishing, 2004.
Allison, Deborah. *The Cinema of Michael Winterbottom.* Lanham: Lexington Books, 2013.
Anderson, Benedict. *Imagined Communities: Reflections on the Origin and Spread of Nationalism.* London: Verso, 2016.
Ashworth, Jenn. *Fell.* London: Sceptre, 2016.
Ashworth, Jenn. 'Old Trash'. Coxon, Dan. *This Dreaming Isle.* London: Unbound, 2018.
Asquith, Mark. 'Hardy's Philosophy'. Mallett, Phillip. *Thomas Hardy in Context.* Cambridge: Cambridge, 2012.
Backman, Sven. *The Manner of Ghosts: A Study of the Supernatural in Thomas Hardy's Short Poems.* Goteborg. Sweden: Acta Universitatis, 2004.
Barnes, William. *A Glossary of the Dorset Dialect with a Grammar of Its Word Sharpening and Wording.* Memphis: General Books LLC, 2012.
Baudrillard, Jean. *Symbolic Exchange and Death.* London: Sage, 1995.
Beasts. Dir. Nigel Kneale. 1976.
Beer, Gillian. *Open Fields: Science in Cultural Encounter.* Oxford: Oxford University Press, 1996.
Bellah, Robert. *Beyond Belief: Essays on Religion in a Post-Traditional World.* New York: Harper & Row, 1970.
Bennet, Bruce. *The Cinema of Michael Winterbottom.* London: Wallflower Press, 2014.
Berrong, Richard, M. and Tzvetan Todorov. 'The Origins of Genre'. *New Literary History* 8 (1), *Readers and Spectators* (1976): 159–70.
Berry, Liz. *The Guardian Review: Orlam by PJ Harvey Review – Musician's Vision of a Curious Childhood.* 29 April 2022. 8 May 2022. https://www.theguardian.com/books/2022/apr/29/orlam-by-pj-harvey-review-a-musicians-vision-of-a-curious-childhood?msclkid=79fc2f9ccee411ecb43886999f2cc51d.
The Blood On Satan's Claw. Dir. Piers Haggard. 1971.
Booth, Naomi. 'Sour Hall'. *Hag.* London: Virago Press, 2020.
Campbell, Ramsay and Dan Coson. *This Dreaming Isle.* London: Unsung, 2017.
Cardwell, Sarah. *Adaptation Revisited: Television and the Classic Novel.* Manchester: Manchester University Press, 2002.
Caughie, John. *Television Drama: Realism, Modernism and British Culture.* Oxford: Oxford University Press, 2000.

Chapman, James. 'Downton Abbey: Reinventing the British Costume Drama'. Lacey, J. Bignell and S. Lacey. *British Television Drama: Past, Present and Future*. 2nd edition. Basingstoke: Palgrave Macmillan, 2014. 132–42.
Chatman, Seymour. 'What Novels Do That Films Can't (and Vice-Versa)'. *Critical Inquiry on Narrative* 7 (1980): 121–40.
Cooke, Lez. *British Television Drama: A History*. London: British Film Institute, 2003.
Coulson, John. *Religion and Imagination: In Aid of a Grammar of Assent*. Oxford: Clarendon Press, 1981.
Coverley, Merlin. *Hauntology: Ghosts of Future Past*. Happenden: Oldcastle, 2020.
Cox, Ailsa. *Writing Short Stories*. Abingdon: Routledge, 2005.
Cox, Tom. *Help the Witch*. London: Unbound, 2018.
Cox, Tom. *Villager*. London: Unbound, 2022.
Coxon, Dan. *This Dreaming Isle*. London: Unsung, 2017.
Dad's Army. Dir. Harold Snoad & Bob Spiers David Croft. 1968–77.
Deliverance. Dir. John Boorman. 1972.
Derrida, Jaques. *Specters of Marx: The State of the Debt, the Work of Mourning and the New International*. London: Routledge, 1994.
Dessner, Lawrence Jay. 'Space, Time, and Coincidence in Hardy'. *Studies in the Novel* 24 (1992): 154–72.
Devine, Christine. 'Hardy and Social Class'. Mallet, P. *Thomas Hardy in Context*. Cambridge: Cambridge University Press, 2013. 167–76.
Dillion, Jaqueline. *Thomas Hardy: Folklore and Resistance*. California: Palgrave Macmillan, 2016.
Doel, Geoff and Fran Doel. *Folklore of Dorset*. Stroud: Tempus Publishing, 2007.
Donnelly, Kevin and Louis Bayman. *Folk Horror: Return of the British Repressed*. Manchester: Manchester University Press, 2023.
Doughty, Ruth and Christine Etherington-Wright. *Understanding Film Theory*. Basingstoke: Palgrave Macmillan, 2011.
Draper, John and Jo Fowles. *Thomas Hardy's England*. London: Bloomsbury, 1989.
Drew, Elizabeth. *The Novel: A Modern Guide to Fifteen English Masterpieces*. New York: Norton, 1963.
Dutton, Denis. 'Authenticity in Art'. Levinson, Jerrold. *The Oxford Handbook of Aesthetics*. New York: Oxford University Press, 2005.
Eagleton, Terry. 'Preface'. Goode, J. *Thomas Hardy: The Offensive Truth*. Oxford: Basil Blackwell, 1988. vi–vii.
Edgar, Robert and Wayne Johnson. *The Routledge Companion to Folk Horror*. London: Routledge, 2023.
Elliot, Kamilla and J. Marsh. 'The Victorian Novel in Film and on Television'. Bratlinger, P. and Thesing, W.B. *A Companion to the Victorian Novel*. 3rd edition. Oxford: Blackwell, 2007. 458–77.
Elliott, Kamilla. *Rethinking the Novel*. Cambridge: Cambridge University Press, 2003.
Far From The Madding Crowd. Dir. John Schlesinger. 1967.
Faulkner, Laura. 'That's Convenient, Not to Say Odd: Coincidence, Causality, and Hardy's Inconsistent Inconsistency'. *Victorian Review* 37 (2011): 111–14.
Finchman, Tony. 'Far From the Madding Crowd: Directed by Thomas Vinterberg'. *The Hardy Society Journal* 11 (2) (2015): 111–14.

Firor, Ruth A. *Folkways in Thomas Hardy*. New York: A.S. Barnes & Company Inc., 1962.
Fischer, Bob. 'The Haunted Generation'. *Fortean Times*. June 2017.
Fischer, Bob. 'Where Ghosts Gather'. *Fortean Times*. November 2019.
Fisher, Mark. *Ghosts of My Life: Writings on Depression, Hauntology and Lost Futures*. London: Zero Books, 2015.
Fisher, Mark. *The Weird and the Eerie*. London: Repeater, 2016.
Fletcher, Tom. *Witch Bottle*. London: Jo Fletcher, 2020.
Flint, David. *Tales of Folk Horror*. London: Hungry Eye Books, 2020.
Folk Horror Revival. *Folk Horror Revival and Urban Wyrd Project*. n.d. 16 April 2022. https://folkhorrorrevival.com/.
Ford, Mark. *Thomas Hardy: Half a Londoner*. Cambridge: Harvard University Press, 2016.
Foundas, Scott. *Variety: Film Review: Far from the Madding Crowd*. 2 April 2015. 21 April 2018. https://variety.com/2015/film/reviews/far-from-the-madding-crowd-review-1201464632/#!?msclkid=0da26502cece11ecb209e58338966196.
Fox, Alisia. *Writing Short Stories: A Routledge Writer's Guide*. Oxford: Routledge, 2005.
Freud, Sigmund. *The Uncanny*. London: Penguin, 2003.
Frow, John. *Genre*. London: Routledge, 2014.
Gibson, James. *Thomas Hardy, Interviews and Recollections*. London: Palgrave Macmillan, 1999.
Gilbert, Zoe. *Folk*. London: Bloomsbury, 2018.
Girard, Rene. *Violence and the Sacred*. Baltimore: Johns Hopkins University Press, 1977.
Gittings, Robert. *The Older Hardy*. London: Pearson, 1978.
Gittings, Robert. *The Young Thomas Hardy*. London: Little Brown, 1975.
Gregor, Michael Irwin and Ian. 'Either Side of Wessex'. Butler, L. St John. *Thomas Hardy and Fifty Years*. London: The Macmillan Press, 1977. 104–15.
Hall, Sarah. *Wolf Border*. London: Faber and Faber, 2015.
Hardy, Evelyn. *Thomas Hardy's Notebooks*. London: The Hogarth Press, 1955.
Hardy, Lucie McKnight. *Dead Relatives*. Liverpool: Dead Ink, 2022.
Hardy, Lucie McKnight. *Water Shall Refuse Them*. Liverpool: Dead Ink, 2019.
Hardy, Thomas. 'Barbara and the House of Grebe'. Hardy, Thomas. *A Group of Notable Dames*. Gloucester: Alan Sutton Publishing, 1986.
Hardy, Thomas. *Collected Poems*. London: Macmillan, 1960.
Hardy, Thomas. *Desperate Remedies*. Oxford: Oxford World Classics, 2003.
Hardy, Thomas. *Far from the Madding Crowd*. Harmondsworth: Penguin, 1979.
Hardy, Thomas. 'A Few Crusted Characters'. Hardy, Thomas. *Life's Little Ironies*. 1894.
Hardy, Thomas. 'The Fiddler of the Reels'. Hardy, Thomas. *The Distracted Preacher and Other Tales*. Harmondsworth: Penguin, 1981.
Hardy, Thomas. *The Hand of Ethelberta*. London: Macmillan, 1979.
Hardy, Thomas. 'Introduction'. Hardy, Thomas. *Wessex Tales*. Harmondsworth: Wordsworth, 1999. vii–xviii.
Hardy, Thomas. *Jude the Obscure*. London: Macmillan, 1969.
Hardy, Thomas. *The Literary Notebooks of Thomas Hardy Vol 1 and 2*. Ed. Lennart A. Bjork. London: Macmillan, 1995.

Hardy, Thomas. *The Mayor of Casterbridge*. London: Macmillan, 1972.
Hardy, Thomas. 'The Melancholoy Hussar of the German Legion'. Hardy, Thomas. *The Wessex Tales*. Harmondsworth: Wordsworth, 1999.
Hardy, Thomas. *The Norton Anthology of Modern Poetry*. Ed. Richard and Robert O'Clair 1988 'Thomas Hardy' in *The Norton Anthology of Modern Poetry*, [Norton: New York]. [Ellmann. New York: Norton, 1988].
Hardy, Thomas. *A Pair of Blue Eyes*. London: Macmillan, 1975.
Hardy, Thomas. 'Postscript'. Hardy, Thomas. *Jude the Obscure*. London: McMillan, 1969. v–ix.
Hardy, Thomas. 'Preface'. Hardy, Thomas. *The Wessex Tales*. Harmondsworth: Wordsworth, 1999. xxx–xxiii.
Hardy, Thomas. *The Return of the Native*. Harmondsworth: Penguin, 1981.
Hardy, Thomas. *Selected Poems*. London: Penguin, 1993.
Hardy, Thomas. *Tess of the d'Urbervilles*. Harmondsworth: Penguin, 1985.
Hardy, Thomas. *Thomas Hardy: Selected Poems*. London: Penguin, 1978.
Hardy, Thomas. 'The Three Strangers'. Hardy, Thomas. *The Wessex Tales*. Harmondsworth: Wordsworth, 1999.
Hardy, Thomas. *The Three Wayfarers*. London: Scholars Facsimilies & Reprint, 1999.
Hardy, Thomas. *Under the Greenwood Tree*. London: Penguin, 1998.
Hardy, Thomas. *The Wessex Tales*. Hertfordshire: Wordsworth, 1999.
Hardy, Thomas. 'The Withered Arm'. Hardy, Thomas. *The Wessex Tales*. Hertfordshire: Wordsworth, 1999.
Hardy, Thomas. *Wessex Poems and Other Verses*. London: Portable Poetry, 2020.
Harvey, P. J. 'Let England Shake'. By P. J. Harvey. 2011.
Harvey, P. J. *Orlam*. London: Picador, 2022.
Hassan, Nooral. *Thomas Hardy: The Sociological Imagination*. London: Macmillan, 1982.
Hauke, Alexandra. 'Dreaming of Leviathan'. *Revenant*. November 2020: 167–94.
Hawkins, Desmond. *Hardy: Novelist and Poet*. London: Papermac, 1981.
Hayes, Tracy. 'Darkest Wessex: Hardy, Teh Gothic Short Story and Masculinity'. *Victorian Popular Fiction* 2 (2020): 76–94.
Hayes, Tracy. 'The Red Ghost and the No-Moon Man: Masculinity as Other in the Return of the Native'. *The Hardy Society Journal* 10 (2014): 51–8.
Hayes, Tracy. 'When Thomas Hardy Met M. R. James: An Evening of Ghosts and Gothic'. n.d.: 140–5.
Heholt, Ruth and Niamh Downing. *Haunted Landscapes: Supernature and the Environment*. London: Rowman & Littlefield International, 2016.
Hesketh, Ian. *Victorian Jesus: J.R. Seeley, Religion, and the Cultural Significance of Anonymity*. Toronto: University of Toronto Press, 2017.
Hewitt, Andrew. 'Galatea in the Hintocks: Living Statues and Petrified Humans in the Work of Thomas Hardy'. *The Thomas Hardy Journal* XXXII (2016): 83–103.
Higson, Andrew. *Film England: Culturally English Filmmaking since the 1990s*. London: I.B. Tauris, 2011.
Hirst, Richard, V. and Dan Coxon. *Writing the Uncanny: Essays on Crafting Strange Fiction*. Liverpool: Dead Ink, 2021.
Holmwood, Leigh. *The Guardian: BBC Period Drama Is 'Going Downmarket'*. 29 September 2009. 27 April 2018. https://www.theguardian.com/media/2009/

sep/29/andrew-davies-bbc-period-drama-downmarket?msclkid=4f0ce47ccece11ec8403090765c6c72f.
Hook, Sarah. 'A Literary Man with a Pencil: Thomas Hardy and His Illustrated Book, Wessex Poems'. *The Thomas Hardy Journal* XXIX (2013): 68–90.
Hurley, Andrew Michael. *Devil's Day*. London: John Murray, 2018.
Hurley, Andrew Michael. *Starve Acre*. London: John Murray, 2020.
Hurley, Andrew Michael. *The Loney*. London: John Murray, 2014.
Hutton, Ronald. 'Ronald Hutton on Folk Horror'. *Hellebore Issue* 1 (2019): 33–7.
Hutton, Ronald. 'Witches and Cunning Folk in British Literature 1800–1940'. *Preternature: Critical and Historical Studies on the Preternature* 7 (2018): 27–49.
Ingham, Patricia. 'Introduction'. Hardy, Thomas. *Desperate Remedies*. Oxford: Oxford University Press, 2003. viii–xxvi.
Inside Number 9. Dir. Reece Shearsmith and Steve Pemberton. 2014–present.
In the Earth. Dir. Ben Wheatley. 2021.
James, Louis. *The Victorian Novel*. Oxford: Blackwell, 2006.
James, M. R. *The Ghost Stories of M.R. James*. London: British Library Publishing, 2018.
Johnson, Daisy. *Fen*. London: Vintage, 2016.
Johnson, Wayne and Keith McDonald. *Contemporary Gothic and Horror Film: Transnational Perspectives*. Liverpool: Anthem Press, 2021.
Jude. Dir. Michael Winterbottom. 1996.
Keating, Peter. *The Haunted Study: A Social History of the English Novel 1875–1914*. London: Fontana, 1991.
Keetley, Dawn. 'Defining Folk Horror'. *Revenant* (5) (2020): 1–32.
Kellaway, Kate. *The Guardian: Interview - Dorset Is Light and Dark, Ecstasy and Melancholy*. 24 April 2022. 8 May 2022. https://www.theguardian.com/music/2022/apr/24/pj-harvey-poetry-dorset-orlam-interview?msclkid=677e8b03cee211ec900b09070b14047a.
Keys, Romney T. 'Hardy's Uncanny Narrative: A Reading of the Withered Arm'. *Texas Studies in Literature and Language* 27 (1985): 107–23.
Kill List. Dir. Ben Wheatley. 2011.
Koeslter, Arthur. *The Ghost in the Machine*. London: Arkana, 1989.
Kroll, Alison Alder. 'Hardy's Wessex, Heritage Culture and the Archeology of Rural England'. *Nineteenth Century Contexts: An Interdisciplinary Journal* 31 (2009): 335–52.
Kryzywinska, Tanya. A Skin for Dancing in: Possession, Witchcraft and Voodoo in Film. 2000, n.d.
Larrington, Carolyne. *Hag*. London: Virago, 2020.
Lawrence, David and Steve Brotherstone. *Scarred for Life*. Liverpool: Lulu, 2018.
The League of Gentlemen. Dir. Steve Bendelack. Perf. Mark Gatiss, Steve Pemberston, Reece Shearsmith Jeremy Dyson. 1999–2002.
Levine, George. *Darwin and the Novelists: Patterns of Science in Victorian Fiction*. 2nd edition. Chicago: The Chicago University Press, 1991.
Lidholm, Charles. 'The Rise of Expressive Authenticity'. *Anthropological Quarterly* 86 (2013): 361–95.
Littler, Richard. *Discovering Scarfolk*. London: Ebury Press, 2014.
Littler, Richard. *Scarfolk & Environs: Road & Leisure Map for Uninvited Tourists*. London: Herb Lester Associates, 2020.

Littler, Rciahrd. *The Scarfolk Annual*. London: William Collins, 2019.

Liu, Max. *Andrew Michael Hurley on Starve Acre: 'A lot of this book's about parenting, the guilt you feel'*. London: The Guardian, 1 November 2019.

Lively, Penelope. *Astercote*. London: Dutton, 1971.

Lodge, David. 'Thomas Hardy as a Cinematic Novelist'. Butler, L. St J. *Thomas Hardy after Fifty Years*. London: McMillan, 1977. 78–89.

Lowry, Elizabeth. *The Chosen*. London: Riverrun, 2022.

Major, John. *John Major Archive*. 4 April 1993. 8 April 2022. https://johnmajorarchive.org.uk/1993/04/22/mr-majors-speech-to-conservative-group-for-europe-22-april-1993/.

Mallett, Phillip and Jaqueline Dillon. 'The Evil Eye: Looking and Overlooking in the Return of the Native'. *The Thomas Hardy Journal* XXXI (2015): 89–107.

May, Charles. *The New Short Story Theories*. Athens: Ohio University Press, 1994.

Maynard, Christopher. *The World of the Unknown: Ghosts*. London: Usborne, 1977.

McFarlane, Robert. 'The Eeriness of the English Countryside'. 5 April 2015. *The Guardian*. 6 January 2018. https://www.theguardian.com/books/2015/apr/10/eeriness-english-countryside-robert-macfarlane.

McLean, Will. *The Apparition Phase*. London: Penguin, 2020.

McNay, Lois. *Foucault*. Cambridge: Polity Press, 1994.

Mengham, Rod and Sophie Gilmartin. *Thomas Hardy's Shorter Fiction: A Critical Study*. Edinburgh: Edinburgh University Press, 2007.

Midsommar. Dir. Ari Aster. 2019.

Mieville, China. *The City and the City*. London: Tor, 2009.

Miller, Lucaster. 'A Hygenic Bathsheba'. *The Guardian Review*. 25 April 2015: 17.

Millgate, Michael. *The Life and Work of Thomas Hardy*. Basingstoke: Macmillan, 2015.

Millgate, Michael. *Thomas Hardy: A Biography*. Oxford: Oxford University Press, 1985.

Millgate, Michael (ed). *The Life and Work of Thomas Hardy, by Thomas Hardy*. Ed. Michael Millgate. London: Macmillan, 1984.

Millgate, Michael and Richard Little Purdy. *The Collected Letters of Thomas Hardy, 7 Volumes*, Oxford: Clarendon Press, 1988.

Morgan, Rosemarie. 'Staging the Native: Aspects of Screening Return of the Native'. Wright, T. R. *Thomas Hardy on Screen*. Cambridge: Cambridge University Press, 2005. 108–23.

Mozley, Fiona. *Elmet*. London: Algonquin, 2017.

Myers, Benjamin. 'Folk Horror, a History: From The Wicker Man to The League of Gentlemen'. *New Statesman*. 12 July 2017.

Myers, Benjamin. *The Gallows Pole*. Hebden Bridge: Bluemoose, 2018.

Newland, Paul. *British Rural Landscapes on Film*. Manchester: Manchester University Press, 2017.

Niemeyer, Paul J. *Seeing Hardy: Film and Television Adaptations of the Fiction of Thomas Hardy*. North Carolina: McFarlane and Company, 2003.

Norman, Andrew. *Thomas Hardy: Behind the Mask*. Stroud: The History Press, 2011.

Paciorek, Andy. *Cursed Earth: Landscape and Isolation in Folk Horror*. 21 May 2021. 11 April 2022. https://folkhorrorrevival.com/2021/05/21/cursed-earthlandscape-and-isolation-in-folk-horror-an-essay-by-andy-paciorek/.

Paciorek, Andy, Grey Malkin, Richard Hing and Katherine Peach. *Folk Horror Revival: Field Studies*. 2nd edition. Durham: Wyrd Harvest Press, 2018.

Page, Norman. *Jude the Obscure: The Norton Critical Edition*. New York: W. W. Norton, 1978.

Parnell, Edward. *Ghostland*. London: William Collins, 2020.

Perry, Sarah. *Melmoth*. London: Serpent's Tail, 2018.

Perry, Sarah. *The Essex Serpent*. London: Serpent's Tale, 2016.

Pierce-Jones, Roy. 'Screening the Short Stories: From the 1990s to the 1990s'. Wright, T. R. *Thomas Hardy on Screen*. Cambridge: Cambridge University Press, 2005. 63–75.

Pite, Ralph. *Thomas Hardy: The Guided Life*. Yale: Yale University Press, 2007.

Platten, S. 'They Know Earth-Secrets: Hardy's Tortured Vocation'. *The Thomas Hardy Journal* XXX (2014): 13–33.

Porter, Max. *Lanny*. London: Faber and Faber, 2018.

Rebecca. Dir. Ben Wheatley. 2020.

Reynolds, Simon. *Retromania*. London: Faber and Faber, 2012.

Riquelm, John Paul. 'Dissonance, Simulacra and the Grain of the Voice in Roman Polanski's Tess'. Wright, T. R. *Thomas Hardy on Screen*. Cambridge: Cambridge University Press, 2005.

Robin Redbreast. Dir. James McTaggart. 1970.

Rodgers, Diane A. 'Something "Wyrd" This Way Comes: Folklore and British Television'. 2017. *Sheffield Hallam University Research Article*. 11 April 2022. https://shura.shu.ac.uk/23108/3/Rodgers-SomethingWyrdThisWayComes%28 AM%29.pdf.

Rose, Steve. 'Bloats from a Scandal'. *The Guardian Review*. 22 September 2017. 21.

Sapphire and Steel. Dir. Peter Hammnond. 1979–1982.

The Scarlet Tunic. Dir. Stuart St. Paul. 1998.

Schaffer, Anthony. 'The Wicker Man'. *Script*. 1973.

Scott, James F. 'Hardy's Use of the Gothic'. *Nineteenth Century Fiction* 17 (4) (1963): 368–80.

Scovell, Adam. *Folk Horror: Hours Dreadful and Things Strange*. Liverpool: Auteur, 2017.

Scovell, Adam. *How Pale the Winter Has Made Us*. London: Influx Press, 2020.

Selby, Keith. 'Far from the Madding Crowd in the Cinema: The Problem of Textual Fidelity'. Wright, T. R. *Thomas Hardy on Screen*. Cambridge: Cambridge University Press, 2005. 96–107.

Selby, Keith. 'Hardy, History and Hokum'. R. Gittings and E. Sheen. *The Classic Novel from Page to Screen*. Manchester: Manchester University Press, 2000. 93–113.

Seymour-Smith, Martin. *Thomas Hardy: A Biography*. London: Bloomsbury, 1994.

Shakespeare, William. 'Henry VI'. Shakespeare, William. *The Complete Works*. London: Michael O'Mara Books, 1992.

Sharp, Andy. *The English Heretic Collection: Ritual Histories, Magical Geography*. London: Repeater, 2020.

Shaw, Katy. *Hauntology: The Presence of the Past in Twenty-First Century English Literature*. London: Palgrave Macmillan, 2018.
Sinyard, Neil. *Filming Literature: The Art of Screen Adaptation*. London: Routledge, 1986.
Sklower, Jedediah and Sheila Whiteley. *Countercultures and Popular Music*. London: Routledge, 2014.
Slater-Williams, Josh. *William McGregor on the 'Slow Burn, Anti-Capitalist Folk Horror' of Gwen | BFI*. 17 July 2019. https://www.bfi.org.uk/interviews/william-mcgregor-gwen-interview
Southwell, David. *Hookland: High Weirdness from Britain's Lost County*. 2019. 11 April 2022. https://hookland.wordpress.com/.
Southwell, David. 'Re-enchantment Is Resistance'. *Hellebore Issue* 1 (2019): 61–3.
Spencer, Herbert. *The Principles of Psychology*. 3rd edition. London: Williams and Northgate, 1881.
Stafford, Mark and David Hine. *Lip Hook*. London: Self Made Hero, 2018.
Strong, Jeremy. 'Tess, Jude and the Problem of Adapting Hardy'. *Literature - Film Quarterly* 34 (3) (2006): 195–203.
Sumner, Rosemary. *A Route to Modernism: Hardy, Lawrence, Woolf*. London: McMillan, 2000.
Sweeney, David. 'A Lost, Hazy Disquiet: Scarfolk, Hookland and the "Haunted Generation."' *Revenant* (5) (2020): 92–108.
Taylor, Charles. *A Secular Age*. Cambridge: Harvard University Press, 2007.
Taylor, Charles. *Dilemmas and Connections: Selected Essays*. Cambridge: Harvard University Press, 2011.
Taylor, Charles. *Hegel*. Cambridge: Cambridge University Press, 1975.
Taylor, Charles. *Sources of the Self: The Making of Modern Identity*. Cambridge: Harvard University Press, 1989.
Taylor, Richard H. *The Personal Notebooks of Thomas Hardy*. London: Macmillan, 1978.
Tess. Dir. Roman Polanski. 1979.
The Third Day. HBO. 2020.
The Thomas Hardy Society. *The Hardy Society*. July 2021. 16 April 2022. <https://www.hardysociety.org/oxo/370/hardy-meets-mr-james-an-evening-of-ghosts-and-gothic/>.
Thurgill, James. 'A Fear of the Folk: On Topophobia and the Horror of Rural Landscapes'. *Revenant* (5) (2019): 33–42.
Thurgill, James 'Literary Geography and The Spatial Hinge'. *Literary Geographies* 7 (2021): 152–6.
Thurgill, James. 'Strange Permutations, Eerie Dis/locations: On the Cultural and Geographic Specificity of Japanese Folk Horror'. Johnson, Robert Edgar and Wayne. *The Routledge Companion to Folk Horror*. London: Routledge, 2023.
Todorov, Tzvetan. *Genres in Discourse*. Cambridge: Cambridge University Press, 1990.
Toelken, J. Barre. 'A Descriptive Nomenclature for the Study of Folklore Part I: The Process of Tradition'. *Western Folklore* 28 (1969): 91–100.
Tomalin, Claire. *Thomas Hardy: The Time Torn Man*. London: Penguin, 2006.
Toon, Frances. *Pine*. London: Transworld, 2020.

Troost, Linda. 'The Nineteenth Century Novel on Film: Jane Austen'. D. Cartmell and I. Whelehan. *The Cambridge Companion to Literature on Screen*. Cambridge: Cambridge University Press, 2007. 75–86.

Turner, Paul. *The Life of Thomas Hardy: A Critical Biography*. Oxford: Wiley-Blackwell, 1998.

Tylor, Edward Burnett. *Primitive Culture: Researches into the Development of Mythology, Philosophy, Religion, Art and Custom*. 4th edition. London: John Murray, 1903.

Udal, John Symonds. *Dorsetshire Folklore*. Guernsey: Toucan Press, 1970.

Voights-Virchow, Ekhart. 'Heritage and Literature on Screen: Hemet and Heritage'. D. Cartmell and I. Whelehan. *The Cambridge Companion to Literature on Screen*. Cambridge: Cambridge University Press, 2007. 123–37.

Walsh, Brendan C. 'Colonising the Devil's Territories: The Historicity of Providential New England Folklore in the VVitch'. *Revenant* (5) (November 2020): 144–66.

Waring, Edward. *Ghosts and Legends of the Dorset Countryside*. Devon: Compton Press, 1977.

Weber, Carl. 'Introduction and Notes'. Hardy, Thomas. *The Three Wayfarers*. New York: Facsimilies and Reprints, 1943.

Webster, Roger. 'From Painting to Cinema'. Wright, T. R. *Thomas Hardy on Screen*. Cambridge: Cambridge University Press, 2005. 20–36.

Wells, Richard. *Damnable Tales: A Folk Horror Anthology*. London: Unbound, 2021.

The Wicker Man. Dir. Robin Hardy. 1973.

Widdowson, Peter. *On Thomas Hardy: Late Essays and Earlier*. Basingstoke: Macmillan, 1998.

Williams, Raymond. *The Country and the City*. London: Paladin, 1973.

Wing, George. *Hardy*. London: Oliver and Boyd, 1963.

The Witchfinder General. Dir. Michael Reeves. 1968.

Woodcock, George. 'Introduction'. Hardy, Thomas. *The Return of the Native*. Harmondsworth: Penguin, 1981. 11–36.

Wright, T. R. 'Introduction'. Wright, T. R. *Thomas Hardy on Screen*. Cambridge: Cambridge University Press, 2005. 1–7.

INDEX

Apparition Phase, The (Will Maclean, 2020) 18, 120
Arnold, Matthew 38

Bakhtin, Mikhail 81
Barnes, William 109, 112, 130
Barrie, J.M. 94, 122
Beasts (Nigel Kneale, 1976) 17
Blood on Satan's Claw, The (Piers Haggard, 1971) 13, 153
Bockhampton 22–23, 48
Brown, Martha 128–129

Calcraft, William 129, 134
Cockerell, Sir Sydney 122–123
Communist Manifesto (Karl Marx and Friedrich Engels, 1848) 56
Conjurors 112–13, 129, 130–1
Coxon, Dan 7
Crowley, Aleister 108–9

Darwin, Charles 52–3, 56, 58–60, 125
Davies, Andrew 139–41
Derrida, Jaques 22
Detectorists, The (Mackenzie Crook, 2014–2022) 161
Discovering Scarfolk (Richard Littler, 2011) 114
Distracted Preacher, The (Brandon Acton-Bond, 1969) 153
Downton Abbey (Julian Fellowes, 2010–2022) 140–1, 144

Eerie 87, 93, 110
Egdon Heath 2, 3, 110–12, 114, 126, 130, 139, 140
Eliot, George 92

Far From the Madding Crowd (John Schlesinger, 1967) 137, 143–4
Far From the Madding Crowd (Thomas Vinterberg, 2015) 144
A Field in England (Ben Wheatley, 2013) 109
Fischer, Bob 17, 120
Fisher, Mark 18, 22, 25, 29, 73, 87, 93, 106, 110, 116, 130
Folk Horror Chain 19, 87
Folk Horror Revival 19
Folklore 2, 7, 8, 12, 14, 15, 19, 20, 29, 35, 68, 73, 75, 76, 80, 82, 88, 109, 110, 111, 112, 119, 120, 123, 126, 128, 162
Freud, Sigmund 54, 105, 115, 126

Gallows Pole, The (Benjamin Myers, 2017) 12, 20, 95
Ghostland (Edward Parnell, 2020) 2, 8
Gifford/Hardy, Emma 23, 36–42, 44, 96
Good Life, The (BBC TV, 1975) 160
Gwen (William McGregor, 2018) 9

Hag-rid 13, 113, 129, 130
Hanging 127–8, 133–4
Hangman 31, 127–9, 161
Hardy Society, The 2, 18, 114, 117
Hardy, Thomas: 'An Indiscretion in the life of an Heiress' 90
Hardy, Thomas: *Barbara of the House of Glebe* 31, 154–7
Hardy, Thomas: 'A Changed Man' 127
Hardy, Thomas: 'Claim, The' 152
Hardy, Thomas: 'Darkling Thrush, The' 50

INDEX

Hardy, Thomas: 'Dead Man Walking, The' 43
Hardy, Thomas: *Desperate Remedies* 90, 95
Hardy, Thomas: 'Distracted Preacher, The' 127
Hardy, Thomas: 'Dynasts, The' 91
Hardy, Thomas: *Far From the Madding Crowd* 25–6, 91–2, 94, 110, 137, 142–6
Hardy, Thomas: 'Fellow Townsmen' 127, 154, 157
Hardy, Thomas: *A Few Crusted Characters* 24, 127
Hardy, Thomas: 'Fiddler of the Reels, The' 10, 14, 17, 107, 110, 116, 119
Hardy, Thomas: 'Grave by the Handpost, The' 110, 121
Hardy, Thomas: *Hand of Ethelberta, The* 87, 91–3, 96–7, 108
Hardy, Thomas: *An Imaginative Woman* 154
Hardy, Thomas: 'In a Wood' 30
Hardy, Thomas: 'Interlopers at the Knap' 127
Hardy, Thomas: *Jude the Obscure* 28, 58, 81, 104, 110, 124, 146, 152
Hardy, Thomas: 'Lament' 41
Hardy, Thomas: *Late Lyrics and Earlier* 82
Hardy, Thomas: *Life's Little Ironies* 127
Hardy, Thomas: *Mayor of Casterbridge, The* 14, 27–8, 97, 100, 113, 117–18, 121, 130, 137, 143
Hardy, Thomas: *Melancholy Hussar of the Germain Legion, The* 127, 154, 155
Hardy, Thomas: 'Nature's Questioning' 53
Hardy, Thomas: 'One We Knew' 80
Hardy, Thomas: 'Oxon, The' 50
Hardy, Thomas: *A Pair of Blue Eyes* 95, 96, 100, 138, 127, 155
Hardy, Thomas: 'Phantom Horsewoman, The' 40
Hardy, Thomas: *Poor Man and the Lady, The* 88–90, 92–3, 108, 152
Hardy, Thomas: *Return of the Native, The* 12, 27, 52, 77, 79, 84, 101, 107, 110–12, 114–15, 125, 135–6, 138–9, 143, 153
Hardy, Thomas: 'Ruined Maid, The' 130
Hardy, Thomas: 'Something Tapped' 122
Hardy, Thomas: 'Spell of the Rose, The' 37–8
Hardy, Thomas: 'Standing by the Mantelpiece' 34
Hardy, Thomas: *Tess of the d'Urbervilles* 28, 30, 52, 99, 101, 103, 106, 113, 119–24, 130, 138, 143–4, 152, 155, 157
Hardy, Thomas: 'Three Strangers, The' 10, 31, 87, 94, 127, 132–5
Hardy, Thomas: 'Three Wayfarers, The' 94–5
Hardy, Thomas: 'Time's Laughingstocks' 43
Hardy, Thomas: 'A Tradition of Eighteen Hundred and Four' 127
Hardy, Thomas: 'A Tragedy of Two Ambitions' 154, 157
Hardy, Thomas: *Under the Greenwood Tree* 28, 112, 124, 142–3
Hardy, Thomas: 'Voice, The' 39
Hardy, Thomas: *Wessex Poems and Other Verses* 102, 106
Hardy, Thomas: *Wessex Tales* 13, 80, 127, 131–4, 142, 154
Hardy, Thomas: 'Withered Arm, The' 2, 31, 79, 84, 112, 127–31, 134, 154, 162
Haunted Generation, The 17
Hauntology 15, 18, 22, 42, 57
Henry VI, Shakespeare 114
Heritage 135, 139–42, 146, 151–2
Hurley, Andrew Michael 2, 9, 18, 136

Jaspers, Karl 66
Jude (Michael Winterbottom, 1996) 142, 146, 150–3

INDEX

Keetley, Dawn 1, 5, 7, 11, 36, 54
Kill List (Ben Wheatley, 2011) 95

*League of Gentlemen, The (*BBC TV, 1999–2017) 159–60
Littler, Richard 17, 18, 114
Lombroso, Cesare 55
Loney, The (Andrew Michael Hurley, 2014) 10, 122
Lovecraft, H.P. 16, 87–8
Lowry, Elizabeth 36

Machen, Arthur 9, 16
Manet, Edouard 104
Max Gate 36, 42, 123
Mayor of Casterbridge, The (BBC TV, 1978) 144
Mayor of Casterbridge, The (David Thacker, 2003) 137–8
Midsomer (Ari Aster, 2019) 14
Moule, Horace 32–5, 41, 44, 48, 49, 51, 88
Mummers 77
Myers, Benjamin 2, 12, 17, 20, 55, 77

Old Trash (Jenn Ashworth, 2018) 18, 95, 122
Origin of the Species, The (Charles Darwin, 1859) 52–3
Orlam (P.J. Harvey, 2022) 3, 161–3
Our Exploits at West Poley (Diarmuid Lawrence, 1986) 153
Overlooking 112–14, 129

Paciorek, Andy 6, 10
Parnell, Edward 2, 8
Pastoral realism 88
Polanski, Roman 105, 142,144, 146–9, 151
Pride and Prejudice (Jane Austen, 1813) 139, 141
Psychedelia 109

Rainbarrow 52, 111, 114
Reddleman 27, 115–16, 138, 143
Return of the Native, The (Jack Gold, 1994) 139
Ritual (David Pinner, 1967) 122

Robin Redbreast (James MacTaggart, 1970) 17, 95, 102, 153, 160

Scarred for Life (Steve Brotherstone & David Lawrence, 2017–2023) 17
Schlesinger, John 143–4
Schopenhauer, Arthur 59–61, 74
Scovell, Adam 9, 19, 28–9, 87
Simulacra 10, 87, 160
Skimmington-rides 117–20
Sleaford Mods 109
Spatial Hinge 10
Spencer, Herbert 54–6, 58
Spiritualism 22
Starve Acre (Andrew Michael Hurley, 2019) 2, 95, 102–3, 131
Stinsford Church 102, 123
Surrealism 105–6

Taylor, Charles 2, 61–3, 65–76, 84
Tess (Roman Polanski, 1979) 105, 142, 144, 146–9, 151
Tess of the D'Urbervilles (David Blair, 2008) 101, 149
Thackeray, William Makepeace 89
Third Day, The (HBO, 2020) 7, 10, 95, 117, 122
Thomas Hardy Society, The 16, 124
Time Machine, The (H.G. Wells, 1895) 54, 56
Todorov, Tzvetan 19
Toelken, J. Barre 15
Tomalin, Claire 6, 21, 23, 29, 31, 36, 39–42, 45, 89, 100, 123–5
Trishna 152
Turner, William 103–5
Tylor, Edward Burnett 76–8

Udal, John Symonds 109, 113, 118, 121
Uncanny 115
Usborne World of the Strange: Ghosts (Christopher Maynard, 1977) 18

Water Shall Refuse Them (Lucie McKnight Hardy, 2019) 14, 18, 114, 117
Weird 87, 90, 93, 106, 116–17

Wessex Tales (BBC TV, 1973) 153
Wheatley, Ben 95, 109
Wicker Man, The (Robin Hardy, 1973) 11, 13, 26, 95, 122, 153
Winterbottom, Michael 104, 142, 146, 150–3, 160

Witchcraft 131
Witchfinder General, The (Michael Reeves, 1968) 153
The Withered Arm (Desmond Davies, 1973) 154–8
Woolf, Virginia 77, 99